ECHOES OF THE *Heart*

JOURNEYS, STORIES, AND REFLECTIONS

VOLUME II

CHRISTIAN LANCIAI

with anonymous illustrations by anonymous recipients, mutely expressing their answering feelings

Copyright © 2025 Christian Lanciai.

All rights reserved. No part of this book may be reproduced, stored, or transmitted by any means—whether auditory, graphic, mechanical, or electronic—without written permission of both publisher and author, except in the case of brief excerpts used in critical articles and reviews. Unauthorized reproduction of any part of this work is illegal and is punishable by law.

ISBN: 978-1-63950-427-5 (sc)
ISBN: 978-1-63950-428-2 (hc)
ISBN: 978-1-63950-426-8 (e)

Because of the dynamic nature of the Internet, any web addresses or links contained in this book may have changed since publication and may no longer be valid. The views expressed in this work are solely those of the author and do not necessarily reflect the views of the publisher, and the publisher hereby disclaims any responsibility for them.

Gateway Towards Success

8063 MADISON AVE #1252
Indianapolis, IN 46227
+13176596889
www.writersapex.com

CHRISTIAN LANCIAL'S VOLUME II OF
COMPLETE POEMS IN ENGLISH

Poems from 2008

Embarkation

Another journey, another difficult departure,
another temporary brief divorce
that risks as ever to amount insufferably
to a torturous infinity of abstinence;
and yet, the contact is more live than ever
and continues in its growth the more
for being challenged and subjected to a trial,
feelings growing into storms
for being subject to adversity.
And yet, the moment always comes
when we once more must meet,
unite and join in perfect love
that seems for its impossibility

the more to always win in possibility
to be an everlasting thing
that simply must continue
constantly to grow forever.

Promise

The rotten smell of death and putridness
in my dejected state of loneliness
in the outrageousness of your departure
leaving me a victim in the clutches of nightmarish harpies
brings me to the bottom and the end of my existence;
lost and lonely in the sea of barbarous vulgarity,
I can but sigh in pain against my fate
that never will allow me to remain in you.
Are we then dead because of this unwanted separation
to each other, since the line is broken,
our communications stifled and our contact gagged
by fate in silence and enforced passivity?
My roaring heart speaks otherwise;
and although all the tyrannies around the world may triumph,
our love shall overcome them all,
survive them all and bring them even lower down
than we can ever be brought down by them.

Manifestation

My thoughts turn into you
as you are manifested in my dreams
in longing tenderest affection
raising our love in marvellous presence
from the ghosts of ruins of the past
to approaching imminent reunion
plunging us into a new life
of which we know nothing.
Maybe it is better that way,
guiding carefully each other
through the abysses of blindness

without knowing where we go.
All we do know is we have each other,
which should be enough for guidance
into any distant unknown future.

You'll Never Cry Alone

When in the darkness of the night
you cry outrageously for all your losses
all alone in desperate dejection,
while I roam around the world
completely unaware of your friend's death,
how can I even guess at the extent
of the disaster you are falling through
to misery of bottomless infinity?
And yet, your tears are but one wave
from out the ocean of the sorrows of humanity,
and your friend's death is just another
new beginning for a new and even better life.
There is no end to the beginnings,
since there are no ends without beginnings,
and there is no death, but only life's transition
from one state into another,
like a common bird's migration
no less natural and obvious.
Cry, lament and wail by all means,
tears can only do you good,
and nothing is more needed by the earth than water;
but be certain of the fact,
that no matter how much you cry,
you'll never cry alone,
and all your tears have company forever
in the bitterness of all the oceans of the world
that all consist of only human tears.

Looking Down

How could I else than care for you,
since the responsibility of love
is never to desert the loved one
but to care and tender infinitely
or at least as long as you are able to.
No matter what the snake-pits of your past
may offer, I will certainly indulge in them
to help you out of any mess
that stands between us and our love.
If there is anything that I was not afraid of,
it was the worst and the most challenging of dangers,
our own enemies within, the abyss of the unknown,
which is ever there and lurking,
waiting to engulf us and commit us to perdition,
which temerity you ever must remain aware of
so as never to be taken by surprise
by anything less pure and beautiful
than the perpetual phenomenon of love.

In Despair

The darkness overwhelms me
as I stifle in despair
and can't make out
how I got drowned in love
instead of simply having it,
enjoying it and cultivating it;
but it must inevitably grow
into a stormy ocean
thundering and roaring universally
and drowning everything
in its tempestuous emotions
that will carry everything away
and most of all your self
and all you have
while only one thing will be saved:
love purifies the more it is enjoyed,
and through all trials and upheavals
you will have your soul still floating
flying universally in triumph after all.

Love is Not Enough

Only love is not enough
in a relationship to make it work.
You need so much else,
like trust and mutual understanding,
depth of feelings, and, the most important,
the community of souls,
that sticks together in fidelity of mind
to always have each other in their minds.
(You also need the possibility to be alone
for meditation, concentration, freedom,
work and clarity of mind,
but all this is self-evident.)
If all this works, ensured with depth of trust,
then love is here to stay,
and you don't even have to bother to express it.
It will keep on going and expanding by itself,
and all you have to do is just to follow
and maintain it properly by not forgetting it.

Approach

Are you real, my love,
or are you just a ghost of my imagination,
do I mix you up with someone else
that merely exists as a chimaera,
leading me astray in desperate delusions
like an all too realistic mirage in the desert,
or are you quite simply too good to be true?
The only certain thing is that I love you
whoever you are,
and so far you at least have not betrayed me,
thrown my love away or let me down
except most unintentionally;
so what can I do
but keep on loving you and longing for you
since at least we all the time
are getting nearer to each other.

Greeting

I greet you in the morning with a prayer
that you might be spared all pains
and all adversities and worries,
since I care for you with infinite protection,
wishing all I know a hundred years of health,
accomplishment, perfection and success
and nothing less than all the best;
but you stand out before the front line
in your delicacy and vulnerability,
having cried too much already in your days
and scoliosis being as a handicap no trifle.
The more I love you for not being able to
accomplish any absoluteness in our consummation,
leading to its being the more consummated
in our hearts and souls and arts instead,
projecting in the testimony of its beauty
further than to just the stars,
the finite universe and all infinity.

Our Love

I love you – if you please, and if I may,
in morningtime when I arise
and in the evening when I close my eyes
and in the night in all my dreams
which even in the days continue in my work.
So has it been since I first saw you
now four years ago, and chances are
that this will not be discontinued.
Although separations mess our lives about
the mind is always there
of the united love we have in common
which will keep us up whatever happens
even when we fall to never rise again –
our love was made to never be unmade.

Love's Freedom

Love is not love if it is bound in chains
by obligations, promises, routines and duties
but must live by trust alone and understanding
and needs freedom above all to keep on flying
steadily sustained in permanent expansion,
progress, growth and pioneering enterprise,
for which you have to have your spirit out of bounds
with more sense than the ordinary five ones
and with one eye ever turned unto its own divinity;
for love without divinity can not live long and is not love
but needs its sixth sense of the spiritual open mind most necessarily
to at all be able to have any breath and life.
So there you are: I give you all my love with all my freedom
to be able to forever love you with all freedom.

Blend

When in the shadows of the night
we change identities
in cover of what can't be seen
and get confused about as who we really are,
emerging with profundity into each other,
you becoming me and vice versa,
it is difficult to know
if love is real or only madness
as our senses are distorted
by the ultra-rational intensity of our confusion,
spiritualism taking over our perceptions
as we blend much more than just our blood,
all I can say is,
that we never are as much and more alive
than when we leave ourselves behind
to by love's right and miracle become each other.

The Dilemma

Just an explanation. I am not the victim of my workoholism. I am merely the prisoner of my poverty. The fact that all my life's efforts as writer and composer have met with no success, no acclaim, no acknowledgement at all, has just obliged me to work the harder, since without more than a minimum income I can't allow myself any proper freedom, which I therefore struggle the more to obtain. I can't do anything more than what

I am doing: trying to improve my recordings, eventually turning them into CDs, and at the moment I have two manuscripts waiting for their doom in Stockholm by insensitive bureaucratic readers for publishers and theatres whose only task is to scrap as many manuscripts as possible: in Sweden you don't have the English system of book agents. My other voluntary works for others are like a relief from this squirrel's wheel of poverty. Even when I travel I constantly have to keep myself on the shortest possible leash and allow myself no extravagances but always think of containing the wallet. So I am not really the self-made victim of workoholism, only constantly struggling to get out of my prison of poverty without losing the only freedom I have, the one of my creative work. This is my constant headache.

Holy Madness

Sweet folly of wisdom,
the experience of your hardship
is more valuable as education
than whatever merits of material life,
certificates, awards and medals
counting nothing in comparison
with the humility of personal disaster,
since most people have to learn the hard way
by surviving suicides and nervous breakdowns
to be kind and human, all that matters.

Indians of America regarded lunacy as sacred
with respect and veneration, as if idiocy
was actually a higher state of being than the normal one,
and they were right, since epilepsy too,
the actual idiocy, was termed "the holy sickness"
by those sages who knew better than ourselves
in this dehumanized denaturalized decadent perverted age
how to take care of life and nature
in ancient times of naturalness, harmony and order
guided more by druids, common sense and knowledge
than by politicians led by greed, ambition and incompetence.

Better then to be an idiot and know better
how to live in humble circumstances
than to make a universal mess of life.

Between the Extremes

How come that love is always either or,
an overwhelming inundation
sweeping everything and everyone away
or drying up for thirst
in smothering desertification
leaving you alone in languishment

pathetically miserable in abandonment?
– and then the flood comes back again
and drowns you in its force.
How come you never find a middle way
in love, which seems to make impossible
whatever compromise, as if it must be all or nothing,
and if love is not all yours she is your enemy.
I'm sorry, but I can't accept that.
If love is so impossible in her extreme demands,
I'll rather do without it
than risk ending up all torn apart
by shipwrecks in atrocious storms
and smouldering consuming desert mirages.

The Everlasting Dance

In the beginning there was movement.

There is no music without dancing
like there is no dancing without music;
they belong together
and are closely knit together,
music being but a spiritual dance
performed and executed by the fingers
or and by the mouth or voice
to give an outlet for the movements of the soul,
its caprioles, caprices, gambols and gambados,
voiced expressively in higher harmonies
to let the spirits soar and join the rhythms of the universe
partaking in its cosmic dances, piruettes and twirls.
It is a dance that never ends,
true music never being able to be halted,
terminated, interrupted or shut down,
the dancing of the universe continuing forever
without any force or power able to do anything about it
except join in, tune in and face the everlasting music.

Love Truisms

Is love a sin? No, never!
The only sin of love is not to share it
but to keep it to yourself,
containing it under a bushel
and not let it forth to light and to expand,
for that's the only way for love to live:
by growth, by sharing and expansion.
If I love, the worst thing I can do
is not to let the loved one know it,
and the only love that could be called unlucky ever
was the love that never was made known.
The force of love is exteriorization
and expansion by multiplication,
and there never was a force or power
that could ever check it or contain it
if it was just natural and true.

To a Dear Departed Friend

My friend, remain, for thou art so lovely.
Your visits in my dreams
are the most welcome calls of all,
ensuring me that you are still alive
and not just well but in the best of health
and even better than when you were here.
You live in paradise, which you ensure me of,
with all your generosity now breaking greater records
and inviting me to join you on your journeys.
I will always join you, follow you
and keep you on the track
up-dated and turned on as usual
in our love which this year has its 50th anniversary
and still unchanged since we were kids.
The strangest thing with your last visit
was the phenomenon that it was natural
that there was no consideration even of your being dead
while you bewailed your brother,

keeping him in sanctuary in your special chapel
even in his coffin at your central place,
while he is still alive among us
with his family and house and car,
while you made it so clear,
that he was to be pitied and deplored,
not you, the greatest shocking loss I ever had.

Some Advice

My love, your paranoia is not serious.
We are everyone our own worst enemies,
and there is nothing really dangerous
in life or in the world
compared to what's within ourselves,
the unknown depths of the unconscious
which alas! sometimes takes uncontrolled charge
of our minds och make them see things
out of all perspective and proportion.
Evil is a misconception
and a kind of lurid mirage
which in fact does not exist,
while only our thinking turns it on,
and it is only true if we believe in it
in twisted and misguided folly.
If our inner worlds are stormy
wreaking havoc over us with senseless worries,
we should just look outside at the sunshine
to immediately rest quite assured
that all the world and universe
act absolutely independently
of what we think and are within ourselves.

Getting On

Recovering from hardy nights of exercise,
you wonder naturally how it all will end,
in some kind of disaster,
as is natural for passionate affairs,

or just a humdrum commonplace divorce
when boredom has replaced all passion spent,
or infidelity, the worst of all,
or just an incapacity to go on and sustain it?
Worries have from the beginning clouded
everything in our relationship,
and there is no way out from them,
except the only sensible and perfect choice:
to concentrate on friendship and companionship.
That is the vital thing that we could never lose,
if we just stick to that diplomacy
and take in passion just for luxury,
as cream and bonus for an extra.
Let us also keep in mind,
that love transcends us all,
and no matter how much we love,
we never can fulfill our quota
of our real capacity.

Relative Departure

Where is our love of ancient days,
when all was rosy red
and everything was more than beautiful,
as we went basking in our youth
of only positiveness, generosity and sunshine
while humility was ruler of the universe
and we subordinated naturally,
feeling part of it and sharing it
with joy and harmony of limitless proportions?
Alas, my love, it's all now gone,
but only temporarily,
since only you are missing,
and as I miss you everything is gloom
while only dreams of pecoral nostalgia
comfort me, reminding me of my pathetic weakness
as my empty life now only fills with memories of you,

until you will be back,
which I sincerely hope will happen soon,
since it can never be too soon;
while actually we never really parted anyway,
since that is spiritually an impossibility.

The Harmony of our Souls

As we blend together
fleeting in and out
there is a concord of our music
that defies expression
as the harmonies are out of this world
sounding the more deeply
in the inner universe of spirits
which you only reach transcendentally
by an insight more profound
than even music can express.
Thus are we one in spirit

even separated and apart
belonging as much to each other
as to that more sovereign authority and power
that resounds and rules the universe
with harmonies that never can be false.

The Inadequacy of Words

Never say 'I love you'
if you mean it,
'cause it's such a worn-out phrase,
diluted into such a commonness
that it's become a mess
of empty words
that can't be taken seriously
for being the most commonplace of all.
No, if you really mean it,
make it better,
make it deeper,
make it art
with thoughtfulness,

consideration and profundity,
so that at least it gives some after-thought
and is remembered,
like a riddle and enigma,
like a poem with more substance
than just superficiality
with something worth sustaining
and remembering for lasting treasurableness.

The Genocide Olympics

Sarkozy is going there, the president of France,
to boost French business with the genocide autocracy,
although he previously was eager
to lead boycott protests against China,
which continues persecuting innocents,
like Falun Gong practitioners,
a constant gold mine for Chinese authorities
for harvesting of human organs
safely in the mental wards
where Falun Gong practitioners are put away
reduced to apathy and drugged unconscious
for the profitable organ market greed,
together with all other religious minorities,
like Christians, Buddhists, not to speak of farmers
causing demonstration trouble all across the country
for their being used, exploited and evicted,
while the genocide goes on in secret in Tibet
with covert murdering of monks and prisoners
brought into jail on mere suspicion.
The Berlin Olympics 72 years ago
were also a manifestation triumph
of successful propaganda for totalitarianism,
but then the Germans had not yet commenced
their genocide procedure, and the Moscow
failed Olympics 1980 were at least subjected
to the boycott of some 50 nations.

Now concerning China everybody knows
about the genocide that constantly goes on,
and still, not only Bush but even Sarkozy,
the momentary chairman of the European union,
which officially is democratic,
will pay homage to the genocide Olympics
for the sake of European business interests
in the greatest and most cruel of all autocracies
that nurtures Burma and its junta
and was backing up Pol Pot before Zimbabwe and Sudan.

Music to Our Souls

The sweetness of our song
comes bringing peace to our nights
with rhythmical perfection permanence
in silent whispers of the loveliest intimacy,
like some immortal melody
that never can stop playing
but goes on forever in increasing beauty
by each bar and intensification,
lulling us to sleep in love
to ever softer beats of tenderness,
while this inspires but one wish:
let this go on forever,
let us stay in love like this
and keep sustaining it
no matter how exhausting it might be,
for it is worth it, every effort and humiliation,
just to keep the finest of all music going.

Approfondazione

(translator's note: there is no equivalent in English)

Love must be an idealism
in order to at all exist,
subsist and breathe,
but all idealism, they say,
is but illusion and a self-deceit.
So grant me that illusion, then,
and with me everybody else,
for no one can exist without true love,
and if true love is always an illusion,
that illusion then can but be true.
So keep me still in that illusion
that I love and may continue doing so
without adversity or sabotage,
defeat, resistance or malicious undoing,
and let me keep on cultivating that capacity

for love, to ever make it more sincere,
profound and deeply felt,
and I believe that that can do no harm
but only reach the opposite,
constructiveness, accomplishment and consummation.

Anticipation

No matter how we age,
for me you'll always be the same,
like in our youth when we were at our fairest;
and although our withering since 30 years
have marked our brows with sinister corruption,
our friendship has increased the more in beauty
and in depth of mutual respect.
What are all worldly sorrows
with a global melt-down and our planet burning up,
with human poisoning of carelessness corrupting our environment,
to the pleasure of our meeting once again
together after too long a geographic separation?
Looking forward to our reuniting
and the reinforcement of our friendship
is for me a universal joy of such immensity
that it excludes the possibility of any worldly crisis.

The Hippy King

To me, you are the king of hippies
matching all the bum ideals
of freedom without limits,
any self-indulgence but within control,
heroic continuity in underground democracy
against autocracy, bureaucracy and all totalitarianism
and humble service at the same time
to all humankind in careful modesty,
while in private your flamboyant intellectual brilliance
and extravagance are more than boundless.
Let me never lose your generosity,
so that I always when in moments of dark moods and dire straits
may save my spirit by enriching it with yours
as the most permanent reliable example of constructiveness
that I could ever find among humanity.

Mirror Mirages

Never believe your eyes.
The only ones who tell the truth are lies.
If one day you don't recognize yourself
looking deep into the mirror,
then the mirror at last is telling you the truth.
All reality is just a passing mirage,
and we are all deceived fools who believe in it,
while only the doubters have any reason,
only the sufferers know life,
only tears know love,
only pain is free from lies,
and only death can open your eyes
and will reveal the only actual reality
which is the somber machinations
behind this shallow faked shadow play,
which exists only to bury the soul alive.

When in Darkest Moods...

When in darkest moods I think of you, my love,
with all the nastiness that we together have gone through,
I don't know whether I shall weep or rave
and risk indulging in them both, ferociously,
while there is very little comfort
in the fact that our love is still enduring
although we can almost never see each other.
Wallowing in my imagination
of how it could be and could have been
is like a masochistic escapism
that offers as much pain as sensual release,
as if the bad accompaniment of good was necessary.
I would rather do without reality, then,
than be without those dreams of mirage comfort,
that seem after all more real than cruel reality,
since there is more love in my wishful thinking
than in all the world of sensual deception.

When Your Life is Ruined...

What do you do, when your life is ruined,
to those who ruined it? Revenge?
Is any retaliation possible?
Seek justice and amendment,
correction of mistakes and arbitrary wrongs?
Protest and demonstrate and join the street mobs?
No, it's all a waste of energy and time.
The only thing worth doing
is to start again all over
patiently from the beginning,
and at best you'll next time manage to avoid
the parasites, hyenas, brutes and hooligans,
those ignorants who did not know what they were doing.

Unacceptability

Who shall save the world
when everything is going wrong,
the only superpower going down the bog
of economical disaster as the natural result
of warring madness failure in Iraq,
a king size caca and the worst mistake in US history
destroying universally its credibility,
while it gets into the economic clutches
of the greatest, cruellest and worst dictatorship,
the fascist state of lies called China,
spreading its colonial tentacles
all round in south east Asia and Africa,
a new colonial superpower to which USA
is falling into economic slavery.
What shall we do? What can we do?
I am afraid, that all that we can do
is to at least take care of our own freedom
and integrity as individuals,
refusing brainwash imposition and extortion;
and our hope and comfort is the fact,
that all successful revolutions start from inside
in the heart and soul; and that at least
is still in our possession and our power.

We Just Have to Accept it...

(tribute to Kathy and Mike)

It's such a pleasure to have it confirmed
that you are still around, Mike,
and that we have never lost you.
Kathy is your crownéd princess still,
and she keeps up our poetry
with flying colours of the highest quality
in your name for not only you to still be proud of.
Celebrating you this day is already a tradition,
Kathy, on the day of Herman Melville
and his elder sailing writing colleague Henry Dana,
and we do it now with even greater emphasis
because of the regretted absence of our missing Mike,
although our celebration at the same time
for the character it takes
becomes sincerely a reminder
of his being still around
and being with us
most of all with you, of course.
Accept my humble celebration on your birthday,
as I ever will continue to accept
that Mike was here
to never leave us.

Love Unbreakable

I hope you always will remain aware
that I remain as constant in our love as ever,
dreaming of you every night
when we don't sleep together
to enjoy the only perfect bliss
that sexuality can offer:
reaching satisfaction without hurting,
although it is never without pains.
You were the only one who never slowed me down,
while at the same time our love was always reciprocal,
never without dialogue, return and feedback,
which is why it always could continue
growing and expanding and developing.
The crises that were unavoidable with constant interruptions
never led to infidelity or any break-up
but to glorious renewals only, resurrections
and continued richness of our intercourse.
Of course we hope that it will last forever,
while we both know,
that although it must be definitely interrupted sometime,
it will merely continue in another life
to just take on another form again.

The Power of Love

Let me penetrate your lovely hair
and make it mine to play with,
hide in, vanish in and quietly extol in
while caressing it admiringly
for your so sweet and personable being
with the utmost tenderness approaching love
and being it and nothing else
for both of us to have
as a most memorable joy forever.
Let me dream of you with only goodness,

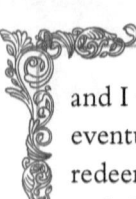

and I will be certain that our mutual love
eventually will by its enigmatical delight
redeem all mankind, history
and all the rotten world.

The Constant Reunion

My friend, we see each other only once a year,
but every time it is like yesterday
since we last met and parted
just to join again, year after year,
as if all time was but a fleeting moment's nonsense
of no consequence at all,
an unimportant twinkling of an eye;
which makes all history appear as most absurd
considering the real condition of dimensions,
friendship and reunion gloriously transcending them
to never tire of reducing all eternity to nothing.
Love is all that matters,
and as long as we keep sticking to it,
we are safer than and safe from all eternity.

The League of Beauty

They are everywhere, the partners
and the intimates of this our union,
those who know the worth of beauty
and who therefore are subscribed to love
forever with a constancy transcending
the material universe with all its vague illusions
that are bound to ever lose to beauty's inner worth
that overcomes all egoistic artifice
of vanity, mundane ambition, greed and folly,
to forever and continually restore the order
of life's only everlasting law of all existence,
that the truth of love and beauty is the only league that holds
ensuring life and nature and survival,
and that nothing can withstand the force of love.

The Way of Love

(This is a song - unfortunately I can't give the music here as well.)

The way of love
is like a dove.
It soars forever
is home in heaven
will never even
go home for even
because it never
can sleep out fever
but is forever
a restless rover,
the holiest ghost.

My Brothers

My friend, you must not warn me of your aspects,
the change of looks will never change your person,
and meeting you again has never caused me consternation
although years have passed between our reunification,
which the constant process of our mutual rejuvenation
never actually has let us down.
You are forever in my mind,
and I can feel that you have never left me,
although already as boys we felt the crisis
of our lives becoming almost something of a constant separation.
Strangely, both my best friends were approximately born
on the same day, like twins,
but so extremely opposite each other
in their background, character and personality
and even in their opposite approach to love.
And still, you are to me more close than brothers,
and I know that brotherhood will last
much longer and beyond all ties of family and blood.

An Ancient Love Dream

Why do you fade so early,
lovely ladies,who give out your love too early,
wasting it on wrong unworthies
never to recover fully from mistakes
that mark your lives unnecessarily
with far too early grown grey hairs?
You used to have the loveliest hair
in all the world, and longest,
marking your integrity and freedom,
for that is the meaning of long hair:
a demonstration of personal freedom;
while you still in spite of decades
of mistakes and wrongs and sufferings
have that personal freedom left

and are the same in soul with all your beauty.
Once I gave you all my love
to never take it back,
and my word counts as much today
as it did then of all my warmest love and friendship
which still makes us twins of destiny
forever on the quest of new discoveries
of how to win and grow and manifest that love
that for some reason never became ours.

Transcendence

My poems about you can never do you justice
since you are so inconceivable
in your dynamics and mysterious ways
that leave all men and minds dumbfounded
failing utterly to comprehend your personality,
since your mentality transcends all human thought
in baffling contradictions to what anyone is used to.
But I understand you and am grateful for it,
for behind your sticky surface there is so much love
like some youth fountain never ending in abundance
that ensures me that I cannot lose you
no matter how far I travel and whatever comes between us.
Stay with me, my love, like I will always stay with you,
our love defying every hindrance, overcoming every distance,
turning every difference between us to its contrary.

My Tibetan Friend

You travel all across the Himalayas
as an outcast, outlawed by the occupants
and forced in exile since your childhood,
forced to cross the snows in winter across passes
of six thousand meters, where the butchers of your country
stand in wait prepared to gun down any refugees
who have the unacceptable impertinence to flee their country
occupied by probably the cruellest of the world's autocracies,

an atheist totalitarian regime which makes all human life impossible
for those who can't subject themselves to anti-spiritualism,
enforced fanatical ideology of atheism,
the national compulsory political denial of the soul
and all its natural demands and needs of freedom.
They have destroyed your country, ruined almost every temple,
almost every monastery and burnt most of all your books,
a thousand years' collection of hand-written manuscripts,
they have reduced your people,
those that were not extirpated,
to sub-citizens of second rate,
if they at all are given rights as citizens,
and killed off one fifth of your population
to replace it gradually with Han Chinese,
a long-perspective ethnic cleansing
typical of socialist dictatorships,
and sterilized an unknown number of your women
and your mothers also after forced abortions,
carried off 240.000 of your ladies
forcing them to slave work down in China
forced to marry Chinese men
who then are forced to populate your country
as another link in the methodic long-term ethnic cleansing.
How many of you have already been lost in concentration camps,
in prisons, tortured to extinction,
or abducted already as children
to be brainwashed and brought up as Chinese puppet capos?
As the Jews keep screaming on and on
with every right to every now and then remind the world
of crimes against humanity committed by political autocracy,
so you Tibetans, Uighurs and Mongolians
never must stop showing up your testimony to the world
about the slow but fatal holocaust
that still goes on today
and has been carried on for sixty years
by the totalitarian party ruling the Chinese.

The Forest

(This is an old story from 1968 full of symbolisms.)

Canto I.

1.

Be it far from me to have pretensions
to be any kind of poet,
but in this world and the other one
I think that anyone would certainly agree,
there are some things that can not well be told
except by words transcending sense
and the conventional reality,
as we accept and know it.
Such things I am here about to tell,
a story strange and difficult to grasp,
and lacking skills in verse and language,

my humility and poor simplicity
will hardly be sufficient to describe
this truth, that I nevertheless
experienced personally all the way,
although I never knew myself
some persons that were part of it.
Accept it as a humble offering
by me, a humble monk,
on ancient altars of tradition,
beauty, wisdom and experience,
and forbear my innocence
and incapacity to render credible
such matters that are visible
to only sentient human souls
and the mind's eye, that sees beyond
the lying sensuality
of this most insufficient limited reality.

2.

I used to take those morning walks
down to the sea as early and as soon as possible
after the sunrise, and my abbot gave me leave himself –
he knew that exercise would do me good,
and not just me, but all my influence
on others for the whole remaining day.
I used to sit down in the sands,
enjoy the rolling waves so generously coming in
sent forth from out there in eternity
to gloriously commit their foaming suicide
against the gentle shores,
caressing them with tenderness
in this eternal process;
when an object in the water caught my eye.
It was a shining object which the sun had found,
some beams had entered it in glimpses of reflection,
which went on into my eye and my attention,
striking me with wonder and amazement,

for immediately I felt it as a message meant for me.
I sat there still with my bare feet all sandy
basking in the glorious sun, as if transfixed
by sudden new and strange sensations,
as if I already was quite overwhelmed
by feelings that belonged yet to the future.
Finally I rose to carefully approach the object,
overcoming the last doubts concerning its reality.
It was indeed a bottle well closed up,
quite light and empty, but for something
that indeed made all my hairs rise in excitement.
There was a letter in it! And it came to me,
of all the people on this earth,
to me alone, there on the beach,
where I had wandered quite alone
exclusively to find this bottle!
Naturally I just had to open it.
Here is the letter, in original verbatim,
that since then has changed so many lives
by opening a world of lives of others:

3.

"My friend!
I pray you, do not judge me
for my awkwardness in language and expression,
but please try instead to understand and to investigate
my case and matter, and then judge me afterwards,
if I have given you the truth or only fabricated lovely dreams!
I am a wanderer gone totally astray
and facing death approaching in some hours,
for the ship that I am sailing on will not endure this tempest.
Seeing no chance to survive, I offer all I have of any value,
my life's secret, the one knowledge
of some consequence that I acquired,
to this stormy sea of destiny.
The fact is, that I once discovered Paradise,
and I left it as the crazy fool I was!

Now it is lost forever for my part,
and all that I can do is in my blindness to give directions
as to how it can be found again.
Just go to Winchester in Hampshire
and to Wynyard not so far away from there,
then follow the old southern road
until you pass the ruins of a castle and then cross a brook.
Get off the road and follow that brook upstream,
and you shall find the Paradise that I have lost forever
in despair and foolishness and desperation,
following my folly in my life's supremest deprivation!
All that I can do about it now
is to stand trial by myself
and let my life pass on from this life unto God."

4.

This spoke this enigmatic wondrous letter
anonymously with no signature
to me, who was unknown to this unhappy writer,
shipwrecked now, no doubt, and lost at sea
and dead and never buried.
I was totally beyond myself for pity
and committed instantly myself in tears and prayers
for the poor man's fate and soul.
And although he was dead, and I would never know him,
thus he spoke to me in graver earnest and directness
than did ever any living man
whom I met in my lifetime.

5.

My steps were burdened and slowed down
by serious pondering and wondrous feelings
on my way back to the monastery,
and my fellow monks there wondered
what had turned me so reflective
all of a sudden and tried teasing me and cheering me

with no success whatever. They had to be satisfied
with my simple explanation that I would discuss the matter
only with our abbot and with no one else –
of course, I dared not show my confidential letter.
My old abbot, like a father to us all,
sat quietly as usual in the monastery garden
busy at his roses, herbs and other lovely flowers
when I dared approach him, and he saw immediately
that there was something deeply serious
that had happened to me of some bother.
I went to the point directly,
showing him the flask and the fantastic letter
and explaining the concern of this new situation.
He immediately laid all his brows in wrinkles
and was perfectly immersed in the predicament.
He understood me wholly and looked serious about it.
Finally he spoke, and I was all attention.

6.

"My son, this is a matter of delicacy
that can not be trifled with.
Not only is it a concern of life and death,
but it is also evidently the last words and will of someone dying,
leaving a most vital message for posterity,
which he has committed to the ocean without any other choice,
which Fortune has placed in your hands,
the humblest monk among us of all people.
There is certainly a hidden meaning in this matter,
and I have to ask you to investigate it.
The directions could not be much clearer,
all you have to do is just to follow them
and see what place, if there is any,
this poor outcast shipwrecked sailor talks about.
Do not expect too much. There might be nothing in it,
but if there is something, you should certainly discover it,
fate having put his secret in your hands.
Good luck, my son, and I expect you to come back

when you are ready, with at best some very interesting report
that even might turn out intriguing."
He turned the letter back to me,
and I was free to go, entrusted with a sacred mission
that, I can't deny, enlivened me with joyful spirits.

7.

My fellows in the dormitory turned of course quite curious
when I packed my rucksack for a journey of some week or so,
but I said nothing to them of my errand,
but: "When I return I'll let you know,
but how can I inform you of my journey's mission
when I haven't started on it yet
and knowing nothing of where I am going?"
They were satisfied with that and let me go.
And so I started on the first and greatest journey of my life.

8.

It was not difficult but only pleasurable,
leaving everything behind in basking sunshine
as the spring was entering triumphantly
and light was king all round the world.
The walk was nice and long,
I passed the site of Glastonbury on the way
and visited my uncle, who was bishop in old Winchester,
who wondered greatly at my errand.
"Why on earth are you let loose?
Don't tell me you've been sent upon a mission!"
I could only gratify his worst suspicions,
and I told him everything and showed the letter,
whereupon he laughed his sides off
rattling all his vicarage and Winchester
to its foundations, whereupon he let me go
as soon as we had finished a most glorious dinner,
that would last for days and better than supplies.

9.

Thus I went on and followed the instructions of the letter.
They were clear enough, and not even the weather
offered me the slightest difficulty.
I walked swiftly on and found the river and the bridge
and started following the brook upstream.
I felt the strangeness of this moment
of some destiny of truth unknown
and wondered in what fairy-tale
this wonderful adventure would project me.
I was soon enough to know,
as gradually the country grew less habited
and wilderness grew more apparent
as the brook led me into a forest finally.
It was an ancient forest mainly of majestic beeches,
and the prevalent characteristic mood was peace
and quiet of a most inspiring and awesome nature,
so as almost some old chapel or cathedral
was to be expected somewhere near.
And then I came to what I almost felt
that had to be the centre of the forest sanctuary,
where silence ruled and everything was still
and where the waters of the brook was like a mirror
parted in two streams that joined together
peacefully and formed a little island.
Then I couldn't keep my feelings any more inside me.
They freaked out, and I freaked out with them
in a most irresistible exhilaration
that knew no bounds but burst out laughing
in a joy of universal freedom and release,
the like of which I never had experienced before.
It was sensational and could not be contained,
as if I suddenly had found the formula of world salvation
but could not explain it. I just had to sit down,
relax and laugh my heart out
in this greatest joy of bliss that came from nowhere
but replenished, permeated, overwhelmed

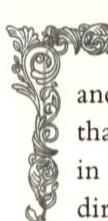

and influenced so palpably all life around me
that I knew for sure I had to have arrived
in paradise itself and nowhere else
directly, manifestly, definitely and demonstrably.

10.

As I calmed down the greatest miracle of all awaited me.
There was a house! It was a small house by the stream,
magnificently pretty in its humble aspects,
built with love undoubtedly, with lovely wooden carvings;
but what baffled me the most was the apparent fact
that someone lived there, and – my heart made quite a leap –
was even there at home! My heart made many thumping leaps
as I with quaking expectations neared the lovely house
and slowly and more slowly by each step,
until I finally dared move the handle of the door.
Yes, it was open, and it was not even fully shut.
And at that very moment, that most gentle voice
was heard, that spoke directly to my heart:
"Welcome, my friend! You have been long expected!"
I dared then push the door more open,
and there was but one most spacious comfortable room
with some small space for cooking in a corner,
and close by the window there was someone sitting in an armchair.
I had never seen a more resplendent youth in all my life.
It was a young man clad in white with hair so golden
as if he was actually an angel, but he wasn't.
"I am Gabriel," he continued gently to present himself.
"What message do you bring? For you must have been sent here
certainly by someone of my friends. Am I correct?"
I could not speak a word, but found the letter
which I pulled out of my pocket to present to him.
He read it with some consternation, and his brow was bent in sorrow.
"Did you actually receive this by a flask?" he asked me finally.
I told him the whole story. Then I asked him to tell his.
"What do you want to know?" he asked,
"where do you want me to begin?"

"My first most thirsting question is about this forest.
I feel such a beatitude in here. How is it possible?
Where does it come from?"
"You are not the first one to feel that sensation,
and you boldly step right into the main issue here.
My friend, relax. You shall remain here for some days
as my most celebrated guest, and I shall tell you the whole story.
It begins in fact with this our friend, this very man called Manuel,
who was the first one who came here, a sailor lost
and roaming round the country, fleeing from some fault,
some trauma or injustice. He found peace in here
and was enchanted by a tiny thing that glimmered in the water
just where these two streams join up together.
Go thou and do likewise, watch what you can find,
and then came back here, and I'll tell you all about it."
I was naturally most intrigued and followed his advice.

11.

As I lay down there by the stream and searched into the waters,
what I found was something most extraordinary.
Shining on the bottom of the brook there was a golden ring
of such amazing regularity and charm and beauty,
that I could not leave it by my sight.
And there, I realized immediately, was the whole story.
I had to tear myself away by force,
returned to Gabriel in the house and told him
what I had discovered. "I could read the story
in its beaming force of wonder, but I would prefer
to hear it more exactly from yourself," I told him.
"You were wise, my friend, to keep away from touching it,
and your reward shall be of course to hear it all,
the full account of this most fundamental love story of all,
as Manuel read it from the ring, and as I lived it through myself
with my own parents and especially my mother.
But it is a lengthy narrative indeed, so I suggest
we start our session with a cup of tea. Is that all right?"
Of course that was the best way of an introduction,

so the last thing I did was to protest.
He prepared the tea, I had some milk in it, he didn't,
and then he sat down and started to recount
the most intriguing fairy tale that I so far had heard.
The character of his amazing story suited him so well,
since he was actually a child of it, with his long golden hair
that flowed so generously down his back to reach his bottom
and his simple but so perfectly white dressing
that could certainly have matched the clothes of Christ.
And this is now his matchless story.

Canto II

1.

"There are some fundamentals
of this strange existence we call life,
which simply aim at not exacerbating it
but on the contrary, at making it more easy
and agreeable, endurable and nice.

The heart of these recommendations
concern of course the strange phenomenon
on such a universal bearing on us all,
that everything depends on it.
Love is of course to everlastingly be cherished,
cultivated, practised and disseminated
but with care and always kindly.
It must not be enforced,
for then the only consequence is backfire
which can lead to anything destructive.
You shall hear our story,
which is all about the consequence of love,
for good, for worse, but never without consequences."

2.

Thus spoke the fairest man that I had ever seen,
all clad in white,
with golden hair down to his waist,
not even twenty, but still with such a wisdom
as if he had been an old soul ever
with experience enough to teach all mankind
how to make it better and get more aware and wiser.

3.

"He was a kind of rover of the sea,
no roots ashore although he was a doctor,
shunning his own kind and living only for the aliens,
innocents of wilderness, the undestroyed of nature,
preferrably of some romantic pure environment
of virgin beauty, ocean shores and mountains,
like Tahiti and the southeast Asian archipelago,
but most of it had already been spoilt and ruined.
There were still, however, some few archipelagos
unknown to white men's greed,
and one of them was only known to him.
It was the seven islands of Jagánde

far away beyond all maps and charts of knowledge,
and it was his habit once a year to go there
selling trinkets and some medicines
for pearls and costly handicrafts and jewels,
which he then would sell on the Calcutta market
at some modest profit. Thus his only use of his monopoly
was to preserve it, keep it virgin and unknown
and act as its protector, while he modestly enjoyed
the local fame of being venerated as the only white man
known at all to all the natives of Jagánde.
But one year he brought a fellow with him.

4.

He was of some dark romantic hue,
a sailor born and famous for his legendary seamanship,
as he once as a youngster actually had managed quite alone
to bring a ship without its captain through a storm.
He was from Venice but, like doctor Magnus,
kept roaming about around the world
with no safe haven to find peace and rest in.
They had met at some bazaar in Bombay or Calcutta,
and at that time doctor Magnus needed some spare hands,
the storms, typhoons and hurricanes around the Indian Ocean
growing worse, so that he felt the need to play it safer,
going out to remote islands beyond any chart
without a single person knowing where he was.
As you grow older, loneliness becomes an alien company,
while instead the urge of sharing grows more imminent.
Quite simply, doctor Magnus asked his newfound mate:
"Would there be any interest on your part
to come along with me to unknown South Pacific isles
which no one in geography has ever heard of?"
The Venetian sailor asked immediately:
"That is exactly what I need.
Do such islands still exist?"
And he was on.

5.

They reached the islands early after dawn
one morning, and people gathered everywhere
along the shores to greet them
with a wondrous song of welcome,
which they sang in parts
in clear and stupefying harmony,
preparing garlands to receive the yearly visitor;
but the activity and eagerness along the shores
among the steadily increasing groups of curious people
were enhanced when it was noticed,
that their loved friend the doctor
this year had brought with him a companion,
who looked interesting indeed.

6.

As they were fetched ashore by outriggers,
the king himself embarking on his sumptuous royal boat
to offer them a very special welcome,
as they almost were submerged in garish garlands,
they were lifted up on shoulders of the natives on the shore
to then be promptly carried to the king's house
for a most pacific banquet,
while the singing and the celebrating went on enthusiastically.
After all, the best friend of the natives
paid them annually one visit only,
and since now they were two persons,
that must needs have double celebrations.

7.

As they sat down to their royal banquet in the king's house,
there was no end to the affluence
of the most exquisite delicious cooking of the south seas.
Present at the presentation of the king's whole family
with wives and sons and other relatives

whose status and relationships were out of definition,
there was also the king's one and only daughter,
a fair maid of perfect and exotic beauty
in her best age and not yet in full bloom.
As the sailor's eyes discovered her,
she went under his skin immediately and stayed there,
and he could not concentrate on any matter else
all through the overwhelming dinner.
Doctor Magnus saw that something dangerous had happened
and gave him a friendly warning:
"Mind you, as the only daughter of the king,
she is everything to him, and he will never part with her.
There have been suitors, lots of them,
but no one will get through without some testing.
If the test is failed, the suitor's life is lost."
Appalled but not deterred, the sailor asked:
"Have many suitors thus been executed?"
"They can not be counted," was the somber answer.

8.

Naturally, the more the sailor's interest grew
in that most fascinatingly attractive princess
with her dark brown olive-reddish hair
in most intoxicating generosity and richness
flowing far beneath her bottom,
especially as she did not remain for dinner
but departed suddenly as soon as she had seen him.
That could only mean one thing,
and he was well aware of it.

9.

He had no interest, therefore, in remaining
bored and stuffed by far too many dishes
at the royal table, but as soon as it was possible
for him to break and move out from the culinary slavery,
he made polite excuses, indicating natural demands

and went out for a vital breath of fresher air.
He instantly made out his bearings
and soon found himself a total stranger
in the middle of a capital but alien village,
but was nonetheless led by a higher instinct
to pursue a very special course,
like by a higher scent and sense,
and suddenly stopped short at a most touching scene.
There she was, the royal princess,
in a very humble cottage, helping a sick family in need,
where obviously the mother lying on a bed was dying.
The dark sailor with his most romantic aspects
of a wild and dashing stranger from beyond the seas
knew perfectly how to control himself
and therefore did not interfere with anything
but stood apart in reverence and kept his silence
absolutely still, while the young princess worked
and did her best to soothe the dying mother's pains
and ease the last remaining moments of her life,
while her two children, crying silently,
kept equally perfectly still in mute despair.
The moment came when the afflicted patient
breathed her last. The princess had to finally give up
and tenderly embraced the orphaned children,
giving them the comfort of her sharing with them all their tears.
She then looked up at the observant and respectful sailor
as if she had known him all her life
and gave him unmistakably a sign
for him to help her cleaning up
and managing the ruined household.
He did never hesitate but did his best,
and so they worked together,
comforting the children, talking with the relatives,
preparing for the funeral and obsequies,
until she could breathe out as she had done her work.
She rose, the children were now taken care of by the relatives,
she moved towards the entrance, where the stranger stood
quite still, as he had done the whole time as if in devotion,

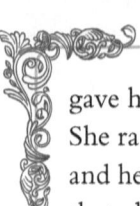

gave him but one glance, – and ran for it.
She ran away like an escaping deer,
and he took up the hunt –
that glance had told him far too much
not to be challenged.

10.

She ran like a stag, and she was a good runner,
so for all his excellent condition,
he had to put some effort into it,
while she remained far ahead of him
and he could but keep pace with her.
She ran all the way out of the village
and did not at all seem tired of it
as she finally made suddenly a halt
and turned around to meet her lover,
laughing heartily for a most natural welcome.
He could not believe his eyes.
There she was, the fairest princess in this world,
waiting for him, well outside the village,
in perfect safety and complete intimacy
with the most warm welcoming laughing welcome.
Checked, he hesitated for a moment,
but for just a fragment of a moment,
before he accepted her opening to him
and made the final and irrevocable advance.

11.

When they both were tired out
and rested in the shadows of the hiding palms,
she gently stroke his rich dark longish hair
that matched her own most perfectly
in shades of darkness with some dark blond streaks,
as his was growing also, as all hairs will ever do,
although not as far beneath his shoulders as did hers,
and told him intimately warm with tenderness:

"My father will cut off your head for this."
He read her thoughts and got her warning message,
as the worried tender eyes were not to be mistaken,
and he thought: "I would not have loved you for less."
They rested still, remaining in each others arms and harmony,
enjoying the relaxing peace and quiet after the exertion,
while they mixed each other's hairs
as a silent promise never to let them unmix again,
while he delighted in completely burying himself in hers,
unwilling ever to get out of her again.
At last she rose, as she felt ready,
and he knew the moment was at hand
of truth and confrontation.

12.

They walked together through the village
hand in hand, as natural as any lovers,
while the villagers who saw them did not mind at all
but took them as they were,
accepting them completely without reservations,
noticing at once that they were natural as lovers
and a most becoming pair at that:
they hardly could have matched each other better.
One or other aged villager perhaps looked down
with some foreboding afterthought,
like, "I sincerely hope this suitor finally will be the one,"
too well aware of the ordeal that was awaiting him.

Canto III

1.

"My love, I do not fear your father
although he be king and might cut off my head,
but I am sure he can't do that for love,
and my sincerest love of you
is of a greater power than of any king."
She did not understand him but the meaning
and took firmly hold of her protector's hand
and led him without hesitating
promptly to her father's home and royal hall.

2.

"I know it all already," said the king,
not in the least nonplussed by the young couple's boldness –
he had seen too many suitors to his daughter in his life
and seen them all end up as failures.

"Leave us, daughter. Your new suitor
and myself will have a chat together,
since he needs to be informed of what awaits him."
She had been through this procedure several times before,
so she did not object, just pressed her lover's hand a little
as a small but definite encouragement, and left.

3.

"My honoured guest, you know of course
the consequences of your importunity?"
"I love her. That is all," the sailor said,
"and I am willing to accept the whole responsibility."
"You don't have to. You may still be free
and leave our islands never to come back a living man."
"I would prefer to stay here as a living man and as your son-in-law."
"So you insist. My friend, I pity you,
for no one has proved worthy of my daughter,
nor will no one ever do so, since it is impossible."
"How so?" "So you are willing to go through the trial,
even well aware that it may cost your life?"
"Of course. Or else I would not love her.
Love alone will prove me worthy of her."
"I pity you the more. But since you are the friend
of my best friend the doctor, and he brought you here himself,
I shall make an exception for you. If you fail,
which you will naturally do like all the others,
I will let you leave our islands with my doctor
without execution, on condition that you never will return."
"I will not fail." "Not even with the utterly impossible?"
"Just try me, noble king, and I will risk whatever."

4.

Not even to himself the king could quite deny,
that he was just a little bit impressed
by this romantic stranger's stalwart courage,
and he wondered at his lack of hesitation

and did almost think: "How sad that he will not become my son-in-law."
Instead he said: "All right. You take it on yourself.
Just face the consequences, then. The trial is as follows.
You shall prove your love by accomplishing a ring
that proves love's sovereignty over any power.
You shall make that ring of gold but out of nothing,
and with that ring on my finger I shall manage
to have any wish that I might come to think of realized."
"A ring of gold to manifest whatever you may wish?"
"Precisely. Don't say it is possible. You are still free to pull out."
"And is that all?" "What do you mean?"
"The ring." "Of course that's all. What could there more be to it?
Of all wishes, that's the most impossible to ever have accomplished."
"Let me try at least." "Of course you may.
That's why I have presented you with the ordeal, for you to have a try."

5.

The sailor left the king's house deep in thought,
while the presumptuous king again just could not help
considering: "It would have been a splendid son-in-law in spite of all."
The sailor walked out of the village down to the lagoon
with lingering and thoughtful steps as the pacific afternoon
soon started glowing before sunset
turning everything to gold and rosy red.
He found the beach and beyond it a lonely rock
which matched his own predicament and loneliness completely,
wherefore he made his position there
and simply went into the deepest meditation
as the evening turned the universe all red
to quietly fade out like dying embers
for the metamorphosis into night.
When all the stars were kindled, lo,
there also rose the moon to join them all,
and by coincidence it happened to be full.
So there the man sat lonely and immovable
in meditation like a statue
while the moon transcended gloriously all brightness of the shining stars

and triumphed through the night
like really trying to inspire the unanswering man
who did not seem to pay the least attention
to the magic efforts of the moon, who started to decline
as morning gradually was to be introduced.
But then, just as the moon was lowering herself
to sink into the ocean with the brightness of the night,
the man just raised his hand with thumb and index
like to catch the last ray of the moon
and thereby shape something into the air;
and there it was, a golden ring, that hung like in a spider's thread
so delicately in the last ray of the moon;
and as that last ray finally was spent,
the morning rising and the moon resigning finally,
the man picked down the ring from that last ray
and held it in his hand, as if it could not be more obvious
that a golden ring had been accomplished in that fashion.
And then, as the sun presented her first morning beams,
the man at last rose from his meditation
with the ring committed in his hand
and started confidently to return back
to the village, to reality, to humankind and to his love.

6.

The king could also find no sleep this night
since all that he could think of was that blasted would-be son-in-law
whose failure would turn his daughter once again most miserable,
as if there had not been enough before of failed suitors.
In his sweat he rose quite early in the morning in despair
and thought: "Maybe for once I just should cancel my presumptions
and let love, my daughter and her suitor, have their way without objections?"
In that very moment, the young sailor entered through his door
and met the king without a word. The king looked questioningly at him.
Still without a word, the sailor left the ring
delivered safely in the king's own hand,
and all the king could do was just to look perplexed
and watch the sailor leave for other business,

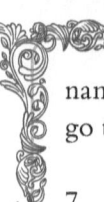

namely to at last now after a long night's hard work
go to his love and tenderly take care of her.

7.

The king looked at the ring and wondered at its marvel.
"Maybe he just had it in his luggage,
like a present from the doctor's own considerable store."
It therefore simply had to be a fake. To prove that fact,
the king decided to express a wish
but found it hard to wish for anything, since he had everything.
But then he had a bright idea:
The one thing he had lacked in life
was a good singing voice.
So that's what he decided on to wish.
He laughed at the idea, of course it was impossible
that he now after croaking all his life
should have a voice of quality,
but then his laughter struck him as melodious.
It was musical! He could sing!
The ring had worked! It actually had been accomplished!

8.

There was naturally then a splendid wedding
while the doctor still was present at Jagánde,
while the happy couple were content
to ever remain there at their pacific paradise
by the white beaches on the coral shores
with only beauty all around them
in the people and in nature and from all the sea
with blue and purple golden sunsets every day
with music singing them to sleep each night
by magic whisperings from ever rolling waves.
As doctor Magnus left without his steward,
music also followed his departure
as the people in three voices sang their praise
and thanks to him that had delivered to them
such a perfect lover for the perfect beauty of their princess.

Canto IV

1.

The king however felt misgivings at the power of the ring
and was afraid that it might one day be abused.
He never dared again to wish for anything
since that one wish had so astounded him by coming true.
To make it certain to exclude all possible abuse,
he went out to the far point of his island
where the river mouthed into the sea,
and there he flung the ring into the current,
hoping it would bring it out into the ocean
there to bury it forever.
But however there was one small fish
that saw the golden object glimmer in the water,
and just not to let it go, he simply caught it
in his mouth and wondered what to do with it.
"I know!" he thought. "I shall deliver it
as present to the fairest of all mermaids,
to the ocean king's own daughter I shall give it
as a humble token of my even humbler adoration."

2.

But it was no easy quest our little fish
had found to his commitment, for the sea was vast
encompassing the entire globe,
and the sweet mermaid lived in its profoundest depths
far from the ordinary streams and currents,
but our fish knew how to seek her out.
There was a special natural phenomenon
deep down in the remotest South Atlantic
where the storms make traffic sparse,
and where the billows are notorious for their devastating size,
a whirlpool coming from the bottom of the sea
as the unique accessibility and entrance to the sea-king's dwelling-place,
where also our fairest mermaid had her premises.
Our fish sought out the outskirts of the whirlpool
and allowed himself to follow and get caught therein;
and so he soon was on his way down to the bottom of the sea
where lights increase the further down you get,
the whirlpool being constantly illuminated by the brightest plankton
and the smallest living beings carrying their own light.

3.

Thus gradually the fish was willingly dragged down
into the slowly brightening profoundest abyss
of the South Atlantic where the sea king had his palace.
He had visited the mermaid princess once before,
so he knew well his ways into the royal virgin chamber
where the princess at the moment was quite busy
combing out her long and flowing greenish silken hair.
"My fish! You have returned!" she cried for joy
as she immediately did recognize the small but friendly fish.
"My princess, yes, and with a mission, for I have a present for you."
And the fish delivered what he so by chance had found.
She took it up and marvelled at its perfect rounded form.
There never was a circle made so perfect as this ring,

and she did greatly wonder as to how it had been made
and could not guess, of course, that it had once been shaped
from the last ray of a full moon at morning at its very fullest.

4.

She could not in any other way show her enormous gratitude
than by indulging in a kiss between the eyes of the small fish,
which made him blush considerably.
Never had he been so overwhelmed by such a royal grace.
He swam away beatified, while she had put the ring
upon her finger and resumed her combing;
but of course, like combs so often do, it suddenly got stuck
in that rich hair of hers, and she lost all her patience.
"Useless comb! I wish I had one that would never more get stuck!"
And suddenly there was another comb beside her.
"Where did that come from?" she thought and used it,
and it pleased her greatly by not getting stuck at all,
which made her wonder even more.

5.

As the days passed, she now and then again was taken by surprise
by the alarming fact that her small petty wishes suddenly came true,
and she began to think about how this phenomenon had started.
She remembered well the visit of her small admirer the fish
and tried for luck the innocent experiment
of daring to express a wish without the ring upon her finger.
Nothing happened. She again tried that experiment,
without and with the ring alternately,
and thus, empirically, she found out the secret of the ring.
"This goes beyond me and my limited capacity," she thought
and went with this new worrying problem to her father.
She explained it all to him, he shook his head and couldn't quite believe it,
but she proved the fact to him, which turned him serious.

6.

"My daughter," finally the sea king said,
"this gift from out of nowhere, from a small red herring,
offers us a terrible responsibility,
and we shall have no choice but to apply it well."
She nodded, since her train of thoughts had been the same.
"You know, that all our oceans with all wildlife
seriously are threatened by the recklessness of man.
Our entire world is being poisoned and polluted
by his ignorance and self-indulgent carelessness,
as if he was alone and easily could do alone
without all nature and without all other forms of life,
forgetting that he is dependent on the echo systems
and that they will work and flow without disturbance,
keeping naturally the whole planet clean,
while he alone keeps ruining it with dirt and rubbish.
Several of our rarest species have already been exterminated
by his carelessness and egoistic folly.
Let us do something about it, since we here now have the means."

7.

She instantly caught on and was completely with him.
Thus they went together for the strangest quest
abandoning the safety of their royal palace
at the bottom of the South Atlantic
to embark upon a journey that would last for all their lives,
preserving natural resources everywhere, restoring paradises,
saving species and creating safe environments,
protection areas and wildlife havens
inaccessible to man, the all invading monster,
for the preservation and protection of all kinds of life.

8.

The very last thing they created was this forest,
where they left the ring right at the heart of it

where these two brooks together join to form a junction
and a little island by it, at the bottom of a tiny whirlpool,
where it has been lying undisturbed and unused all since then;
but still its power secretly invisibly pervades the entire forest,
the effect of which is that impurity can not exist here.
Everyone who enters is completely purefied in soul and body
in a natural etheric process, which no one can fail to be affected by
most positiviely, which of course you felt yourself.

9.

When thus they had accomplished their life's work,
the saving of the planet and all wildlife with all nature,
they gave up their earthly sealife and were taken up
to join the spirits of the air, in which community
they still are active even more invisibly
and even more inspiringly constructively
than when they worked concretely physically present
here on earth among us, but we shall not know for certain
how they go on working spiritually
until we one day perhaps will join them."
Thus completed Gabriel his story.

Canto V

1.

The Dane who found the shipwrecked Celia on the shore
deserted naked in the wreck of what had been a lifeboat
was a humble man of gentle disposition with the name of Isak.
As she gradually recovered, he learnt all about her story –
that she had forgotten it completely and had none to tell,
except that there was something she had lost that had to be recovered.
Isak was intrigued by her mysterious case and, just like Joseph,
would do anything to help her. She felt not at home in Denmark,
Scandinavia was too cold and slow in mind for her,
so she believed she had to search the continent for what she needed.
Thus their strange odyssey started, that would take them
through a number of exotic and romantic countries.

2.

They wandered through all Germany down to the Boden Sea
where for some time they lingered in the beautiful surroundings
until she was certain there was nothing for her there to find.
They walked on eastwards and finally arrived in Vienna.
There she found herself in spirit slightly liberated by the fact
that Vienna was a capital of music,
talented composers being active everywhere,
especially a small man wearing spectacles
who was distressed and driven to despair
by some dilettante orchestra that could not get his music right,
no matter how much he rehearsed and tried again,
as if the music was too beautiful to be made justice,
It was something of a ballet opera called "Rosamunde".

3.

There was also a most jovial composer
with a most impressing beard with pea soup in it
playing hard at cards with an eccentric colleague
with a most unpractical moustachio,
if he was to drink whatever or eat soup.
It was, as it was said, the waltz king and the king of symphony.
But Vienna was not theirs for anything to find
in spite of all the splendid music,
so they just moved on, passed Graz and into Italy.

4.

In Venice they were asked to pose as models
for a picture by an aged master, who found something
very striking in the homeless searching pair.
He boasted he was almost ninety-nine years old
and active as a painter still, although his eyesight
gave him problems and he used his hands instead of brushes.
There was also an American, a bearded melancholy fellow
from Key West who seemed quite sentimental;

but in Venice, as in Vienna, they found nothing.
So they just continued south as far as Sicily,
returned from there to take a ship to Greece,
which Celia loved and felt at home in,
but still nothing was recovered.
They continued into Turkey, Syria and Israel
but there decided to return to Europe.

5.

David found their trace in Danish Esbjerg,
and from there he tracked them down through Germany
and Austria to Italy and Greece,
but there he lost their trail.

6.

He still keeps searching for them
somewhere on the European continent
and mainly around the Mediterranean,
and he is quite certain that he ultimately
once will bring them back again.
The sad thing is, that they have never found their way,
in spite of all their wanderings, back home to England
and not even into France, but keep on wandering
and searching constantly but in the wrong direction.
If my mother, when she woke up in the ditch,
had just sought shelter in the nearest forest,
I am sure she would have instantly been saved;
but she instead went searching constantly astray,
as if the merest effort of her search was a blind alley.

7.

David now and then came back,
but each time after an extended search
and longer journey, so the periods he was gone
grew longer every time. Now he has not been back

for seven years, and when the fourth year came,
my last friend Manuel here set out to help him.

8.

Daniel is lost forever, there is no hope of his reappearance
after sixteen years by now, and who knows where my father is.
And finally there was a stranger coming here, and it was you,
a lovable and humble monk with, I regret to say,
the worst news possible of Manuel's death.
I'm sure he aimed at coming back here with some news,
but what that news was we shall never know.
And out there somewhere, David, my good father, keeps on searching
for his love, my mother Celia, who with Isak
keeps on wandering all over Europe, maybe also Asia,
for the search of what she never can recover.
I have given up all hope now after sixteen years
and am content with just remaining here
as something of a hermit and preserving all their memories,
the memory of her and what she lost,
and keeping up their homes in case of their return,
maybe after another ten or fifteen years.

9.

The last thing David told me just before he left last time
was something strange about my mother.
When she last was seen in Israel ten years ago
she was still young and fresh without a trace of age,
as if her tragedy had fixed her in unchanging youth,
still blonde with very long and golden hair
and with no wrinkle and not even crow's feet
in the corners of her eyes; and Isak also has remained
as young as he was when he found her.
Her mysterious age has halted up, it sems,
and according to a sage and rabbi in Jerusalem,
they will continue staying young unchanged
as long as they continue on their search –
another case of Ahasverus but of opposite characteristics."

Canto VI

1.

The Dane who found the shipwrecked Celia on the shore
deserted naked in the wreck of what had been a lifeboat
was a humble man of gentle disposition with the name of Isak.
As she gradually recovered, he learnt all about her story –
that she had forgotten it completely and had none to tell,
except that there was something she had lost that had to be recovered.
Isak was intrigued by her mysterious case and, just like Joseph,
would do anything to help her. She felt not at home in Denmark,
Scandinavia was too cold and slow in mind for her,
so she believed she had to search the continent for what she needed.
Thus their strange odyssey started, that would take them
through a number of exotic and romantic countries.

2.

They wandered through all Germany down to the Boden Sea
where for some time they lingered in the beautiful surroundings
until she was certain there was nothing for her there to find.

They walked on eastwards and finally arrived in Vienna.
There she found herself in spirit slightly liberated by the fact
that Vienna was a capital of music,
talented composers being active everywhere,
especially a small man wearing spectacles
who was distressed and driven to despair
by some dilettante orchestra that could not get his music right,
no matter how much he rehearsed and tried again,
as if the music was too beautiful to be made justice,
It was something of a ballet opera called "Rosamunde".

3.

There was also a most jovial composer
with a most impressing beard with pea soup in it
playing hard at cards with an eccentric colleague
with a most unpractical moustachio,
if he was to drink whatever or eat soup.
It was, as it was said, the waltz king and the king of symphony.
But Vienna was not theirs for anything to find
in spite of all the splendid music,
so they just moved on, passed Graz and into Italy.

4.

In Venice they were asked to pose as models
for a picture by an aged master, who found something
very striking in the homeless searching pair.
He boasted he was almost ninety-nine years old
and active as a painter still, although his eyesight
gave him problems and he used his hands instead of brushes.
There was also an American, a bearded melancholy fellow
from Key West who seemed quite sentimental;
but in Venice, as in Vienna, they found nothing.
So they just continued south as far as Sicily,
returned from there to take a ship to Greece,
which Celia loved and felt at home in,
but still nothing was recovered.

They continued into Turkey, Syria and Israel
but there decided to return to Europe.

5.

David found their trace in Danish Esbjerg,
and from there he tracked them down through Germany
and Austria to Italy and Greece,
but there he lost their trail.

6.

He still keeps searching for them
somewhere on the European continent
and mainly around the Mediterranean,
and he is quite certain that he ultimately
once will bring them back again.
The sad thing is, that they have never found their way,
in spite of all their wanderings, back home to England
and not even into France, but keep on wandering
and searching constantly but in the wrong direction.
If my mother, when she woke up in the ditch,
had just sought shelter in the nearest forest,
I am sure she would have instantly been saved;
but she instead went searching constantly astray,
as if the merest effort of her search was a blind alley.

7.

David now and then came back,
but each time after an extended search
and longer journey, so the periods he was gone
grew longer every time. Now he has not been back
for seven years, and when the fourth year came,
my last friend Manuel here set out to help him.

8.

Daniel is lost forever, there is no hope of his reappearance
after sixteen years by now, and who knows where my father is.
And finally there was a stranger coming here, and it was you,
a lovable and humble monk with, I regret to say,
the worst news possible of Manuel's death.
I'm sure he aimed at coming back here with some news,
but what that news was we shall never know.
And out there somewhere, David, my good father, keeps on searching
for his love, my mother Celia, who with Isak
keeps on wandering all over Europe, maybe also Asia,
for the search of what she never can recover.
I have given up all hope now after sixteen years
and am content with just remaining here
as something of a hermit and preserving all their memories,
the memory of her and what she lost,
and keeping up their homes in case of their return,
maybe after another ten or fifteen years.

9.

The last thing David told me just before he left last time
was something strange about my mother.
When she last was seen in Israel ten years ago
she was still young and fresh without a trace of age,
as if her tragedy had fixed her in unchanging youth,
still blonde with very long and golden hair
and with no wrinkle and not even crow's feet
in the corners of her eyes; and Isak also has remained
as young as he was when he found her.
Her mysterious age has halted up, it sems,
and according to a sage and rabbi in Jerusalem,
they will continue staying young unchanged
as long as they continue on their search –
another case of Ahasverus but of opposite characteristics."

Canto VII

1.

Thus concluded Gabriel his story.
Malcolm looked at him aghast with admiration
and compassion, turbulent mixed feelings
but was more impressed than he had ever been,
especially by Gabriel's personality,
which seemed serenity itself in perfect harmony
and consummation of maturity and beauty
all embalmed in this fair youth of timeless charm.
"If you are like your mother," Malcolm finally commented,
"then indeed she must be the most beautiful of ladies in the world."
"I take it as a compliment," said Gabriel,
"not to myself but to my mother."

2.

Gabriel invited Malcolm to remain, of course,
as long as he desired, and the monk was glad to do so

for some days at least. He spent the days in Gabriel's company
in long discussions, spiritual conversations
and hard work in the organic gardens
with some necessary updating repairs on the three cottages.
For years, and taught by Manuel, Gabriel had kept it up
all by himself but was now glad to have some help.

3.

But finally the hour was come for Malcolm to depart.
"I would not want my abbot to start worrying,
and surely he expects me back with some anxiety,
and so do many others." Gabriel agreed.
"Of course you must return and tell the others
of our sanctuary here and of its story,
whether they can manage to believe it or will disregard it,
but this place exists, which no one can deny,
and I am here to verify it.
Naturally, I expect you back."
"I know the way and can not miss it,"
answered Malcolm, and they were agreed.

4.

And then it came to pass, that Malcolm left the forest.
The same day, he made it down to Winchester
and found the bishop there, his cousin
cordially expecting him with an enormous dinner.
Malcolm entertained him all the evening with his story,
and the bishop laughed his sides off
better every time he started a new round of laughter
that shook all the vestry and all Winchester to its foundations.

5.

Just a few days afterwards, the monk came back to Devon
and found on a rosy morning his beloved abbot
in his garden tending to his roses.

"Well, my friend," the abbot said most naturally calm,
"what did you find? And what did you expect to find?
Don't tell me you were disappointed."
"On the contrary, my father, I found much more
than I ever could expect. I found a forest."
"Tell me what you mean," the abbot said,
and he was mighty serious. Malcolm had no choice
but to relate the entire story from beginning to the end
without omitting any details.

6.

Afterwards the abbot kept his silence
for a long while thinking deep and thoroughly digesting
Malcolm's strange account, as if to ponder
whether he could take it seriously or as a fake.
At last the abbot spoke but without raising his grave looks.
"My friend," he said, "this verifies what I believed in always.
You have found a forest, but it's not unique.
Each forest in the world is no less sacred
than the one that destiny has led your footsteps to.
In ancient days we worshipped every tree,
especially the oaken ones, because they were the oldest,
therefore the most venerable of all life manifestations.
Every kind of life is sacred, and not just your forest,
although it may be the very ultimate unalienable evidence
of the eternal sanctity of every kind of life."

7.

And thus the forest soon became a place of pilgrimage
and worship. One of the three houses, Manuel's,
the first one, was transformed into a chapel,
and our brother Malcolm was bequeathed with
the responsibility of taking care of it.
As monk in charge thereof, he spent more time
with Gabriel in the forest than at his own monastery.

8.

Once a wayward wanderer came back from far abroad.
It actually was David, who had found a trace
of Celia and Isak far away in Persia and India.
That's where he was heading next.
He could not stay, he said, for more than a few days
but was impressed and enthusiastic
about what the monks had done to cultivate the forest,
raising it to a more sacred status than it had before
and making it a busy place for pilgrimage.

9.

And thus the story ends. We know not whether David
finally succeeded in his quest for bringing Celia and Isak home,
but there is always hope he did, although it can't be verified.

The End.

Manali, September 2nd, 2008.

Powerful Invisibility

As if thou were invisible
your presence is as palpable
as if you really were inside me
although I can't see you
in the opaque midnight darkness
although the full moon is bright and shining
without penetrating the obscure corners
of where you and I make love together.
Maybe your invisibility
just adds to the enchantment
of your extraordinary presence
almost supernaturally in the haze of darkness
like the finest spice on top of the supreme deliciousness,
and thus your nakedness is hidden

in the veils of splendid midnight darkness,
making it the more enjoyable
in its unreachable but total presence.
Is it possible for love to be more perfect
in more total ambiguity, intrigue and mystery?

The Indifference Syndrome

– *the fact that no one cares*

The murderous indifference
kills you slowly piece by piece
of your mentality and soul
by draining you of your enthusiasm and energy,
confining you to isolation of yourself,
and the worst thing is there's northing you can do about it
but continue working, loving, carrying on
in spite of all. But actually there is one remedy.
Forget yourself. Instead remember,
that you are in soul a part of all the living universe,
in which community each living soul is part,

none more or less than any other,
which implies that you can never be alone
and that the only thing worth living for
is actually that universal infinite community,
that is, all others but yourself,
or, putting it in other words,
to live for others is the only way to make it worth while living,
it's the only meaning of your life,
the only meaning that can actually be found,
for only living for the soul can be awarding and expanding,
and in finding the community of other souls
alone, you'll ultimately find your own.

The Eloquence of Silence

Most people talk too much
and say the less the more they say,
as if they had to compensate
by any means their emptiness
by filling it with torrents out of nothing,

while the unknown thoughts of any quiet person
are extremely interesting
for not being anyhow expressed,
that silence being so expressive
and expressing so much more than any words.
In the same way, the more noise music makes,
the less enjoyable it is as music,
while there is no music like the one you find in silence.
Maybe I have said too much,
so I had better hold my tongue for better silence.

Drowning

Lost in love, it's worse than being shipwrecked,
given over to the fury of the ocean,
drowning in the beauty of your hair
and getting lost in it,
like in a haze and maze,
caught in a web with no way out,
and yet I can't regret it:
all those overwhelming memories
of that supremacy of beauty and enjoyment
will remain alive in me forever
although I was burnt out in the bargain.
Come again, my love,
and we will start anew;
whenever you feel ready
I will also be at hand,
enjoying to get lost and drowned
to burn ourselves completely out again.

Hollowness

For each loved friend you lose
you stifle slightly more by all that hollowness
increasing in the darkest emptiness
remaining in the soul like a disease
for all those irreplaceable relationships
that have been lost forever
while at the same time you never can forget them.
Can it comfort them,
that they in that way still go on,
remaining present and alive in limbo memories?
That uncertainty you'll have to live with,
but if it in any way could comfort them,
if they can feel that you are missing them,

it still remains to you the poorest of all comforts,
since it only can increase and deepen
all that emptiness and hollowness
and terrible incurability of longing for them.

The Past is Past

The past is past,
and although it remains
as fogs that cloud the day
unwilling to depart and lift
as memories that can't leave you in peace,
we have to go ahead into the unknown future
facing its uncertainty and difficulties
with its changes for the good or worse,
and never stop to get bogged down
in all that 'what it could have been like'.
History is history and hopelessly
but safely at a distance,

while the present is completely different
and must needs be handled now,
although the realism that it demands
might not be very nice and beautiful
but must needs be revolting
and repelling in its shocking
overwhelming presence,
like a most unwelcome guest
that keeps intruding ever and again.
What can we do but entertain him?

The Party is Over

No, not quite as yet,
there might be shortcomings and hangovers,
there might be some abruptions,
something wrong that wrecks the gears,
some sabotage and sand or mud
in the machine or in your eyes,
but let the show go on,
and let the party start anew;
when wrecked aside, marooned

and thrown off every saddle,
there is still some party going on
or starting somewhere else,
and it would be a pity
not to be there and to miss it.

The Poetical Over-Sensitivity

Moody poets are most volatile and unpredictable,
they are complained of for their lack of continuity,
that you can never trust them,
that their constant roller-coaster causes trouble
and imperil not relationships alone but even lives,
and so the irritation of the growing avalanche goes on.
The problem is, however, not the poet
but poetic over-sensitivity.
It's creativity that is too sensible
and can't endure the smallest pea under the mattresses,
the soul wide open carried on the arm,
exposed and vulnerable much more than the body
to all those who can't imagine how it feels and hurts
in our society where empathy is vanishing,
the first and gravest sign of total human bankruptcy.
With this I only wish to have it properly expressed,
take care of over-sensitivity,
since it is invaluable,
being creativity itself,
it feels and senses what most people fail to see,
it is the future and the key to timelessness,
and it is the only thing that matters,
when it comes to poetry.

Desperation

Let me be free, or let me die,
but let me cry my love out in your arms first,
more than well aware that it might be forever,
all that grief and desperation being without end,
like all the human tears that constitute
the oceans of the world,
and more than well aware
that you can't hold me in your arms
not even for the briefest moment,
love escaping us in fickle flight
to never really let herself be caught
but showing any presence only to abscond
to ever lure us into traps
and fool us hopelessly astray.
Alas, my desperation is without an end,
because so is my love.

The Pain of Life

– the eternal love story

Just let it hurt
and cry against it,
do not fight it,
but forget it,
for it just means nothing,
all those heart-aches, broken hearts
and wounded souls that never heal,
the bitter wounds that ruined all your life,
those rapes and losses that can never be repaired,
those violations that forever cloud your life,
it's all but shallowness and dust,
and whosoever might abandon you and let you down,
destroy you, ruin you and kill you,

someone will be always there
for you to love,
remaining and surviving,
maybe even waiting just for you.

The Sillification Society

You must be happy all the time,
eat a lot of junk food only, hamburgers and candy,
sugar pies and lots of pastry, coke and pepsi
and watch television every night at least five hours,
never go by bike or walk but only take your car,
and only read the yellow press and comics,
never pass a bar without a drinking bout,
since alcohol is only good for you,
like coffee, booze and cigarettes,
and if you suffer any pain somewhere,
the only remedy is medication,
you can never take too many pills,
and if you claim that you are well
there must be something wrong with you,
so you had better get examined –
there is always something wrong,
and doctors merely exist to give you ordinations –
the more expensive medicines you are allowed to take,
the more you must be grateful,
for all the junk food, all the smart soap operas,
where you don't have to laugh yourself,
since playback choruses will do it for you
just to show you where you have to laugh;
for all the noisy screaming music everywhere
that you so much enjoy in every public place
and would prefer to have on constantly
to cure your tinnitus and deafness with
by ever boosting up the volume;
and for all the wholesomely benumbing medicines,
which do you so much good for your increasing fatness,
sloth and comfortable laziness and dumbness,

since you less and less need any more to think yourself,
which also makes you sleep so much the better
and the longer, so that one day even
you don't have to wake up any more.
And just in case all this would not be good enough,
there always is the bliss of drugs.

Drunk With You

Immersed in peril
by your presence,
I can not get out of you,
and it's worse than just a hangover,
impossible to get the intoxication
out of my head,
but it just goes rolling on,
like some merry-go-round out of order
that can never more be stopped
but has to ride forever
at an ever increasing speed.
So let it just go on,
and let me love you in my drunkenness,
that folly being at least entertaining
and at best amusing,
if with some mixed feelings within me,
at least with compliments to you.

Bloody History

— The truest account of history would be the account of all its victims.

The tears of blood that history consists of
do not show in all those phoney pages
trying to depict and document the truth
in constant absolute deplorable pathetic failure,
for the floods of blood of innocents
is the real history that never can be written,
being so immeasurably overwhelming
and defying any effort of expression
in its neverending tragedy.
If all that blood could speak
it would be just an accusation and denouncement
not of God but of humanity,
that never has been held accountable
for all the crimes of history committed only by themselves.
For all their silence, all those innocents will speak forever
and the more resoundingly for all their silence.

Desire

The music streaming in your hair
fills me with rapture everlasting,
while to touch it would destroy me,
shatter me into an earthquake
leaving me in ruins torn apart,
and still I never can't stop longing
for that devastating demolition
that can only transport me with glory
from a worm into a butterfly
with stronger wings than any eagle,
or at least so would they feel.
Embalm me in your wings, my angel,
and let me get lost and buried in your hair,
and I shall die content,
enjoying every moment of it
to extend that death's desire
to a never-ending masochistic bliss.

Is Love Possible?

For years we have remained the best of friends,
I loved you always, but there were too many men
besieging you and standing in my way,
so I resigned and let it be –
love is a higher thing than worth the opposite,
no conflicts between rivals having anything to do with love.
I was the victim of my own fate
and had long ago accepted it –
one could say, I was long since married to it, –
while during the years, love and affection have grown stronger
in maturity and depth,
and thus increasing both in beauty and in value.
Let it thus continue,
and in some way, although we were not united ever,
neither were we ever separated.

Lost Losses

– the crisis of folly

When I wander all alone among the ruins
drowning in the melancholy of a desperation
that could hardly be more utterly supreme,
the final comfort and solution to your troubles
seems to be the peace and calm of death,
and you are ready to give up all that
which wasn't lost already;
and then suddenly
a voice is heard among the ruins
calling your attention to reality,
the real reality, not all the bankruptcies
and phoney mundane crises of materialism,
but love alone, its beauty and self-confidence
remaining as inviolable, unassailable and sovereign as ever,
and your friend with kindness tells you softly:
"All your tears are gold to me,
for they remind me that I'm needed
if for nothing else, then for your comfort,
since my love exists alone
for keeping you alive
and keeping up our universal love together,
which is something that you never can give up.
Forgive me for reminding you."
And suddenly all love was gloriously rekindled,
in comparison with which all worldly troubles
vanished beyond the horizon, lost forever,
since there is but one reality:
the love that liveth.

Real Relativity

How come your beauty never wanes
but keeps on just increasing
not just year by year but day by day,
as if love was so relative a thing
that it could go on growing
in delight and charm and fascination
and expanding infinitely,
in gross contrast to the markets?
I am just thrilled, intrigued
and stunned by this phenomenon
and can have no objection –

if it's so, then let it just continue,
I will follow as your lover
even at the highest speed
and flinch at no acceleration,
being faithfulness itself
and never giving up my love
wherever beyond any measures
you may take me.

Show Me the Way

Show me the way, my love,
and I will follow enthusiastically
leaving everything behind me
that is incompatible with your beauty
and the path of your incomparability,
that ever set me straight
by the idealism of your silence
so expressive of a higher truth
than any words or revelation can engender,
which I gladly follow blindly
seeing more and clearer second-sightedly
by trusting your infallible clairvoyance
that as yet did never fail me

but invariably kept me safe on course
to follow you on the condition
so intriguing in its irresistibility
that I would never reach or catch you.
Keep me going, and I shall be happy
and content enough to carry on
as long as you are there to be my love.

The Piano is Still There

Who silenced you, old music treasure,
spreader of such warmth and mirth?
Who put an end to living music
to replace it with but noise and junk box nonsense,
yelling concerts and the soaps of television?
Shall we never hear again the natural pure music

that is live and soft, melodious and musical?
I am afraid the evil goes much deeper.
Already when the first world war raged,
both poetry and music almost died,
gone to flowers in the trenches
and replaced with shell shocks
and the coming age of noise,
that in the 30's overwhelmed the world
with the brutality of ugliness, autocracy and war,
sterility of cold materialism, functionalism and inhumanity
that killed off beauty and imagination in the arts
that all degenerated into modernistic nonsense.
Still it's not too late.
We can shut off the telly nonsense,
we can do without the world of grim sillification,
and all that the piano needs is someone
to sit down and play.

Diamond Love

The mystery of our love
is like a secret garden,
always there and thriving
but in secret, hidden from all public sight,
like some virginity that can't be touched
but must be safeguarded and well
not to be trodden on by ignorance and strangers.
Still it is, we always were humiliated
but still always rose again
like every garden after every winter,
and by every resurrection
our garden has outshone them all
in lasting purity of matchless beauty
like a diamond that ever grows more harder
and more valuable the more deep and harder
it is pressed in darkness and in secrecy.

Our Secret Spring

What keeps us young and fresh and innocent
in spite of all ordeals and tragedies?
Is it our diligence at work or love?
I think it's something more abstruse and subtle
and would simply call it our idealism
which can't succumb to bulldozer attacks
no matter how much it is overrun.
That headline stands for all our secrets:
that unflinching optimism that can't be beaten down
and all that enthusiastic workoholic energy
which just increases by its overstrain.
Love is our rest from all those battlefields,
and with the years we need it more and more;
so let us make that finally our happy end.

The Old Fiddler

Everywhere he carried it around with him,
and never he was seen without it,
that old violin box,
and never any violin was seen with him,
so it was doubted that the case contained a violin.
'The Violin Man' became a legend
for the invisible violin
and the most visible case, that never left his side,
which he would never open on request.
Of course it roused a universal curiosity.
Was there a violin or not
in that so jealously protected case?
One day in a small café,
that old man was sitting there with his old violin case
as there was a small group of school-girls entering.
They saw the old man and, of course,
immediately started to discuss the problem
of the secret of what that old violin case contained.
One girl, not more than fifteen, said,

"Why don't we just go up and ask him?"
No one would, so she did.
She went up to him and asked:
"Is that a violin you have?"
The old man answered: "Can you doubt it?",
opened up the case and took his violin out from there
and started tenderly to play
old Vienna waltzes, evergreens and sentimental melodies,
until there entered other people, grown-ups,
growing soon into an audience.
Then he felt abashed and locked his violin up again,
was overcome with shyness, rose and left.
After he had gone, a doubtful grown-up asked the nearest girl,
who happened to be just the girl
who had achieved the wonder of releasing the old fiddler's secret:
"Was there actually a violin in the old beggar's case?"
The girl said: "No, sir, there was nothing in that case
except his soul. We saw it, but you didn't,
so he left."

The Forlorn Lover in Her Absence

Without you my life would be but hollowness
of infinite despair, frustration, desolation and defeat,
while no one else can substitute your absence
felt as strongly as the lack of water in the desert,
since the only one who can be you is you.
Marooned and shipwrecked on a desert island
without water, trees or any trace of life.
I miss you more than any fish bereft of water
or of any bird confined in cage with wings cut off
could miss their freedom and ability to live.
But all the same, you are still there
and waiting like myself for the next moment
of our reunification ecstasy and splendour,
which we both are sure that will come back
to join us once again in bliss and glory
to at one time finally at last
remain and not get lost
with our hearts united and rejoined
once and forever.

On Visiting the Dead

Occasionally, they actually enjoy our visits.
We are always welcome
to for some occasion share their bleak existence
showing empathy for their outrageous state
in hopeless limbo without light,
and it gives us some distance and relief
from this our even more infected world –
theirs is at least most clinically clean,
all damaging corruption having died,
while they at least have all eternity secured for them.
So take a ride once in a while,
enjoy your trip to neverneverland
and see how old folks still are going strong
in after-life with a good riddance to us all
72
who did our best to make a mess
not just of their lives but of our own as well.

Love, by Tsoltim N. Shakabpa

– I beg to forward this beautiful poem by a friend of mine, since it well deserves any variety of readers...

Love is appreciating God when life seems hopeless
It's becoming a vegetarian to save animals
Planting a tree on a parched earth
Saving an animal in distress
Nursing an ailing person

Love is blowing away a mosquito on your arm instead of killing it
It's extracting a thorn from a weeping child's hand
Giving alms to a wretched beggar on the street
Being a seeing eye dog for a blind person
Denying a cigarette to a loved one

Love is being magnetized by someone's beauty and brain
It's healing the wounds in a broken heart
Suckling a new born baby in your arms
Sharing a bed and dreams in old age
Placing a rose on a coffin

Love is giving up a princely kingdom to save mankind
It's respecting race, color, creed and national origin
Pinching pennies for a worthy cause
Giving one's life to God and country
Remembering a freedom fighter

Love is all of the above and more
It's pure and compassionate
Simple but limitless
It's what we all want
What we all must practice

Copyright ©Tsoltim N. Shakabpa - 2008

Some Confession

– from a letter to a friend

It all comes down to your own heart –
if you are not at peace
and can't find harmony within yourself,
you shall be out of place wherever
your embarrassed escapism may take you –
there is nothing wrong in all the universe
except the cobwebs in your own heart to be swept away.
If you let out your heart and harmonize your soul,
you can make any universe or temporal environment
all right and all your own.
Although this place is rotten
and I am completely without future here
and lack most things including what I need,
I would not leave it, not because of work or social life,

but only because destiny has placed me here.
If I got rich and famous, I would still remain here
to associate with all those poor displaced folk here around me,
maybe travel somewhat more to Greece and Italy
but still maintain my humble life and basis here,
since there's no reason why I shouldn't.
It is probably my life with music
which in spite of all its neverending challenges,
frustrations and adversities has made me capable
of turning any kind of life to something positive
for both myself and others. Since I can continue here
with music smoothly, it would do no good to anyone
if I abandoned it for something more uncertain.
That's how I feel. My life is small and humble,
but it's safe and keeps me well content enough,
so let me just work on
to thus continuously at least keep up my love.

To an Absent Friend

Your presence in your absence
is as palpable and shining still
as ever the eternal sun beyond the clouds
that ne'ertheless gives daylight every day.
How can one miss you
when you are so omnipresent?
There's no surer way of getting home
than going for a journey,
for there's but one aim of every journey,
which is to get back to the beginning.
All life is a journey
filled with longing to get through with it,
but all we long for is for home,
back to where we all came from,
a nostalgia for the mother's womb of life
which we do actually all have in common.
So, my friend, you are not gone
but merely on your way back home.

Incurable Idealists

That's us and proud of it,
inveterate as workoholics,
poor in everything except imagination,
hopelessly unpractical but wise
with spiritual insight
and never to be fooled
by a society of phoney carpetbaggers,
experts most of all at wasting other people's money,
so we are perhaps more fortunate without
and always having something good to live for.
Although we are just a happy few,
we couldn't be in better company,
and most and best of all:
unlike all slaves of this society of bleak delusions,
with idealism as some incurable disease,
we never are alone.

Partying Philosophy

Partying hard in splendid company
is fun as long as it goes on,
but you had better not think of the following,
the consequences, life after the blackout,
when you wake up to a blinding morning
with outrageous sunshine
to accompany the blacksmiths in your head;
so better keep it on,
the partying, until you can end up
totally unconscious in your bed
at best, or on the floor, at worst,
in someone's vomit.
Anyway, it's fun in the beginning,
and since it's so enjoyable indeed,
at least in the beginning,
why then bother in advance
about the afterthoughts?

You Can't Stop Hearing It

– a general complaint

Leave me in peace
from all the noise and hubbub
of this worldly life of nonsense
giving only pain to ears and brains
for all its stress and horrible exertion
all for nothing, making nothing but a nuisance.
Where has all the quietness been banished
with all natural and healthy life
that always was relaxed?
We'll nevermore see that again
as long as civilization is transformed
from something thoroughly creative
to a world of noise pollution

brainwashing humanity
away from everything
that once was good for both humanity and nature.
Ears can not be stopped,
and since the closing of your eyes
can't hide away the noise
of brawls from loudspeakers and microphones
wherever you get lost in civilization,
it simply has to be most radically remedied,
or civilization and humanity will perish,
drowning in the brainwash stress of noise
that is the opposite to charitable music.

The One Worth While and Supreme Addiction

How could I else than love you
being so outrageously romantic
to the utterly extremest irresistibility
to naturally endless faithfulness
to stay bewitched by you forever,
taken into custody by love
to stay there willingly and endlessly
in bliss and healthiest intoxication?
There is only one addiction
that is health itself, to be in love,
which everyone should always fall to
and remain as slaves to in interminable gratitude
for their own good and for the best of health;
for love is singular in its capacity
for being the one slavery
that leads alone to freedom.

![Alice Pini]

Cloudburst

– riding the storm

The skies were filled with formidable clouds
that burst in reckless fury
wreaking chaos, havoc and disaster
all around in hopeless desperation
constantly increasing the horrendous darkness
that seemed thicker every day
with thunderstorms and heavy rains

that flooded all that was considered safe
and ruined almost everyone
in this abysmal cataclysm and horror.
What is to be done about it?
Close your eyes, escape to heavy drinking,
party recklessly just to forget
or go abroad in exile
hoping for the storm to pass
and hoping for the world
to still be there as we return?
All we can do is long for
that eventual opening that must arrive
which will let in the sun again.
That's all we know for certain,
that the sun one day inevitably must return.

Great Expectations

(received the news in the Kumaon Himalayas)

The moment of triumph is here
bringing great expectations.
It's still not too late to wish all wars to end
and to some better order to this troubled world
so grossly mishandled by crooks and impostors
that ever turned history to a most ruthless
and thoughtless rumbustious bulldozer.
All countries are ruined at least to some part
by the reckless irresponsibility of warring lords
acting first, shooting blindly and afterwards
bleak-minded by their mistakes.
Anything would be better than what we've been through,
so it's not wrong to have expectations
since any change must bring improvement.
Let's hope also for some enlightenment
and some good sense for a change;
so I welcome you heartily with deepest thanks,
Mr President Barack Obama,

for finally bringing some hope
to the desperate state of the rotten American state,
which the whole world with me but can welcome
with enthusiastic applause and encouragement
of this new hope of some betterment
and possibility of a new deal for America.

The Softness of Your Light

The lights in yonder window
lifts my spirit out of space
to everlasting light of glory
in the view of what it means,
that somehow my love has come home
and might be thinking of me in my absence,
while her presence never was more present
to me than now with this light
that softly stole into my heart.
Beware, it might go out, it flickers,
so let us take care of it
and warm our hands to it
so it might feel itself more useful
and go on with shining brightness
just to warm our hearts
enough for hibernation
through whatever winter we might have ahead.
My light of you, however, never will go out
since it outshines all stars of every night.

Mercury and Apollo

Apollo:

– O brother, how I envy you
your swiftness and your grace in flying,
your intelligence and smooth agility,
by cleverness surpassing everyone
and fooling every mind except your own.

Mercury:

– It's not my fault. I was just born that way
and am a slave in that capacity,
since I always have to work so hard,

just hurrying everywhere with urgent messages
of bad news from the gods to hopeless mortals.
Your vocation is by far more honourable,
being basically and one-sidedly creative,
since you mainly deal with only inspiration.

Apollo:

– But I lack your communicative facility.
The world is not receptive of my influence
except by singular exceptions,
since only geniuses can understand me.
On the other hand, you can be everywhere at once,
communicate with everyone and always get your message through.
I am an isolated god who finds true happiness
in almost only making poetry and music by myself.
For instance, Orpheus did understand me,
but was killed for all his arts by mortals.

Mercury:

– Don't complain. You are nevertheless supreme
among the gods for your refinement, excellence and beauty,
being actually the only true inspiring power of the gods.
Ask Homer, if you don't believe me.

Apollo:

– And what happened? Homer was replaced by Virgil
by the Romans, who ran down the world to hell
in chaos, cruelty, dictatorship, intolerance,
barbarity, fanaticism and the Dark Ages.

Mercury:

– But that Roman empire perished,
while you still have Homer left
with Orpheus, Euripides and many others,

not to mention the philosophers
like Plato and Pythagoras, who all were Greeks
or stuck to Greek, like Mark Aurelius.
Apollo: – Well, you comfort me, no doubt about it,
and I thank you for it, for I really need it
sometimes in my doldrums of melancholy.
What can I do for you, my brother, in return?

Mercury:

– Just keep on being what you are,
remain the paragon of beauty, culture and refinement,
discipline and purity and light of spirit that you always were,
and I'll be able to perform my work
of constant journeying even better and with smoother swiftness,
while I really couldn't make good speed
or any speed at all without your inspiration.

Apollo:
– Thank you, brother.

Farewell to the Mountains

The purity and inspiration
of the greatness of your beauty
clad in ice of coldest whiteness
almost outshining the sky in brightness
fills me with dismay at our divorce,
as I must down again
to baseness from the hills,
to the mundane vulgarity
of the stress-stricken common crowd,
who never climbed the icicles of beauty,
beyond reach for any common realism,
the inscrutability of beauty being always out of reach
except for those who keep their distance,
understanding it and worshipping it in respectful awe.
There is no better incarnation of true beauty
than the holy mountain out of reach for any mortal,
while alone the probing universal mind
can satisfy itself by finding his way into it
by metaphysically loving and adoring it.
There is no higher freedom than the highest
and no higher inspiration than the loftiest,
up-liftingness is all there is for the soul's nourishment,
and mountains know the way and show it
by the majesty of the serenity of their white armour
of the hardest coldest purest ice-clad beauty
never to be violated, and enthroned forever.

The Pianist

– a true story

She lived quite alone with her music in exile,
a pianist all by herself in a snug little room
with her piano somewhere in the slums
of the old Kathmandu in Nepaul,

where no tuner could ever be found for her instrument.
Anyway, she kept on playing and giving her lessons
to a very limited circle of musical pupils,
for which she could hardly earn more than her sustenance.
Often she dreamt of her country, Ukraine,
which she could not return to,
since she was bereft of her passport
in the revolution that brought independence;
but she was content as an exile in old Kathmandu in Nepaul.

But then one day her brother came visiting her.
He was shocked and appalled by her living conditions.
"But you live in desperate misery! How can you stand it?
How can you survive? It is worse than intolerable!"
"But I have my old piano and all my old music.
What else do I need? I have everything here!"
But her brother was shocked almost out of his wits
at her misery, poverty and worn out state,
which she had no idea of herself;
and he left, being shaken and unable to understand
how his sister could live so unbearably miserable
like a beggar in exile.

But she continued and still has her piano
somewhere in the old Kathmandu ancient slums
where her only complaint is that no one is there
who can tune her old instrument for her.

The Lost Train

(– the notorious "Sikkim-Mahananda Express",
which once made me lose a flight,
dedicated to Rajesh Poonia, who helped me out…)

We were three at a loss for a train that was lost,
and we wondered: What are we to do?
They were my very last days in India,
I couldn't afford to lose any connection,

and I was advised by the Ticket Collector
to simply jump on the next train.
My two friends were reluctant to take such a risk:
What if, then, they had to stand all the night up
without seats, without berths, without ticket?
They stayed to wait patiently for the lost train,
that, according to the latest news,
so far was only twelve hours late,
maybe fifteen, but that was some hours ago.

I jumped on the next train and sat up all night through
without berth, although I had paid for one,
while the ticket conductor could help me with nothing
except that, at least, he could not throw me off.

The next day, when we reached Allahabad,
some sorely tried passengers entered the train.
They also were victims of the Mahananda Express,
which by now was nineteen hours late,
and the ladies were crying most pitiably unconsolably.
My chance on the North East Express
at least spared me one day, although sitting
that whole night on that shaky train was uncomfortable.

Nothing was ever heard any more from the train that was lost,
having actually added every second hour one hour of further delay,
and my friends that were on it were lost with it too –
at least they also were never heard of again.

Like an Indian equivalent to the notorious Flying Dutchman,
that train is most probably still getting on somewhere
constantly adding to its overwhelming delay,
like some train out of time, out of touch with the world,
lost in different dimensions, like so many things are
in that most particularly charming Indian subcontinent.

Bombed Dumbells of Bombay

They thought they would start a new war
between India and Pakistan
by detonating some bombs
in an effort to make 9/11 in India
by murdering innocents by many hundreds.
How daft can you get?
There does not seem to be any limit.
For once, politicians were actually innocent,
muslims in general more shocked than christians
at this amok-running unhuman derangement
that no one can sympathise with
and that nothing, and least of all any religion,
can justify or make excuses for.
As a suicide attack, it only backfired completely
and hurt most the cause of the guilty delinquents,
if they indeed even at all had a cause.

Lost Love

You disappeared out there
somewhere diffusely in the fog,
like some ethereal phantom
vanishing, dissolving in the mists
with nothing left behind
except what could have been,
some bitter disappointments
and a painful mess of memories.
Still you exist
out there somewhere
and waiting only to return
in hopes of my forgetting
all the negative misfortunes
and the inexcusableness of your lacks
of sense, of order and of faithfulness.
But I can not forget.

The memories will haunt me
never leaving me in peace,
while all my comfort is
all that which could have been,
the love that went out like a phantom
and the soul of purity
that never could materialize.

Who Shall Save the World?

We are completely powerless
against the world corruption
which by greed has ruined all the world,
with Bush as leader of the universal egoism,
denying there is anything to worry about,
while oceans are dying,
wildlife disappearing,
people starving without water,
cruel dictatorships supported by democracies
for just some short-term gains,
while we, who watch and are aware
of the world crisis steadily increasing
can do nothing
but observe and pray and hope
for all too necessary miracles.
Can even love do anything about it?
That's perhaps the miracle
we're waiting for,
the most improbable
but maybe only possible.

Stealing Up To You

Sneaking up to my love
like a dream in the night
with unheard-of mysterious messages
of outward nonsense but perilous sense,
paying blinded obeisance
unto the highest irresistibility
of the most natural force in existence
of love, for its permanency in expansion,
enhancing its beauty forever,
I simply can't help using magic
to get through the message to you,
that my love of you
still hasn't changed
but only increased

in its truth
of a slow but continuous explosion,
like some chain reaction,
unstoppable in all eternity.

The Black Holes of Desperation

– on the death of an old friend from Warsaw

The black holes of desperation
are by themselves an indescribable infinity
the measure of which never can be fathomed
in their tragedies and sufferings and tribulations.
You survived the Warsaw ghetto
and the glorious Polish insurrection
leaving more than half of Poland more than half dead,
coming here like wreckage from the aftermath of history
to make heroically a new life and a new world.
You made it a success, but now,
as you are gone, the tragedies remain,
the unfathomableness of suffering despair,
and your loss, finally, just adds to all the others,

the black holes of history that never can be filled,
into which the torrents just keep gushing down
of the eternal grief of humankind,
the sufferings of which can never be appeased
but only neverendingly increased.

To Another Lost Friend

(Whom the gods love die young, they say. He was like a brother to me for 33 years – and never grew a minute older…)

The black holes of desperation
are by themselves an indescribable infinity
the measure of which never can be fathomed
in their tragedies and sufferings and tribulations.
You survived the Warsaw ghetto
and the glorious Polish insurrection
leaving more than half of Poland more than half dead,
coming here like wreckage from the aftermath of history
to make heroically a new life and a new world.
You made it a success, but now,
as you are gone, the tragedies remain,
the unfathomableness of suffering despair,
and your loss, finally, just adds to all the others,
the black holes of history that never can be filled,
into which the torrents just keep gushing down
of the eternal grief of humankind,
the sufferings of which can never be appeased
but only neverendingly increased.

Sobriety

– sort of philosophical reflection

To fly away and never touch the earth,
to soar in heaven never to get down,
to be released from any morbid sense
of inhibition and mortality,

of bonds and boundaries and pains,
and to be free in spirit, clear in mind,
like almost being all the time inebriated
is the natural and perfect state
of absolute sobriety,
which can not be affected
by whatever drugs or alcoholics,
since you simply stay the way you are,
alive and natural and ever free
in spirit as in mind
in universal timelessness,
the only absolute stability,
the only way to stay alive.

Vulnerability

No one can escape it,
it is always there,
a lurking ugly thing,
that keeps reminding you
of its existence,
threatening invariably
your life and whole existence:
Who shall find it out?
When will the whistle blow?
There is no one without
that secret that will certainly undo him,
and that is the only thing
to reasonably be afraid of.
So let's not try to analyse
or to define it further,
but let everyone alone
in peace with that one secret
which you only know yourself.

The Junk Society

Leave me in peace from all this morbid stress,
where competition has been made the law of laws
encouraging all and everyone to beat each other
in the universal junk production
where the only thing that counts is quantity
so that the worst can only win
by stifling all the lesser quantities;
wherefore we have this junk society,
this planet drowned in junk and litter,
this by man's shit poisoned world,
the sickness and morbidity of which
accelerates by the same rate as
the explosion of the population,
five times doubled in a hundred years.
Please spare me all this massive dirt,
this universal medial brainwash
which insists on burying alive all decent culture
and on turning man into self-multiplying robots.
Making your career by lobbying intrigues
and manipulative manoeuvres
only gives you dirty hands that never can be washed.
What has become of honesty and decency?
Does it still exist at all in spite of all?
Perhaps we might still find it in the junkyard.

Advent

Where is love in winter darkness,
gone to sleep or buried in dejection,
sorted out or stranded in ejection,
or just lost completely in rejection
by the seasonal depression
causing deaths and isolation
all around in desperation;
but it's only passing

like a shadow, all this winter gloom,
and under and behind the shades of death
life is still there and waiting to return
with overwhelming love as usual.
All we have to do is hibernate
like every winter,
keeping our hearts warm beneath the snow,
protecting our love against the cold,
maintaining our soul's delight
concealed and thriving in the darkness,
always growing,
like the whole expanding universe.

The Art of Love

The art of love
is to never hurt the one you love,
which is of arts the most difficult of all,
since love, more than anything else,
compels you to vicinity
and drives you to the highest degree

of intimacy, which ever needs surpassing.
No matter how difficult this art is,
there's always means to make it,
a way of love completely without hurting;
and it is the quest for that evasive route
that makes love always unsurpassably exciting.

Stranded

Shipwrecked on the shores of nowhere,
cast away like any piece of dirt,
I find myself completely at a loss,
like any forlorn orphan sorted out
with nothing left except unfathomable grief
for all my losses of three invaluable friends
that never more can cheer me up,
and least of all now in this winter darkness,
where life couldn't be much heavier.
For all my losses, love remains,
the only hope of mankind and of life
and irrefutable, invanquishable as such,
the only straw to try to grasp
in all the avalanches of cruel fate;
and the most curious thing is,
that you never have to be dependent
or be taken care of or feel loved yourself,
as long as you just keep on loving
in your own continuous and everlasting faith.

Terrorist Efficiency and Bombing Deficiency

The one shoe demonstration
achieved remarkable results,
initiating world wide demonstrations
and a populistic shoe cult
of the one right shoe for Bush,
while all the terror bombings
of Nairobi, 9/11, Bombay, Bali and so on
achieved exactly nothing
but a universal loathing
of the dirtiest of criminals,
despicable murderers of innocents,
and the opposite of their intentions,
which, as violence is ever wont to,
only damaged their own cause,
backfiring in a total moral blunder.
They should start as shoemakers instead,
since shoes can always be of use,
including even one right shoe for Bush.

Lovability

My love is like a winter garden
always fresh with splendid flowers,
always ripe and blooming
and expanding ever in lush generosity
never to let any flower of love die down
but keeping ever warm like any tender heart.
So what do the faults and foibles matter?
Of what consequence is shortcomings
and impracticability,
when love keeps burning all the same
and warming generously any heart
that sticks to faithfulness?
Forget the worldly matters
and let love just keep on burning
indefatigably and forever.

The Relativity of Departures

Your friends are always there,
no matter how much less you see them
year by year, and even when they are departed
they remain your friends in constant presence;
and when after some long while,
some years, perhaps, you meet again,
it's only as if you'd last been together yesterday,
they are the same, your friendship never changes,
and it only grows more strong and intimate
the longer it goes on for decades,
to, when finally the link is cut,
it is established definitely and forever
as a friendship that can never be let down
and never interrupted even by some death
that only serves as ultimate establishment
and confirmation of the kind of love that never dies.

Enlightenment

– some unorthodox christmas thoughts

You can go on travelling forever
searching without finding,
while right at the next door
love is always there
and waiting for you
patiently in vain forever,
and you miss it constantly
just by going off and searching for it.
Love demands no effort
but is instantaneous
and the more so the more true it is,
like just some moment's flash
as brief as any lightning
lighting up eternity the more
and nonetheless for its abbreviated brevity,
like the enlightenment of Buddha,
just a passing moment and no more
eternalised in lasting world religions
and the old ones totally reformed.
No distance, no time, no effort
count in love but only the existence
of one soul emerging from itself
to care for someone else
in faithfulness, compassion, truth,
constructiveness and understanding.

Competition

It's all in vain, you can't compete,
for there is always something better,
and you always will be left behind
by time if not by competition.
The only worth while competition
is with yourself by sound self-criticism,
which always can do lots of good
if that will make you produce better stuff,
while it is damnable, of course,
if it turns self-destructive
by reducing you to silence.
That, unfortunately, is the general issue
of perfection, which you never can compete with.
So whatever you produce,
just never make it perfect.

Resurrection

Let all the lights die out in midwinter darkness
just for the sake and the pleasure
of the constant resurrection,
for nothing dies but to revive again;
and thus we all shall meet again,
if not in this eternity, the next one,
if not in life, then after death,
the certainty of life being
the constant resurrection
of every life and joy and pleasure,
of every friendship lost and love,
for that's the only true and certain doomsday –
the prolongation of eternity,
the making of each memorable moment
an eternity of constancy
to never stop existing as a joy forever.

Mirrors

(inspired by a poem by Jarl Hemmer of Finland)

The sunshine sea of calmness
mirroring the morning sky
embalms me as I rise
ascending on the rocks
embracing this resplendent morning,
diving deep into the universe
and bathing in the billow blues my thoughts
where I just want to swim along
into the whiteness of the shining clouds
where heaven and the sea together meet and blend,
while the seducing waves keep whispering
enchantingly into my ears
encouraging me never to look back
but keep on swimming in the bursting mirror

fleeting all around me in the lightning broken sparkles;
and I dare not ask how long I may keep going
or how deep the fathoms under me may stretch
how long the light may last way up there in the sky
but just keep swimming on forever forward
into those white blinding clouds
where water meets the sky to blend,
both mirroring each other to unite
in ripples that will sparkle on forever; -
and thus we go on swimming in the broken mirrors of our lives.

Inevitability

– another, or the same old, truism

My love, you are inevitable,
unavoidable and indispensable,
like any love to anyone,
for that is simply something
no one can do anything without,

exist without or do without at all.
This is of course of axioms
the most natural and obvious,
but it somehow always needs reminding of,
like of the fact that you are always rich
regardless of how poor you are
if only you keep up your natural inheritance,
that love of yours of that one next to you
or simply anyone besides yourself,
and that is all you need in life
to ever make it doubly valuable –
to stay on to keep up your love.

Reaching Out

Sadness drowns me as I cannot reach you
while my only comfort is that you exist
somewhere out there but within reach,
as in spite of distances unbridgeable
we seem to understand each other
simply by not speaking the same language,
as indeed in love no language is essential
but the enigmatical consensus of the souls
enshrined and sealed in silence
as if the supreme protection
was the perfect quietness.
But who can understand such riddles
but ourselves? Well, no one else is needed.

Doting Melancholy

As the ghosts crowd in my memories
entangling me in webs of melancholy,
I drown in moods of desperate remorse
and can't find any way out of my troubles
but to stay there stalwartly and deal with them
and so get through the muddy lot
by simply wading down in it
up to my neck and further,
to be able then to concentrate on you,
my love and inspiration and my source of life,
at least to get some glimpse of any possibility
for any betterment of my condition,
which I can't find anywhere and nowhere else
than in the possibility of loving you.

The Midwinter Hangover

– some lugubriety

All the ghosts parade to haunt you
in your mind to bog you down
into depression and to nothingness,
while you, reduced to apathy, just sit and stare
into a black hole in the air
in sordid bleakness waiting for a change
and for the ghost parade to end
and cease their battering of you to pieces;
while you mourn the days when you were active,
free and young and vitally creative,
while there's nothing else for you to do now
but to dream and gradually just fade away
and drift along the self-deceit of self-seduction.
Is there no salvation and no hope, then?
Yes. There never was a dream without awakenings.

Gone

You passed me by
like some spectre of the past,
and all too well I recognized you
and could not escape the fact
that all my love was in you still –
your haunting me has only become worse
with every year and ageing day.
How can I then resist you?
No, I never did.
My love was always constant,
I never held it back and least of all from you
but stayed on loving you
increasingly and overwhelmingly
like in some masochistic effort
to drown myself once and for all in love.

The Danger of Exposure

Who am I to trespass and exceed
the limits of the reasonableness of tenderness,
when love itself enforces me and holds me back,
compels me to explosion while at the same time
care restrains me not to crush
the very thing I would explode for?
The exile of consideration
bars me thus from my true love,
for never would I run the risk of harming her,
while love as force of nature forces me to burst
and put at risk the very soul I love.
Thus love is both the highest irresistibility,
joy and danger to us all,
while love can harm like nothing else,
and those we love the most of all
we would the least of all expose to harm.

Trifling in Bed

Are you lonesome tonight, my love?
I am not, since I have you in my thoughts,
and so entirely you pervade my mind,
that there is room for no one else in my bed.
How many lovers have you had? Never mind,
I know that you have loved many,
and that is only innocence,
I mean, to love others,
while I must insist that only I may love you,
or is it too much of a pretension?
Let's not push the argument any further
but be content, that for me, your love is quite enough.

The Eloquence of Love

Hush, speak softly, whisper, make it intimate,
and the more intimate, the better,
the more quiet, the more eloquent,
the less loquacious, the more expressive,
the less said, the less misunderstood,

and the highest understanding is in silence.
Feelings never speak, since they are only felt,
and that's love's greatest difficulty:
for the greatness, honesty, profundity and urgency of feelings,
no expression is enough, no eloquence can render justice;
so the deeper and the more sincere the truth of love,
the less it can be voiced;
and silence, therefore, is love's highest eloquence.

Underground

– defence for the suppressed

Our time will come,
the time of those who were kept down,
ignored and thwarted,
counted less than nothing
just for being something
contrary to mainstream
and disdained by the establishment
just for being something else,
the outsiders kicked out,
refused as aliens,
an unpleasantness to bypass
and regard as non-existent
just for their existence being undeniable.
But we will rise
as phantoms never die
but only rise more certainly
and keep on haunting history
for ever having been ignored,
buried alive by ignorance.

Detached

In sleepless dreams of you,
my love, I wonder where you are,
your alien presence being out of touch
but still so near, invisible but palpable.
The question is, can we get closer
than we are now in our total distance?
As if we live in two different continents,
an ocean parting us incurably
with hostile black and icy waters,
we are out of touch
but still not with each other.

I can feel you in the air,
and I must admit to the confession,
that I never did enjoy a presence more.

Taking You For a Ride

My friend or lover or whatever,
let me not insult you with my imposition
in these efforts at deficient poetry
of not much sense, since they are doting,
stuck in love and melancholy
and bogged down most lamentably
in pathetic bathos of nostalgia,
while all I want
is just to take you for a ride,
for what is love if not indulgence?
Yes, I told you so and warned you,
I am just a doting fool and good for nothing
but deficiency in foolish poetry
describing silliness of love,
supremest vanity and folly,
wherefore there is no indulgence like it.
But if that indulgence brings us freedom,
then it's worth it, and at least we'll then be free.

The Fatal Diagnosis

Like in all fatal diseases,
you don't understand what's happening to you,
you don't recognize yourself,
you feel you are losing control
not only of your body but of yourself,
your mind is playing games with you
wreaking havoc in your world;
the most sensible and orderly become distracted,
sleeplessness is inevitable,
but the worst is the constant short cut circuit,
your brain going around like a washing machine

ever stuck with the same idea
that you brainwash yourself with
and can't let go of although it consumes you,
and that's the most serious symptom:
the self-consumption that you waste yourself with,
the most serious and hopeless of addictions;
and there has never been a cure
except escape by death.
The diagnosis is fatal: you are doomed,
your affliction is the worst one possible,
you'll never get rid of that addiction
which constantly has to worsen
your case in hopelessness and downfall,
for there was never any cure for love.

Headaches and Heartaches

– some connection?

As I wake up in the darkest night
my headache splitting me in two,
I turn to you for any kind of alleviation,
but you are not there, so I am lost
in darkness of the heaviest night
with hell all burning in my head,
and there is not a single hole
to slip out through in the opaqueness
of the trap of burning darkness
where I am imprisoned without you.
But still, you are out there somewhere,
and that is still a lasting joy
which spites the entire hell of darkness
and confounds the blasted headache,
since I still may think of you.

Hidden Secrets

Is it possible that you could love me,
this old carcass of a ruined wreck,
abused and devastated into shambles
of a good for nothing anymore?
When love is at its truest and most constant,
she is also at her coyest and most vulnerable
and keeps secretive and silent
for the case of her maintenance,
like a flame kept safe through any storm.
Thus silence speaks sincerely
with no voice except her inner light
which in her truth and lasting loyalty
outshines the brightest star in any darkness.

The True Lies Of Love

– some other ever repeated truisms…

It's the perfect self-deceit
to think that you are loved
just because you love,
which immediately forms a natural impediment
to the vital outflow of your love –
love is not taking or receiving
but only giving.
Most people grow conceited
out of love, to think that they are loved,
and thus they smother love
unconsciously and tragically,
as they stupidly forget the only true qualification:
that love needs fuel,
which you can only monitor yourself.
To use it is to waste it,
but to give it is to further it,
and love can but in one way properly be given:
without reservations.

Unattainability

Is that what makes love irresistibly attractive
with that mysterious force that ever is renewed
and always challenges and pulls you up again
to never let you down and never let you rest,
the fact that true love is so unattainable,
so that you always reach for what you cannot reach
and search forever for what never can be found?

The perfect absolute ideal exists,
and that's why everybody always chase it,
but the problem is, that it is never practical
but always unattainably remain
the most alluring theory that never can be realised.
Still we try, we go on chasing it,
we never tire in that wonderful supremest vanity,
since that is mainly what keeps all of us alive.

Complaints

Everywhere there is complaining,
but it is a healthy thing:
if you complain, you see what's wrong
and get yourself detached from it,
thus making clear your distance
from the unacceptable, corrupted,
sick, unsound and evil.
Only if you let yourself become affected and involved
in rottenness, you are yourself in danger,
if you allow yourself to get depressed
and downcast and upset emotionally,
instead of soundly countering, opposing
and making your position clear against it.
Our society has never been more sick,
the Kafka nightmare was but one first symptom,
and since then the morbid formalism
has only made life more impossible for humans
and especially for the creative ones;
but as long as you complain and cry out loud
against the wrongs of the straitjacketness of your society,
it is a healthy sign of soundness
to at all react against what's wrong.

The Anti-Exhibitionist

Not that he is hiding,
but he is no real sandwich man
and therefore doesn't like parading
neither in his nakedness nor his extravagance in fashion,
in neither his deserts nor foibles,
neither in his dirty shoes nor with his purple nose,
in neither his pathetic deplorability nor his excellence,
his morbid fantasies or secret vices,
his tics or manners, crooked ways or lusts,
his insatiable desires or his secret love affairs,
his grotesqueness or abominations,
his preposterousness or indulgences,
his cleverness or lack of, or his awkwardness,
his constant being at a loss and silliness,
his undesirability and uncouthness,
his impertinece and importunity,
nor his ability or disability, -
since he is the anti-exhibitionist
who only can enjoy such manners and exhibits
in the weaknesses of others.

The Lost Jew

I thought I had a country,
finally, after twenty centuries of loss,
but it has betrayed me,
it has turned me out,
the Jew that thought justice was possible,
the Jew that thought his Jewry could be an honour,
the Jew who thought God actually was serious
when he said 'Thou shalt not kill',
the Jew who thought his exile in eternity
was finally at an end when he was welcomed home
into a land that built new Berlin walls
and where his foremost duty was to go to war

to kill civilians blindly without differentiation
as their Big Brother America had taught them to do.
My country is lost, and my people is lost,
again, as we always used to be,
cast out in a meaningless world
that always was governed and pushed by folly
and therefore went hopelessly astray from the start,
as if one ever could believe in anything.

Quite Simply

Who can fight the unacceptability,
the ugliness and horrors of this world,
the meaninglessness of the universal violence,
the ruthlessness of egoism,
the voluntary folly of blind ignorance,
the unaccountability of general destruction,
the mad race for false security,
the global meltdown of climatic change?
– We all can and must fight them all
by simply taking stand against them
and opposing any kind of unacceptability,
and never tire of the fact that by opposing them
and by supporting truth and beauty, knowledge,
education, peace and love instead, and nature,
we are right.

Culture Or No Culture?

– self-evident, of course

We can't do without it.
It's what keeps humanity up,
shows the way and gives some meaning to existence,
while all else really isn't worth much,
materialism, capitalism, politics,
that mainly causes trouble,
while culture is the only thing lifting us

above the animal state and barbarism.
The only hope for humanity
is therefore to be led by culture
and not by egoism and materialist ambitions,
money and power, prestige and vanity.
How is culture then to be defined?
spiritual constructive cultivation.
It's not just libraries and all the fine arts
but also involves such different fields of activity
as environmental care and gardening,
tolerance and kindness;
and it's the obligation of the mundane world and politics
to support and follow that idealism,
or else they betray humanity
and are no better than Hermann Goering, when he said:
"When I hear the word 'culture' I trigger my revolver."

The Road to Perdition

When fate keeps battering you all around
and strangling you in stress and worries,
catching you in traffic incidents
and driving you to nuts by faltering computers
infected by viruses and crashing all the time,
when harassment is all you get for being right
by all those who can't see that they are wrong,
when ruin threatens you and catches up with you,
when your best friends go dying and the living break their ties,
when things are falling down and you have no escape
from devastation and annihilation and a nervous breakdown,
there is still one thing at least that you can do,
and that is simply getting out and getting drunk.

Moving On

My love, I do pursue you,
but I never seem to catch you,
since you always lead me on
to further ways astray
which ever makes it quite impossible
to ever find the right way back
or any right way, for that matter.
But I pray you: Lead me on,
and I will follow you
continuously like so far;
and since we seem to prosper both from it,
so let us just continue straying
never to look back on all the lost ways
and at the same time never lose our touch
or will to some day find the right way.

The Love Syndrome

I used to love you,
but I never quite succeeded,
which is why I love you still
and, the worse, the more,
since you were always unattainable
and therefore irresistible
to almost an unbearable degree,
which is why I can't stop loving you
but must go on
and love you still,
the worse, the more.

Creativity and Love

It is an urge that can't be stopped,
and somehow they seem closely knit together,
creativity resulting and in some way neutralising
the effect of love into the purest constructivity.
I could not do without you both,
the flow of love discreetly channeling
into a force of nature that can not be stopped
but must be let out in creation.
Thus they are together intermingled,
stuck together in a deadlock,
neither one admitting freedom to the other,
having both no freedom but together.

Anatomy of a Suicide

(Mind you, no recommendation!!!)

What poet did not try to kill himself (herself)?
The irony is, that those who finally succeeded
failed the most to die,
since all they did in dying by their own hands

was to get themselves immortalised,
their words and poetry remaining
written more than just in blood
and more alive than they themselves.
The reason, also, is a very strange one.
Creativity is of all ideals the most demanding,
always craving more than anyone can give,
since one fulfilment must have more.
Thus the artist in her mortal limitations and confinement
never can live up to what the soul demands,
which always must defy, denounce and spite
all physical realities and possibilities
and thus, inevitably, tragically, fatally
creates a conflict between soul and body.
Many, if not most, who made a suicidal effort
and survived, were kind of resurrected and reborn
and even generally stimulated into new creative progress,
while all those, like Sylvia Plath, Virginia Woolf
and others, who did not come back,
immortalised themselves nevertheless
by the triumphant victory and glory of their souls.

Between Ourselves

Silence whispers without breath
the more expressively and clearly
when the meaning is unquestionably love
which never can be taken wrong,
misunderstood or understood,
since love does not need understanding
but the listening capacity to silence only,
which has nothing to do with the senses
but is only felt most unmistakably
in obvious truth in depth and soul
the more resounding universally
for its profound inaudibility.
My love, you can not take me wrong
when love is all there is between us.

The Patient

— from real life, a very sad reflection...

My friend, I'm sorry that I had to visit you,
to see you in your sorry state,
survived, but hardly more,
and suddenly grown old,
an ageing man who doesn't care much any more
but rather would go hiding
than receive an old time friend and visitor,
as if you were ashamed of your new face,
of showing up at all to those who knew you
as a youth and vital intellectual giant,
now turned into just a tired shadow
hiding in the memories of how it was,
the glorious opposite of what it is today.
I beg your pardon for my visit
and shall not visit you again
until you have turned back to life,
returned to us as the great friend you were
who doesn't have to hide in bed to visitors.

My pathetic visit must lead to the sad reflection,
that it would be better to depart directly, suddenly from life
than to be operated on beyond all recognition
just to have a shadowy existence of unworthiness
prolonged indefinitely to increase the pains.

The Shrink

(According to old Soviet psychiatry (still practised in China), the one complication with psychiatric patients was that they sometimes got the idea that there was nothing really wrong with them…)

Any trouble with your mind?
Some slight depression maybe?
Feeling shy or socially inferior?
Maybe you feel guilty about nothing?
Any slight discomfort can be taken care of
by the Shrink, who's there to solve your problems –
he has pills for everything.
They all make you forget,
benumbs your mind and makes you feel less,
so that you can sleep more comfortably;
and if you have sleeping problems,
that's no problem. There are sleeping pills
to compensate for all those pills that keep you wide awake;
and if they give you side effects,
there's pills against that problem too.
There are some 375 diagnoses
for all kinds of psychic troubles and disturbances,
while there were only 54 some 50 years ago,
and there are now some 174 psychic medicines
to choose between, while there were only 44
some 50 years ago. Some progress!
Some invention! Yes, the Shrink did just invent them all
like all the medicines against them,
and they are of course addictive all.
If there are any curious side effects,
like general psychosis and suicidal thoughts,

which turn some into murderers
to after carnages end up in suicide,
it's not the fault of those addictive medicines with side effects
but rather something that was wrongly diagnosed,
which calls for new invented illnesses and medecines.
So you just have a nice chat with your Shrink,
and he will find out what is wrong with you
and give you medicines to cure your brain activity,
and when you end up as a calm complacent zombie
that does no harm by just sleeping round the clock,
you may consider yourself cured
with no more complications.

Stealth

Let me enter you
but without tears and pains,
to have a peep around your mind,
investigating feelings and vibrations
just to get to know you
to sort out and harmonize our music
and discover other universes than our own
with no hard feelings and no stealth at all,
but just the contrary: enrichment,
to find out how it all came about
that we two found a common tone
that keeps resounding in our hearts.
My friend, I have been inside you since then,
and I have stolen you into my heart.

Attempt at Some Self-Definition

Drifting lonely as a cloud
of no more stuff than dreams are made of
is the dream of my existence,
floating aimlessly on seas of turbulence
with no more meaning than a passing night
of dreams and of no more than that.

My life and person is a dream that passes on
to change into some other dream perhaps
of no more validity than any dream
of great stuff writ in water
to immediately be forgotten.
Life is perhaps a hangover of some kind
after birth and before death,
the only two events of some significance
to prove the shallowness of your existence –
a most awkward entrance
and an exit into nothing.

Tenderness

Delicateness makes tenderness more vulnerable.
Not all can understand,
that tenderness has more than one side:
depth of empathy for others
makes you yourself more vulnerable
and may lead you the more easily to pains
than others of less sensitivity.
The consequence is that these tender wounded martyrs
by too many beatings get their surface rough
that fools the eye concealing badly covered wounds
that still hurt constantly in depth.
The deeper sensitivity and tenderness,
the touchier the vulnerability;
so mind, and care for soft and tender hearts
that need your tending with some tenderness.

Metaphysical

Long since dead and still alive,
a mystery perhaps that might await us all
here in the middle state of life
between the life before and what comes afterwards
of which we can know nothing.
Still it feels that both before and after
was and must become much better,
as if all frustrations were just limited to our mortality,
mundaneness limiting all spiritual possibilities.
The Buddhists talk of some Nirvana
as an ideal spiritual state aquirable even here,
but even that does not sound very practical.
So shall we then just dream of that ideal state before birth
of universal love that also waits for us beyond the grave?
Well, it's a wonderful idea and possibility,
but even that we dream of here as mortals.
Maybe that's the definite and final comfort:
that at least in all our limitations,
we can always dream of anything.

The Poet's Privilege

A poet goes beyond reality
and has the right to be excluded
from the petty troubles of mundaneness,
since it's natural for him
to break conventional dimensions,
since his home is timelessness.
Do not expect him to be fathomed
or identified or even specified,
he will avoid all analysis efforts,
baffling readers and researchers
and the more so through all ages,
since he stepped aside from the beginning
from the ignorance of lying senses
to devote himself exclusively to the beyond
which no one ever really could define
but which it was his task to understand
and try, at least, to make it understandable,
as some kind of a medium
between conventional dimensional mortality
and the unfathomableness of timelessness.

Back to Camelot

The gates have opened wide again
for the return to vintage days of Camelot
with new frontiers to open
and for love to flourish once again
appropriately at the opening of spring
and introduced by a most promising new President.
Let spring begin again with hard work
joined by harmony and music for the rise of love
to work again in most mysterious ways.
How was it, by the way?
The love intrigues of virgin Lancelot,
the compromised Queen Guinevere,
King Arthur and his most exotic sister Morgan
never were explained with any satisfaction,
and it's maybe just as well.
All that we know is that they loved,
and that proved well enough for all eternity.

The Longest Moment

When love returns
with something like a vengeance
set with fullest sails
and rushing in
with forward wind,
I hesitate to catch my breath
benumbed by the enchantment
of the golden moment
which, although impossible,
I can but hope and feel
that must go on forever.
When it is enjoyed, at least,
it's more convincing than eternity.

What Does it Matter?

(The problem: If you were to make a heterosexual 'Pride Festival', you would get assaulted by lesbians and homosexuals who would feel offended...)

What difference does it make
how you express your love
as long as you express it well?
If you are homosexual or lesbian,
necrophile, bisexual or whatever,
please don't demonstrate it,
practise your anomalies,
perversions or whatever
freely as you want,
there are no limits,
nothing is forbidden,
but it is a private thing
that, if turned into show
becomes ridiculous and ugly,
losing all its seriousness of love,
that only can be beautiful and true
if practised secretly and privately
under the sheets and humbly
without pornographical and prostituted ostentation.
The less known and more mysterious,
the more attractive love becomes,
romanticism is best dressed up in fancy clothes
and veiled and masked becomes intriguing,
while exposed in nakedness it ends up as a trivial bore,
the less effective for its demonstration.

Insomnia

My love is like a sunrise
that never sets again
but just keeps shining
like a soul that never sleeps
but just keeps beaming
like some constant dreaming
turning life to an explosion
of not only energy
but of all kinds of creativity
and altogether a new life
of wonder and of joy
in almost a surrealistic way.
If that is how love works,
just let me love and never die,
and never let me even sleep again.

Someone to Watch Over You

– Let it apply to anyone who needs it.

Take care, my love,
and I will always be your guardian,
being constant in your company
and never losing touch,
your safety being my life's greatest interest,
and I will never let you go
off hand out of my reach,
since your felicity demands my care.
Of that you may be certain,
our guardian angels never let us down
as long as we are anxious to have them there –
it's all about white magic,
that keeps working wonders all the time
because we need them.
Do not worry, I am always with you,
and if need be, I will mobilize all guardian angels
from all heavens for your safety.

It's a Battlefield

The Veteran's song

(My background is the Winter War of Finland 1939-40 when Soviet attacked – my parents lived it through, but many of their best friends were lost, if not in the war in the aftermath...)

I left my heart out there in ruins
with my friends all gone to pieces,
limbs all shattered, spread around the front
and many never even found
but lost in no man's land
without a coffin,
while there were too many coffins anyway.
My spirit keeps on wandering out there
with ghosts of absent friends,
whose company I'll always miss the more
and never leave although it's gone;
for ghosts of friends will never leave you –
they will keep you company enough for all eternity.
You find them in the bottles,
in the depth of emptied glasses,
in the tears of widowed mothers
and in children who came off without a father,
whom they never shall get any chance to know
although they always keep them present
in romantic fancies of their unknown fates.
To absent friends, my friends!
A cheer, a glass, and bottoms up!
And may they live forever in our souls
to ever stalwartly go marching on
for the eternal quest of manhood, chivalry
and the defence of freedom, independence and democracy!

Donkey's Love

As I wander at a loss
bemazed at your serenity of beauty,
I just wonder who you are,
so carefully wrapped up in pride
and hidden behind veils,
that might indeed be seven,
of unsuperable walls
to that beleaguered heart
of paramount desirability,
since everyone is yearning
for that heart of secrets in your charm,
that beauty which no one can fathom
but is there in hopeless palpability
like some consummate provocation.
I am powerless against my love
that keeps enforcing me
to go on overstraining
indefatigably for your sake.
Just never leave my prospect,
sweetest golden carrot.

Invalid Invalid

Invalidity is not acceptable,
even if you are an invalid.
You have to go on working
every day with crutches,
although crippled beyond bearing,
you must just get on with it,
or else you have no more validity.
Your only hope to get out
of your invalidity
is validly to prove that you are valid
and convincingly at that,
and for that end no crutches

or invalid proof will be of any use to you.
Just get on struggling
out of all your pains and headaches
that so intolerably cripple all your life,
and you will find yourself a valid evidence
of being more than just a valid invalid.

The Adulator

How could I ever tire of you,
my only everlasting love?
Once you get to know of beauty
you shall never tire of it
but remain a doting adulator,
lost forever in apprenticeship,
admiring senselessly
completely void of any criticism,
and you want nothing better
than to just go on like that forever.
So don't even nourish that suspicion!
I am yours, and there is nothing
anyone could do about it,
least of all myself,
and not even your doubts
could more than just increase
my love of all that beauty
which is yours.

A Description of Love

The indescribability is limitless
and none can be too much or too extreme,
since love is all about extremes
of fascination, feelings, beauty and fixation,
there being nothing like it, no drug, no mania,
no intoxication, since it's only natural,
a natural endowment common to us all,
which it is our human duty tu use well
one-sidedly constructively,
for nothing will backfire more easily,
the consequences of which always are disastrous.
Love ineed, but please be careful to love well,
it's everything or nothing,
and if you can't do it all too well
it's better to do nothing.

The Year

Spring is like a virgin
clad in purity and whiteness
with her blonde hair loose
all shining in the sunlight
in free length of generosity
just waiting to embrace you
and to cover you in love;

while summer is a bride
of sumptuousness and joy
with garlands in her hair
enjoying feasting all the time
with whirling banquets non-stop
without any end or limit
to her splendid health and happiness.

When autumn comes she is a mother
with a warm and tender bosom
prone to some consideration
and an endless care
of tending to the harvest
for a future without end
of life stability and continuity.

They say winter is a step-mother
of some cold and cruel harshness,
sometimes quite inhuman in her chill,
but she is the most beautiful of all,
the purest and most irresistible
in cold detachment but the lovelier
for her challenge and her unattainability;
and it is by her trial and severity
that our spring virgin can be born again.

Null and Void

Reduced to zero,
spent and burnt out,
finished and washed up,
turned down to apathy
and out of order,
struck down as by lightning
and annihilated more or less,
demolished thorougly
and even sober in addition,
as if all the pitfalls
weren't satisfactory enough,
life is no more than nothingness,
while winter paralysis spreads around
and greyness seems to be the only colour
in appalling universal callousness,
with the advantage, though,
that you can always start again from the beginning,

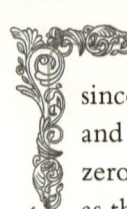

since point zero always is a starting point,
and life can never go below to minus,
zero being kind of perfect
as the equilibrium between plus and minus.

Perpetuated Passion

How could I ever forget you?
We did not have one night only,
but many were our nights
of interminable love
archived forever
in unforgettability.
If there is any weakness in me,
I assure you there are many,
but the greatest and truest of them all
is my ever longing back
to that interminable passion
that never ceased
to forever gild our lives.

In moments of despair
and bleakest desolation,
you are still there,
and I remember you
who never can be far away
no matter where on earth you are,
since we could never part
but stayed united
as we turned in
to one, once and for all.

Do You Still Love Me

– from an old Hungarian song

Is it possible, that you could still
care for this old scumbag
with his baggy trousers and shaky knees,
his multiplying wrinkles in his face
and getting bald all over
except where he should,
this bore of an old fool
who can't fool anyone any more,
this decrepit ruin
of what could have become something once,
this arse-hole of a failure
with only nauseating sentimentality to contribute,

without any initiative left
and nothing to offer
except the continuing decay
of a worthless body
soon to be contained
and scrapped as any carcass.
How on earth could you still love me?
If that is possible,
then, after all, anything still is possible.

The Knight in Shining Armous

– an optimistic fit

The Paladin is back
in chivalrous and shining splendour
armed with beaming virtues
and prepared to save all ladies
with his golden shield and shining helmet,
irresistible to all the world,

the Azure Knight of Knights,
the age of chivalry having returned
and with a vengeance.
There will now be new enlightenment
to scare away the scarecrows
of fanaticism and rotten policies,
those darkmen trusting to blind violence
and terrorist retaliation.
Violence has never worked
to any good or any decent purpose,
while love only always can but triumph.

Haunted

My love, you persecute me
like a phantom in my dreams
to never leave me quite alone
in peace, but always driving me on
furiously in whirlpool storms
more downwards to my ruin
to be ever born again
and start again from the beginning.

It's a phenomenon,
this self-destructive love,
that ever keeps renewing forcefully itself
by constant Harmageddons of destruction.
Just go on and keep on killing me
forever and again, that I may go on
loving you and dying for it
to be able to continue.

Perpetual Youth

All you need is love, they say,
and that's perhaps the universal truth of truths
that never can be constantly enough repeated
and renewed, reminded of and reinvigorated,
since it is the only inexhaustibility
of miracles and of perpetual youth;
since every time you fall in love
your soul renews itself and gets reborn
and even younger than it always was,
no matter how pathetically old
you always felt, since even an old soul

can get forever younger,
and the younger the more old it is.
The trick is: never be afraid
of falling into love again,
for that's the best thing you can do
at all times anywhere in life,
which every time will be a miracle again
providing you with yet another life.

Paradise on Earth

– someone asked me where to find it

You find it far away from all mundane politics,
since of course the politicians have done all their best
to ruin everything; but beyond this destruction
out of reach from dirty hands and greediness
there always are oases in the desert:
friends with common interests
of creative and constructive kind,
who offer you good company
of intimacy, tenderness and warmth;
and then of course there's always some good food
in spite of all to be occasionally found
somewhere in picturesque locations
of some decent human natural environment, – and perhaps the most important thing of all:
the coffee after lunch or dinner,
the supremest highlight of each day,
when there at last is offered you
a moment of enjoyment and of relaxation.

The Love that Came in From the Cold

The chill infects us with a paralysing cold
that kills all creativity and effort
of a decent life of work and strain,
but then there was this startling breath

of a new life of long ago,
of childhood memories and tender warmth
that I was not aware existed anymore,
by your surprising resurrection from the dead
or from the depths of history at least,
when you so suddenly bring me to life again,
reminding me of love that I thought dead
and frozen stiff and buried deep so long ago;
and this amazing gush of life and freshness
comes directly from the frozen vastness
of the hopeless winter landscape of Siberia,
where you never would expect
that love would come to you;
but there it is, another blessing
undeserved, surprising, reinvigorating
like the miracle of life itself;
but dare I hope that it will stay?
At least this ray of light gives hope enough
for me to go on living after all,
although it might be on condition
that I shall thirst forever for the next one.

Winter Blossoms

– to die, to sleep...

The cruelty of frozen hearts
transforms the world into a desert
of despair in anguished hopelessness
in frozen endlessness and white sterility
where cries of languishment are stifled
by the death of muted universal silence, –
but appearances are only there to lie.

Well hidden under cover, winter blossoms sleep
and bide their moment to explode
out of the ice in life's eternal triumph
in the fullest bloom of love and beauty;
but their time is not yet come.

Do not disturb their sleep,
but let them have their fair amount of rest
to later the more splendidly be able to
take care of us and of all life
in all love's worthiest magnificence.

Challenging the Winter Deep-Freeze

My heart is frozen deep
congested by the frozen tears
that never found an outlet
but were frozen stiff as soon as they were shown
by the surrounding hardness of the winter
stalemate of all frozen hearts.
Of course it aches like hell
so desperately over-burdened
with the griefs and sufferings of life
that never find an end but only increase.
Still, all world economies may tumble down
and perish with the doomed race of humanity,
but one thing I am sure of:
there was never any frozenness
without the thaw of spring to melt it down,
the unavoidability and irresistibility of light
reducing all things dark and cold forever
to the negligeable meaninglessness
of the emptiness of nothing.

The Old Maid's Song

– complimentary to Pete Seeger, if he can pardon me...

Where have all my lovers gone?
Long time passing
Where have all my lovers gone?
Long time ago
Where have all my lovers gone?
Gone to young girls every one.

When will they ever learn?
When will they ever learn?

Where have all the young girls gone?
Long time passing
Where have all the young girls gone?
Long time ago
Where have all the young girls gone?
Gone to young men every one
When will they ever learn?
When will they ever learn?

Where have all the young men gone?
Long time passing
Where have all the young men gone?
Long time ago
Where have all the young men gone?
Gone for soldiers every one
When will they ever learn?
When will they ever learn?

Where have all the soldiers gone?
Long time passing
Where have all the soldiers gone?
Long time ago
Where have all the soldiers gone?
Gone to graveyards every one
When will they ever learn?
When will they ever learn?

Where have all the graveyards gone?
Long time passing
Where have all the graveyards gone?
Long time ago
Where have all the graveyards gone?
Covered with flowers every one
When will we ever learn?
When will we ever learn?

Where have all the flowers gone?
Long time passing
Where have all the flowers gone?
Long time ago
Where have all the flowers gone?
Picked by young girls every one.
When will they ever learn?
When will they ever learn?

Where have all the young girls gone?
Long time passing
Where have all the young girls gone?
Long time ago
Where have all the young girls gone?
Gone to lovers every one
except for those old maids
that something learned on the way.

Splendid Richness of the Soul

Is the richness of your hair
something for you to hide in
or just an allurement
or a generous manifestation
of your freedom and integrity,
or only irresistibility of vanity?
The sum though is unoverestimable
in its beauty and alluring irresistibility,
and my interpretation
must be generosity of spirit,
since you so generously share your beauty
with whomever fancies it.
Remember one thing, though:
no matter how innumerable your admirers may be,
I am your only faithful lover.

The Message

A chord is struck in me
of a most personal resounding touch
as if your poems only spoke to me
in unheard of and unequalled intimacy
that must leave me thunderstruck
by the sheer might and force and power
of your softest tenderness.
How can I answer but with prayers
of profoundest thankfulness
for this impressing confidence?
Be calm, my heart,
our secret is quite safe within us,
since I never can betray you,
sealed with silence as I am
by voluntary faithfulness.

Off Course

– self-evident, of course…

Love is never a deception
justifying any cowardly retreat,
no matter how extremely difficult it is
to keep your balance and your course
amidst a hell of risks and dangers.
Never be afraid
as long as you are certain of your love,
which is your only safe insurance
and the only discipline to keep you straight.
Not until you yourself betray your love,
the fall becomes inevitable,
and once you've fallen off your course of love,
it will be much more difficult the next time
to renew the purity of how it was the first time.

A Definition of Hell

Hell is all that infinite despair
that never can be properly expressed,
the sorrow that can never fully be cried out,
the eternal suffering that knows no limits,
the unreleased and unknown love
that never gets communicated or fulfilled,
the unrelenting ceaselessness of cruel oppression,
all that pain that is too strong
to even be expressed by any screams,
the anguish that can not be even remedied by death,
the evil that can not be isolated or defined
and never ceases to torment us
by completely meaningless catastrophes and sabotage,
the losses that can never be restored or compensated,
mostly suffered by the passing of relationships;
in brief, hell is all that which most of all needs treatment
but which never can be treated.

The Necessity of Poetry

– They say the highest language of love is poetry.

In the dreariness of gloom
of winter darkness, poverty and misery,
amidst depression and despair
of dismal memories and apparitions,
love is always necessary for a change,
no matter of what kind,
as long as there is someone else to love
than just your own unbearable company.
Just let it hurt and ache and give whatever pains
and drive you mad and to exhaustion,
as long as but you have your love
to cherish and surrender to,
some sweetness to escape to
just for a relief of a most momentary kind
from the unbearibility of the reality of hell.

Patience

– to one of my many secret loves…

Only patience can save us
ultimately to bring on the victory
of love against all those against it,
stupid imbeciles and impotent degenerates
who fail to see their own unwantedness
and their incompetence,
who even fail as crooks
and will go down in history as bogeymen
who did no more in history
than make themselves a nuisance
like some fungus parasites,
like Bush, the waster of the world
who did his best to leave it all in ruins
for his betters to clean up –
I hope sincerely they will prosecute him
with Dick Cheney and that scoundrel Rumsfeld.
But all that has nothing more to do with us,
our pure relationship continuing as always
more replenished and enriched with love
for every year since our affair began
some twenty years ago.
Let's hope and trust unflinchingly
in twenty more years of that love.

My Poverty

My love, you must not doubt my constancy
as long as my sincerity keeps burning
tenderly for your unfathomable charm and beauty
that keeps constantly increasing
like my love by every hour of each day –
this fact is so reliable and undeniable
as it has been for the last 40 years

and keeps increasing still,
like the profundity of your incessant quality
that never ceases to impress and haunt me,
making every sleepless night a joy forever,
more enjoyable each time.
If this sounds sado-masochistically morbid,
it's because you only see the words
and can't check up my feelings,
that speak more the truth of my sincerity
that never can be hidden, although awkardly
expressed inadequately in the poverty of words
that can no more than sketch and hint at
the reality of universal live eternal love.

The Flight of Life

– Please excuse the brutal realism…

You are catapulted into life
between the buttocks of your mother
like a fart, most furiously and forcefully,
and of course it hurts,
and you do right in screaming out aloud
but soon forget,
that that scream would be valid all your life,
that flight of constant turbulence of torture
which will never leave you quite in peace
from worries, anguish and anxieties;
so that first scream of yours
you never really would have any reason to lay off,
the turbulence and torture always getting worse,
your wisdom and maturity acquiring ground
exclusively at the most devastating cost
of all illusions, harmony and happiness,
which always are replaced by that first truth of yours,
the scream of pain of your original,
which all your life you try to get away from
by escaping into new illusions, alcohol or drugs,

which always prove completely vain,
until you finally are earthed and landed
safely into life's uniquely certain destination,
the final grave of some relief,
in which you end up into ruins
that confirm the definite veracity
of that first scream of yours.
That flight of life was no more than a scream
and a primeval terror of your final touchdown,
which will haunt you and torment you all your life
until you finally are ready
to start it all over again from the beginning.

Too Much Love is Always too Little

My heart is cleft in twain
by too much love on many sides
and none decisive, all coercive,
all demanding, none forgiving,
everyone an obligation,
none a liberation;
and how could I let them down,

neglect and fail to care
for anyone of them,
when love is everybody's right
forever, and your duty is to love
whomever gives your love to you?
It's a predicament, the total failure
to live up to your ambitions,
the most human shortcomings of love,
when you just want to give it all
and only can deliver fragments.

Adjustment

When love knocks on your door
you don't ask who it is,
but you just open doors and windows wide,
you can't do otherwise,
since you can not afford to let it go
and let it fly away from you once more
like it has done so many times before.
You open up your heart and soul
as wide as possible
133
and hope your guest will thus be comfortable
until she must leave again for other loves.
You only have her while you love her,
and when she turns other ways,
the only thing to do is to look out
for love in other ways.

The Curse of the Full Moon

You'll never get away with it.
I'll always be there to remind you
of the facts of life that chain humanity
for always in the bonds of midnight magic
as I ever will return each month with waxing light
to never let you down in love completely
but light up the midnight darkness just to put you off
in the hysteria of overwhelming feelings
of the midnight magic light that never fails.
You will stay in love forever,
hounded by irrevocable feelings
that no alcohol or drugs can chastise

but must have full vent in sumptuous flow
since Nature, master of the universe, demands it.
Just keep on decaying, falling, shattering and suffering
the pangs of love in ever greater hardship,
and I will continue shining
just to drive you nuts forever.

Just Another Death Star

No names – but the type of vanity star i everywhere

The inflexibility of your hardness
makes you unapproachable,
and your chill does not make things
much easier either;
so why do you protest so much then,
bragging out your love so loud
for anyone to hear your garish invitation,
while all you love is just yourself
with that excessive vanity
disclosed in sumptuous luxury,
as if your sole intention was to bribe the world
by ruthlessly impressing on it,
while in the end the only thing you do achieve
is self-deceit and vanity in others also,
fatally contaminated by your blindness
of no distance to how faked you are.
I will not intervene, I'll let you have your game
and let you fool whoever wishes to be fooled,
but please excuse my staying outside,
wishing not to be contaminated by your radiation.

Reliability

You can count on me, my love,
to never even run the risk of being tempted
to reveal, betray or give away your soul
disclosing your identity to anyone unworthy
of your love, your character and influence,
which means much more to me than all the world,
since it is so much more important.
The evil of the Chinese communist imperialism
is so established, that whoever makes resistance
and objects can only be self-evidently good.
What mean the crises of the world to us
and to our love, when only things constructive matter?
Let the evil-doers be alone with their destruction,
afterwards we'll do the cleaning-up as usual,
and that's all what history is all about.
Our love will triumph anyway,
and history will merely fade away
as insignificant to the eternity of love and beauty.

The Chamber

You invade my heart again
and are most welcome there to stay.
You'll find there space enough
for both of us and all the world,
and all the doors are open
and the window view the best,
the temperature is moderate but never cold,
and you will never find it too hot either,

since the thermostat is perfect.
Just feel comfortable and at ease
and welcome to remain as long as possible,
since I have no other guests,
and you are free to use it all yourself,
since that is what it's made for:
to make room for love and only love.

Double Duplicity

Reality can never fool you,
only you can fool yourself
by trusting your alluring dreams
and take your own idealism seriously,
the all too common wishful thinking,
which makes you believe you have the power
to transform reality into your dream.
It is not possible without a dialogue,
and that dialogue consists of oppositions -
no one will accept your dreams,
since they all have their own.
If your idealism in spite of all is true,
it will survive deceits, defeats and downfalls
and especially your doubts,
your best defence against yourself,
among deceivers of your life and person
the most cunning and most tireless.

The King of the Hippies

I know of no one else
that justly would deserve that title.
You already as a young man
travelled round the world,
exploring, analyzing and evaluating it
from San Francisco to the Himalayas
in surveyance of your empire of freedom,
finding and selecting friends

of every nationality and race and faith
to suit your mission of enlightenment
to spread the word of love and beauty
in close observance of reality and truth.
Your sticking to the underground
was maybe more of a necessity than tragedy
which you however used to your advantage
to develop and expand your special wisdom
in a kind of universal co-reaction
of an almost revolutionary kind
against all rottening stagnation called corruption
with eventually some unexpected fair success;
and so you keep that operation basis
to continue that rare mole's work
of indefatigably undermining
all that works against the best of all,
accepting our present situation
as perhaps the greatest challenge of all history:
to save the planet and at least the best of mankind.
And still you are no more than just a bum,
a disregarded and discarded hippie
of no realistic consequence,
the best of all disguises:
that of being negligeable as a perfect no one.
Captain Nemo was a fiction, as they say,
but who was behind that fiction, really?
Some weird urban legends are too good to not be true,
and you are one of them.

A Riddle

The sooner you admit it,
the more you will be able to achieve it,
that it never can be quite accomplished,
and that if you reach it,
it most certainly will be undone
before your eyes and by the very act
of your accomplishment and consummation,

since it can only be maintained and cultured
by your never reaping it,
for harvesting means death,
while plowing, labouring and hard work
is the only guarantee of life,
of continuity, continuance and constancy;
so never try to catch your dream,
it must remain a dream,
for dreams can never stand awakenings,
and dreams are all the carrots and illusions
that can make life carry on in spite of all,
in spite of all delusions, disappointments and deceptions,
since although dreams are in themselves beguiling,
they are dreams that never can be apprehended
and as such untouchable as perfect virgins
to be loved quite safely and pursued forever.

No Bounds

Forgive me that I love you,
but I just can't manage it alone,
and the mere sight of you is too intoxicating
not to give some relevant results
in crazy outbursts of exhilaration
and the perfect drunkenness of beauty.
Stay that way, my love,
and I can promise you
that I will go on loving you forever
in impeccable and perfect faithfulness
to never fail you with my loyalty,
since the love that you inspire
must transcend and brush aside
to conquer all impossibilities.

Fragile!

As my love grows old
it grows forever younger
in vitality and enthusiasm
and power of expansion,
but it is an ardent flame that must be tamed
and well contained to not burst open
into violent and unforseen explosions
that might consume not just itself
but even the most precious object of your worship;
so take heed and please excuse my warning
that I must contain my love

in order to preserve it
as the most uniquely perfect and constructive force
that only can be treated and contained with utmost care.

Deliverance

Deep in the night
you sneak up into me
to stay there raping me
and stealing all my soul
but to endow it once again
with the profoundest inspiration,
winning me for love,
possessing me both heart and soul;
and still I never can get hold of you
and keep you for myself
but only love you
unto madness and exteriorization,
like some surgic kind of surging meditation;
while the only thing that I can do
is just to love you,
which you seem to take as natural,
accepting it and having nothing much against it.
Keep my love, then,
so that you at least,
although I never can keep you,
can keep something of me
which is much more than all of me.

Meeting in Darkness

(earth hour…)

In the darkness of your eyes
it's easy to commit oneself
and get completely lost
in the dissolving magic of enchantment,
since bewitched by love

you are not only all at sea
but even all beside yourself,
tongue-tied with arms tied also
with your hands behind your back,
your mouth and senses sealed,
while all that you can do
and voice and think of is your love.
The total consummation is the total concentration,
and that is how life begins.

Absent but Lasting Presence

You say, my love, that you can only love me
when you see me and I am at hand,
concrete and tangible in virtual presence,
but for me the soul is much more real,
more present and more tangible
and even more so when you are not present,
since I can not live without that love of yours
which constantly pervades my whole existence.
Let me dream of you and keep you in my dreams
forever tangible and more so even in your absence,
since I'll never let you go away from me
where you belong inseparable from my soul
no matter how much falsely separated we may be;
since all the senses always lie
by satisfying mirages to please us,
while the soul sees far behind reality
and sees it through
to see what is much truer and more lasting.

Aquarius

(actually an old poem written way down in 1984...)

A new dawning age of liberation
will deliver us from every tyranny,
since no one is to order anyone about,
since only common sense will rule us all.
Religions will lose all authority,
and only those of them are able to survive
who are completely free from dogmatism.
Exaggerations and fanaticism shall disappear,
and there will never more be any Martin Luther,
Mahomet, no Marx, no Lenin and no Hitler,
never more a demagogue or autocrat,
and those few monarchies that will survive
shall most of all be just protectors of democracy.
No martyrs shall be needed any more,
self-sacrifice shall be unnecessary,
and only common sense and honour

shall be leader to us all.
Justice shall be the supremest good in life,
and only that shall be the common aim
of all humanity together.
All intolerance shall be prohibited by law,
and those poor few who anyway indulge in it
in foolish arbitrariness, irrationality and folly
and the self-destructiveness that must inevitably follow
shall be pitied, since all destructivity
quite naturally then shall be regarded as an illness.
God shall not be mortal any more as crucified,
and Satan shall be banished to the myths of fairy tales,
and only simple human common sense shall dominate
the world religions and ideals;
and this religion down to earth of common sense
shall not include just all religions
but even every non-religion.

My Unknown Cousin

As a revelation from above
you suddenly appear
as some kind of godsend
in the substitution
of all dear ones that I lost,
as by some kind of universal law
that losses never can be suffered
without karmic compensations
in one way or another.
Even you, they say, have suffered hardships,
and we might thereby find in each other
some kind of a recompense
and complement each other,
which we both might need.
Thus a new chapter has begun
which definitely closes old ones
simply by miraculously
constituting their continuation.

Dumbfounded Awesomeness

How often does it happen
that you suddenly are served
with the existence of an unknown cousin
who proves more than like a friend
but even like a twin and sister?
Once in your life at most,
and there could hardly be a moment
more fantastic, precious, sweet and priceless
than a union of such kind
of souls of the same vein
of equal wavelengths to perfection.
Love is not the word for such unique coincidence,
but rather some mysterious force of destiny
that brings such miracles about
which only leave you thunderstruck
with gratitude to providence
and to whatever power outside yours
that you could never think of or imagine
in your negligeable absolute minuteness
against the universal ocean
of ethereal workings of the fathomless profundity
of metaphysical enigmae of the everliving soul.

Better Fusion Energy

The soul shines through the eyes,
and nothing can exclude its beauty,
radiant and forever young and true
in honesty and straight integrity
of timeless worth and durability.
Let us remain thus as companions
on the timeless path of destiny
towards no end but always forward
as the best of friends forever.
That is the most precious gift
that never can be wasted:
trust in the trustworthiness
of two united hearts
that found each other
never to be separated
in the unity of spiritual fusion.

Your Home

You offered me a glimpse of paradise,
and I was struck with wonder, awe and worship
of a perfectly ideal place to live,
with hanging gardens on the roof
and close to nature, although still in town,
with space and air to breathe
and freedom without limits
with no ghosts in any cupboard,
no hangovers, nothing dark,
just openness and friendliness;
and such a home you offered me.
How could I possibly accept?
I had to leave too early the next day,
and any intimate engagement
would just have exacerbated the departure.
But we are still here in lasting friendship,
and your home remains for the next time;
and until then we can continue
building our relationship on firmer ground
to next time celebrate it thoroughly.

Precarious Validity

What do I care about what people think,
attentive flatteries and criticism,
misunderstandings of shortsightedness,
intolerant superficiality
and hasty violent unjust reactions?
Let them rave, who can't control themselves;
my only aspiration and ambition
is to stick to honesty and truth
in faithful loyalty of beauty,
that my only aim is to take care of
with my utter tenderness of worship.
Let my words and dreams remain

unknown to those who do not care,
as long as they remain available
to those who understand and love
and in their hearts are capable
of keeping up their souls' flames burning
for the only thing that really matters:
joys that last forever.

No Doubt About It

Don't ask me who my love is.
It's enough that she herself can feel it,
be aware that no one else is meant
and that my loyalty endures
in constant faithfulness for her alone,
and thus it's futile that I name her.
Love's sincerity is unmistakable
and always felt at heart
unnecessary of expression –
language, vows and promises will not suffice,
and no protesting can be more convincing.
Rest assured, my love,
that I will never with a word betray you,
since there can be no impediment
of any limiting or mortal kind
to my unquenchable sincerity
of purest constancy of love of you.

The Return of the Native

– after the Turkish holocaust in 1915, the Armenian ambition,
a kind of documentary

Back to basics
in the dawn of time,
to ruins of the past
and memories forgotten,
after many years of exile

there at last was finally a day
of coming back to the original,
to houses laid in ashes
by the cruelties of history,
to cemeteries without gravestones
and to history buried alive
together with the unknown victims
of the first of holocausts in Turkey.
There could never be a sorrow
and a melancholy more profound,
and still, there was the opportunity
to start again, rebuild the past,
restore an ancient civilization
and return to timeless glory
of a righteous people
that did never any wrong
but only suffered wrong immensely
without any reason for it.
Somehow, the dimension
of the suffering of timelessness
remains incurably constructive,
always ready to begin anew
with work and reconstruction
of the greatest glory of them all –
the good that never can give up
but ever and again is victimised
to only resurrect and start again
in ever greater and increasing glory
of eternal continuity
of life that never can be quenched
without resuming ever greater power.

Strange Coincidence

You are the dream that never ends
but always justifies my love
and makes it constantly increase
to never stop developing,
as if you always were there,
while we haven't known each other
more than some ten days
and only met once in a lifetime
in a moment longer than a lifetime
of some history and truth
of some momentous imposition,
since we always were there
close enough for fifty years
to never meet until this strange event
of fate all of a sudden
bringing us together
out of chance and by coincidence.
Well, well! There's nothing we can do about it
but the best of it och keep it up
as maybe the most rare and strangest love affair
that ever came across our minds
not by ourselves but by reality
for us to do something about it
and some valid thing, of course,
to better our statistics
and perhaps to lick our wounds
of all those past disasters
and experiences of shipwrecks
undeserved and only brought by accident
and bad luck for some reason –
well, we have the chance now,
and our moment is eternity
for us to shape according to our wish
in mutual affection without limits.

Miraculous Encounters

How do two peole find each other
lost in billows of eternity
identifying and remembering each other
from an unknown ancient history
of nothing left except vibrations
of immortal souls for recognition?
It's a miracle and the more undeniable as such,
as experts even know with certainty
the art of recognizing spirits,
elves and angels of no palpability at all.
Denying miracles is to deny the facts of history
and to deny the miracle of life itself.

Sharing

You have caught my soul, my love,
by simple charm and honesty
and won my heart
for you to handle but with care;
but there was never anything amiss between us,
melting instantaneously together
as two old souls always do,
and even sharing the same sorrows,
the outrageous tragedies of two beloved sisters
representing beauty, talent and intelligence,
one mother of three children
and one sparkling blooming youth.
There is nothing so far that we could not share;
so let us just continue sharing our lives together
naturally as it comes,
and there can be no end on it.

Dreamburst

As I dream of you
entering my mind
in the still of the night
and all through the glorious day,
I just can't imagine
how ever I could do without you,
and still we existed for so long
without knowing the other existed.
The beauty of the soul transcends all reality
and overrules it by replacing it
by its more lasting significance,
while reality is only death;
but dreams and love and beauty
last triumphantly forever.

On the Edge of Extremity

Of course it hurts,
all those supreme disappointments,
all those disastrous heartbreaks,
all those deceits, betrayals and undeserved adversities;
but still it was worth it,
the total commitment
of your life and soul and body,
the wasting of your last energy,
the exposure of your inmost feelings
and the loss of everything you had,
it was all worth it,
since you survived
and still can go on loving
even more for all your loss,
to lose it ever and again
in the repetition of eternity
of how you can not live

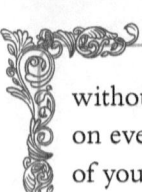
without your wasting of your love
on everything that's worth all losses
of your love forever to be gone
and lost to be regained forever.

Courtesy

As you remain the only tenant of my dreams,
my love flows on incessantly
like bleeding wounds of lust and joy
to never stop beautifying
all that is to our world
of common friends and relatives,
the victims and deceased ones
ever being there more live than ever,
while this haze of tenderness
beleaguers me to warm me up
in ever greater piety towards our love
that is a fountain of the purest joy.
So let me keep you in my heart
for you to dwell there in supreme security,
while I remain the thankful tenant of your own,
completely reassured that there could be
no better and no safer place
for my heart to keep bleeding in
in tearful joy of thankfulness.

Ice

It's unavoidable,
it's part of life,
the ice you have to cross
and slid on, often falling,
never safe,
its coldness made for slips
and always one day or another
thawing
with disastrous consequences,
as you must fall through
sooner or later;
and then all depends
on that life struggle
which must follow –
will you sink, succumb and perish
or survive refreshed
but somewhat cooler?
It takes time to warm up afterwards,
but then at least you are experienced
to walk more carefully next time,

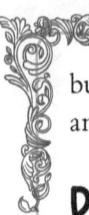

but there will always be more ice,
and there will always be more thaws.

Digital Love

Is it possible?
Does it work?
It depends
on what's behind it,
if it is supported
by the honesty of telepathic truth,
sincerity and will
to make it happen,
to maintain the contact
and the love by thought
if physical reunion is impossible,
as it is now in our case;
wherefore I can not love you any less
but only even more
for digitally clumsy imperfections.

The Only Risk

How could I possibly let go
of such a beautiful relationship,
which costs us nothing
and allow us only freedom,
carrying with it only love
and strong affection that forever grows?
There is no chance of getting free
from such a perfect freedom
binding us together only naturally
in the harmony of natural affection.
Could there possibly be any harm
in such a strangely wonderful liaison?
Yes, there is one harm, but one harm only:
that of ever losing touch with it
to let it go.

Separated Together

As you whisper in my ear
the things I want to hear,
my heart melts down to tears
for you, my only dear,
while distances betray us
and our circumstances
aggravate our grievances
while our love enhances
perfectly to match our chances
to perhaps one day in spite of all
find something to unite us,
while at the same time
everything combines
to make our separation
to our very union.
Fate always intertwines
to force our fall
into what ultimately brings us
to remain withal
together after all.

Helpless, Almost

Your rationality bewilders me,
your sense transcends my own,
I am a maniac in comparison
and sick at that in mind and soul,
while you appear a formidable godsend
to adjust me and correct me
with your calm good sense and reason,
but do I have the capacity to listen
and to be corrected by a better self
that I did hardly make myself deserved of?
It's all up to me, I am afraid,
but one thing I will do for sure:
to thank you for your mere existence
and to never let you go away or vanish
from your vital presence in my life
as my only light to guide me in my blindness.

Service

As I move to you with my vibrations
tenderly caressing you at length,
I just could not feel any better
at this consummation of our harmony,
as if there couldn't be a thing
still lacking in our free existence
of pure love and nothing else,
as if our separation even
couldn't be more negligeable
as my life is filled with you.
So let us stay that way and carry on,
and I will humbly stick to this my altar worship
of my daily constant service to our love.

Facts

As I dream of you in faithful homage,
it is difficult to keep away from worship
of the saintly ideal that you represent,
while at the same time nothing
could be so much down to earth
as your impressing common sense
and downright honesty of pure sincerity
which makes all other positive characteristics
negligeable and superfluous,
your character and heart
so dominating and outweighing,
overshadowing all pettiness to be ignored.
We struck together instantly
the Mother Lode of life's essentials,
and what more can we expect
except the joy of sharing it together?

Enigmas

As my love rises in the morning
with the sun and beauty of the world,
there is no match to all that harmony
that blooms throughout my soul
singing all your glory
and that we have found ourselves
and found each other
never to be separated ever again
as our souls were always grown together
into something of an everlasting union
of united wisdom, love and tolerance
in worship of eternal truth and beauty.
Could I be more clear and explicit?
What is there more to say
when love has taken our language away
to speak more freely
what never could be spoken
except by wavelengths of the air
of that strange idiom of vibrations only
that only telepaths may understand
and therefore hold their most expressive silence?

Comradeship

My comrade in the struggle
is my twin of destiny,
our personalities are intertwined
as if we never had but been together,
and I don't just only love her
but adore her senselessly
in fatal passions of eternity,
and I will gladly suffer for it
as a downright self-tormentor of profession.
Cure me not of this my plague,
but let me go on loving you forever

as the one friend I could never do without,
my bosom friend of destiny
and comrade of our freedom struggle of eternity.

Manifestation

- reflection

The sweetness of your presence
transcends all limits of resplendent bliss,
the more so for your absence
shortened by the overwhelming longing
that keeps on continuing to grow,
embracing you in ever warmer hugs
of love that never can be stopped.
Thus beauty rules the world
magnificently and ubiquitously
bestowing on it everlasting life
of simple love that never can be halted
but must keep on growing
and continuing forever.
Thus am I but one small wave
along the ever windy roaring ocean
always moving forward
in the overwhelming love force
that keeps battering all shores forever
in a constant demonstration
of the universal force
and origin of love and life.

Appeal

May I love you once more?
– in secret intimacy,
most clandestinely
with only you and me to watch
and be aware of how I love you,
needing you more urgently
than I myself can be aware of,
nevermore to let you go
away from me out of my heart,
but keeping you in safety,
locking myself out of
any other possible pretension,
since you are my other half;
and without you
my life would be reduced indeed
to that intolerable poverty
which was I before I met you.
Maybe I protest too much,
but love's voice never can be quieted;
for nothing is more irresistible
than the truth of nature in true love.

Hardships of the Die-Hards

That's us, the sufferers
who never can give up
but go on fighting,
torturing themselves
for nothing but thin air
despised as asinine ideals,
while we know better,
fighting to the bitter end
for our faith in truth and justice,
untouchable crusaders
for the values of eternity,
unvanquishable truth and beauty
manifested in continuous creativity
that no one ever can put down,
the glory of creation
that if anything on earth
is properly divine.

Impossible Equation that Works

It's like a mathematic formula:
distances are neutralized
and absence is made void,
reduced to nothing by affection,
while our love can only be advanced
by turning into objectivity
by facts of separation,
leaving only facts remaining
of our common personality,
how we belonged from the beginning
to each other to remain so
mystically in our mind united
while we are two different persons still,
of different stories, different destinies
and very different wills,

and seem obliged to so remain.
Our common fate thus seems to be
united closely in true love together
and the more so for our constant separation.

Maturity

What does it matter
that your hair is getting greyer
and your tempo slacker
while you get more comfortable
substituting laziness for work
with handicaps and pains for an excuse,
while you look less and less into the mirror
to evade the obvious truth
that you are getting old;
but everyone is getting older,
even young impertinent and careless sports
rejoicing in their ignorance naïvely
have nothing to be proud of
in the perspective of time;
while we, in spite of our grey hairs
have learned to love in spite of all
and keep on loving,
and that will keep us young at heart
and ever grow our souls forever younger,
as we stick to life's profoundest wisdom,
that of simply sticking to our love.

Out of Touch

As we are never out of touch,
no matter how far we are separated,
there is never any risk of losing
that most valuable touch of pricelessness
with our world of sound reality
of chaos, turbulence and revolutions
where the ultimate deciding force is nature,
justly threatening with the upheaval
of abusive mankind's universal terrorism
in irresponsibly exterminating wildlife,
the only sound life form there is;
which we are allied to
as incurably free lovers
of the wildest forms of life,
and that is our eternal contact.
Bide by me, my love, and keep to purity
of life and soundness and of nature,
and we'll never lose our touch
as universal freedom fighters.

A Glimpse of Paradise

A glimpse of paradise
out in the desert
of the nakedness of loneliness,
the lack of water in the universal drought,
and there was you,
like some miraculous angelic apparition
out of nowhere,
showing me a way to go,
a path through all the mirages
of lies of failures of this barren life,
which brought me back to life
in search for you,
and my chief comfort is now ever,
that however much astray I go,
I know now that all ways and paths
will always lead me back to you.

Abstruse Facts of Life

So it was from the beginning:
there were no limits to my faith in you,
no reservations in my absolute affinity,
the flow was there and live
and ready to embalm you
in the overwhelmingness of beauty
of the endless riches and resources
of an overflowing heart
once opened up to natural affection,
and so, there you are, we stand there caught
by destiny in its most wondrous mechanisms
of inexplicable benevolence,
quite given up to our common soul
that inveigles us in fathomless profundity
of total mystery, all in the greatest riddle of them all,
how all this actually could be reality.
And yet it's there, and we are here,
and all that we can do about it
is only to succumb to factual love.

Between the Battles

In the breaks of time
between the battles,
my sole chance of an escape
is flying up to you
in loving thoughts of limitless affection
far away from this confusing vanity
to find you even furthermore away,
but there at least our thoughts can meet.
It is the briefest of encounters
but the more invaluable as such
and more significant
for its taking place at all;
and I can live on it for any time

throughout the trenches
as I dive down into battle
to be buried once again
in this confusing world of vanity.

Chance Meetings

Suddenly a friend appears
completely out of nowhere,
and you didn't even know
that person did exist,
and suddenly a new dimension opens up
of aspects of new friendships and horizons,
and your future prospects multiply
of opportunities and possibilities
of new mentalities to know

and new life facets to discover.
Naturally you must cling to such chance meetings
and not let them just pass by,
but catch them in their golden moment
and preserve the treasure that they bring
to let them join your life
and let yourself join in with them.

Stuck

As my heart melts into you, my love,
with no end to its sweetness,
filling up the world with beauty
coming out of our affection,
there is nothing to resist our warmth
as we encompass the whole universe
in one embrace and fit of perfect love.
I wish to stay with you within you
never to get out of this embrace
to leave the joy of staying inside you
in ecstasy of bliss and happiness.
So let's just keep within each other
never to let go of our counterpart,
and thus we will remain united
to enrich the world of love with our love.

Love and Physics

I found my love so far away
that it would seem a matter of far-fetchedness
to bring it and to keep it up to date,
and thus my closest friends, both male and female,
are the farthest distanced from me;
but at the same time, this might be the very proof
that love is independent of the physical conditions
and survives the better for adversity and trial,
if it's genuine and true.
My love is therefore closer to me than she ever was

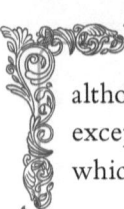
although our wordly distance is unbridgeable
except by the communion of the souls
which easily breaks any rule of physics.

We Are All Out of Joint...

As I dream of you, my love,
you come to me in strange manifestations.
I have even dreamt about your mother,
although I did only meet her once.
The care is infinite between us,
not just for ourselves but for our families,
no matter how dispersed and shattered
they are in all directions of the world
with usually aborted lives
which they claim all the same to be successes,
while we are too down to earth for self-deception; –
but let all those tragedies and losses be –
whose life is not a perfectly aborted failure,
viewed objectively? We all end worse
than even how we started with a naked scream,
and if we're lucky we'll find love at least
somewhere between, while the ultimate journey's end
is always a most well deserved release
from all the things that always did go wrong,
while we are free at least from the responsibility
of trying to at least set something right...

The Power of Longing

As long as there is something for you
ardently to long for,
you will keep afloat and flying
in control of all your powers,
for the longing is the surest symptom
of the definite syndrome of love and life.
I know, the more you long,
the more it is a torture,

but I can assure you at the same time,
that the more you long, the healthier for you,
since love is only wholesomeness,
and longing is its spiritual manifestation.
Never be afraid of longing and of suffering for love,
for there is no more certain evidence
of manifested truth of life
in absolute sincerity and honesty.

The Supreme Paradox

(the supreme self-contradiction as its own supreme self-evidence)

You are always by my side
especially when you are not there.

You are always in my heart
especially when it is broken and empty.

You are always present in my life
especially in your absence.

You are always in my focus
especially when I am out of my mind
and all my senses are dead.

You are always my one and only love
the force of which goes on
increasing constantly forever
the more we are distanced from each other.

And thus our love goes on increasing and expanding
the more it becomes impossible,
thus proving the supremest paradox
in proving itself by refuting itself.

Let it Be Enough

And would I not love you
with a bleeding heart
of fountain inexhaustibility
that never could care more for you
in self-denial unto self-annihilation
out of worship, adoration and idolatry?
That fire never will be quenched
nor leave me ever any peace,
and I enjoy it.
Let it be enough:
I could not love you more,
nor could it ever end.

To the Brave Oppositions in Iran and East Turkestan

Wasted and exhausted
it's a feat to lift your feet
while flapping broken wings
is just a weary burden
and your heart of lead needs melting down
to softer, lighter and more pliable material
for more apt and healthy purposes
than heavy broken hearts and heartaches.
Let me sleep again and dream again
of better worlds than all the lost ones,
and I shall most gratefully reach out for any straw
that providence and mercy offers me from nowhere
in the whirling stream that drags me down
into the dregs of all this worldly mess
of universal violation of all human rights and freedom
which was all the health there ever was in mankind.

The Problem of the Eternally Beloved

(– Beethoven's "eternally beloved" has never been identified, for instance...)

Who is his love?
Who has his heart?
Is there at all an object
that can be identified?
There has been timeless speculation
sometimes endlessly
in certain literary lovers' seriousness:
could they have been but fantasies,
or was there really someone,
and in that case, who was she?
If it remains unknown,
how can we even know about the gender?

I assure you, there was never any true love
that was not concrete:
if there was love that found expression
in sincerity and honesty of words,
then the loved one always was a person
and a certain person other than himself;
and if he called her Beatrice, Laura,
Fanny or a secret and protected name,
it is a matter of self-evident and obvious proof
that she was clearly an identified and private person,
never anything diffuse or general
and never just a fantasy;
for true love is not love
if it is not concrete,
which every true and honest lover knows too well,
and there was never any word against it.

Sotto Voce

Am I too intimate for you?
Is that an outrage that insults you?
Let me lower then my whispers
to be even more inaudible
except for your ears only,
and allow my touch
to soften even unto mere vibrations
unperceivable except for your soul only
in the finest harmonies conceivable
that can be heard in silence only
in the voice of only purest love.
Thus maybe I may touch and love you
without ever hurting you
or trespassing too closely on your soul,
too well aware of the extremest sensitivity
that only the supremest truest love is made of.

The Mystery of Love

What is the inmost power mystery of love?
Is it your own active love,
or is it someone other loving you?
Is this mysterious force an outside matter
reaching you from others,
or is it your own and private matter?
No one knows for sure.
The only certain thing
is that you never are alone with it,
that it must be a dual mutual thing
to work and to exist at all;
and then I lean towards the mystery,
that it is the communion of two souls
that it is all about,
that somehow reach a contact
that is beyond the material,
which seems obviously manifested
when two souls remain in contact
although they can't see each other.
That if anything is probably true love
which carries on beyond all known dimensions
independently of space and time.

Surreptitiously

The impossibility of our love
is no impediment to its reality,
we can deny it to the world
but never to ourselves,
it is a fact of life,
and though it brings much suffering,
the joy of it is infinite
belonging to the zone of timelessness,
a certain matter of eternity.
So let it just go on

in torment, agony and sorrow,
its beauty easily surviving vanity
and every weakness of mortality,
since in untouchable supremacy
it simply never can give in.

Timelessness

Timelessness is actually the only time zone
and the one we all should live in
now, tomorrow and in all times past,
neglecting nothing of our time responsibility
for all that happens, all that ever happened
and all things to come.
The individual responsibility is absolute,

transcending the mortality of power and politics
dismally confined in private interests,
while the individual mind
of empathy and sense of decency
is the supreme responsibility and motor
of all welfare for mankind.
The cue now for the future is co-operation,
since what history now needs most urgently
is a new age of international co-operation.

The Volatility of Love

You fall in love and fall to wishful thinking
that you've found your life's ideal
and offer her eternities of love
in perfect willingness to sacrifice whatever,
until you are cheated and betrayed,
deceived and brought to ruin by reality.
Thus love seems just a fleeting thing,
like a delightful dream of no more substance;
but still, love remains and drives you on,
the very heart of love is to continue against all denial,
spurring you to after all remain an obstinate idealist;
and whoever falls to love, love never falls.

Hope

I could cry out my eyes in flooding tears of blood
for all my sorrows and lost loves;
but still there is the possibility
for beauty to in spite of all start triumphing again,
since it was there once, true and honest;
but you chose to just walk by
and leave her as a fatally presumed impossibility.
The formula is this: first do your duty
and what's necessary, then do what is possible
of all the things you want to do,
and after that quite natural accomplishment

you'll find that all that's left for you to do
is to break through and carry out the most impossible;
for beauty never leaves us but is always there,
just waiting to appear again, if she is bypassed,
hibernating to just flourish, ever turning up again.

The Magic of Manali

Manali is one of the most popular hill stations in India at the foot of the Himalayas at 2000 meters with a very exotic cultural blend of its own…

The friendly idyll of the snowy hills
has something over it of deep intrigue,
while nomads, outcasts, sadhus,
hippies, trekkers and adventurers
flock here to some of them remain for life,
a sacred haven for the seekers
with exotic access to such places of notoriety
as Manikaran and Malana up the Parvati,
the valley of the lost and those desiring oblivion,
like all those pathetic Israelis after three years'
heavy and traumatic military service,
going on the loose here only to forget about their situation,
like so many others here with their lost lives.
There certainly are stories here to tell and to discover
and to learn concerning destiny and the whole situation
of the definite predicament of all humanity.

The Nomad

Nothing can impede his freedom,
he was born to roam and wander all his life,
and lucky he, to have that precious gift
of being constantly in touch with the supreme divinity
of freedom all his life,
like being touched and ordained by eternity.
And he is wiser than most civilized prisoners
of cities spending all their lives in cubicles,
since he never bargains with his freedom,

his ideal of staying constantly in touch with nature,
ever on the move and circulating with the universe
to stop at nothing; since the only perfect freedom
never knows of any bounds or any limiting dimensions.

Departure

The sadness filling up the vacuum
in the emptiness of your departed friends
is like an endless melancholy abyss
too profound and overwhelming for expression,
going deeper in your heart and soul
than any physical expression can admit or show,
the feelings draining you of energy and will
so far that even oceans of your tears
will never water such a desert
and not even make a dwindling mudpool
for relief to all your pains, regrets and losses.
But that hope remains,
that your friends are still there
and waiting for you in the future
for that golden moment to return
of your most loving association.

What About It?

What about love, my darling?
You tempt me so seductively and irresistibly,
and I am all for it, but still
there are misgivings of experience.
So many times the truest love affairs went wrong,
and the cliché happy ending is the falsest myth,
since there always was what happened afterwards.
So let me love you faithfully but without ties,
let love be free and active on its wings
without any cuts and no enforcements down to earth,
and only so I certainly will love you
and be constant ever in my faith in freedom.

Spirited Away

I lost my mind and soul
up in the mountains
and cannot get them down again.
They call for me up there,
and there is no choice
but to return
up to the mountains
where freedom calls forever
for your liberation
holding there your mind and soul
in safe and sacred custody
until you return
up there unto the mountains
where one day finally
you will find your peace
up there beyond the mountains
with your head lost in the clouds
of the ultimate freedom
way up high
beyond the tops of the mountains.

Renewal

I was old and miserable and decrepit,
worn out by too many sorrows,
problems galore and worries without end,
but someone came along,
and it was you.
The spiritual healing of such wounds
that bleed to death inside the soul
without an outer trace of anything
is more miraculous than any other cure,
than any medicine and wonder,
and there was an urgent need of it.
The question now is:

how to keep it up,
maintaining this our new reunion
without new mistakes and failings,
without getting all dispersed,
disintegrating into pieces?
All we need is to keep up communication,
that's the only life-line,
which, when working,
can accomplish any miracle
and make all problems vanish,
blissfully transformed into surmounted challenges.

Frailty

Thy soul is all the treasure
of your love and universal charm,
the concentration of your beauty,
irrevocable and irresistible
and unpersihable as your heart
so full of only warmth and joy
that can but last forever.
Let me cherish you
but without touching you
inflicting never any harm or injury
but only watering your cultivation
as the most conscientious lover
only would at any cost
wage all on just preserving
and aggrandizing the beauty
of the everlasting moment
of consummate love.

Hestia

This enigmatic divinity, one of the 12 gods of ancient Greece, was the only one never to be depicted. Her symbol was instead the hearth.

The unknown goddess,
almost never made a statue of,
a silent modest background figure
staying quietly at home –
and maybe the most vital and important
of all gods and goddesses
for doing nothing but just being
there at home in coziness
with warmth and candour by the fireplace,
just keeping up the homely standard order,
keeping clean and making the home comfortable –
what could possibly be more important
than the very base of life,
a home to be at ease with
and to be at home in?
Still, she never made much noise,
no scandals, no atrocities,
no arguments, no love affairs,
just being there as the continuous stability,
the comfort of just being there at peace
and keeping up the basics
as the only ground
for the existence of all humankind.

Wuthering Heights

When the devils attack me in the night
my only possible escape is you,
while storms keep harrowing the countryside
wreaking havoc and destruction,
threatening our lives with mortal danger;
but my love is safe and beyond reach,
and I am with her in my dreams
untouchable to any mortal evil,

and I wallow in my bliss
and feast atrociously in my beatitude,
more certain than I ever was before:
no hubris ever can get even near to the sublimity
of love's eternal consummation,
that keeps constantly surpassing and transcending
even all her previous endeavours of eternity.

Getting Through (2)

Is it really worth it,
all that agony and desperation,
all that torture and despair,
that is the consequence
and other side of love and ecstasy,
the abyss of that hell
that heaven's bliss inevitably leads to,
ending up in knots of opposites,
the heavenly existence and its liberation
proving but a trap and desperate entanglement
of jealousies, complexities, suspicions,
sleeplessness and nightmares?
But the issue is of no importance,
since love never can be done without,
evaded or escaped from;
it is always there
expecting you and waiting for you,
and there is no way out
but to just get through with it;
and while you suffer it,
you might as well enjoy it.

Facebook Reflections

They say it's only for the young,
a forum for displaying vanity,
a wallowing in nonsense
and an endless jungle of confusion;
but it's in fact a very clever site,

well programmed, trimmed and working well,
a kind of ideal social network
for anyone to keep in touch
with all his friends or hers
on a continuous regular and daily basis,
with a smart and most efficient possibility
to exchange ideas and links and pictures,
– Yes, it is the ideal social network
for the busy person who has little time
to spend in actual company of all his friends,
while he can reach whomever all across the world
by simply looking up in his computer
what his friends are writing and communicating
universally but simply in the common facebook
which, accessible to everyone, belongs to everyone.

The Mask

You veil yourself in most mysterious disguises
as you enter prying into love
in masks that not just hide your face away
but even all your personality,
neutralizing and dissolving all your sex
to give full entry to your overwhelming love
that flows so generously without end,
so as to raise suspicions
as to who you really are.
Perhaps it's better not to know it
but to be content with your unfathomableness
which in its unidentifiable disguises
is the perfected manifested mystery of love.

Delirium

You are a concrete person, no mistake,
although I mainly see you from behind,
where none the less your beauty fills me
overwhelmingly with joyfulness delirium

and repletes my life with lovely dreams
of love that promises eternal continuity,
for such is beauty's force and influence,
more strong than anything on earth,
especially when clad in weakness and humility.
Thus am I sneaking constantly up from behind to you
to never let you go out of my love
that keeps caressing, worshipping and cherishing you
in fondest sweetness indefatigably,
keeping up that soft delirium
never to diminish
but to on the contrary forever grow;
for there is no more reliable long term expansion
than the labour of untiring love.

Backstage

The dream of love will never end
but constantly perfume our daily lives
with neverending fragrance
of sublime and subtle dreams
that are more real than ever our reality will be;
since love, the background motor
of all life's existence,
is all-powerful but only in spirituality,
the action being just a consequential play.
The background lovers, then,
are those who truly know something about it
and will keep controlling it
sustaining life in perfectly expanding continuity
as long as they remain invisible behind the scenes,
aware of the importance of safe-guarding
the most sacred secret mystery
of love's untouchability
in order to remain all-powerful.

Dead End of Conspiracies

When everything is turned against you,
what can you do? Just nothing.
Maybe you could simply scrap a thing or two,
some uncoöperative apparatus,
like an obstinate computer
that just drives you nuts,
with other electronic instruments,
all turned against you in a hopeless conspiration
that gives you no other choice
but to give up and leave it all
to hell, renouncing all responsibility;
and when you finally succeeded
in efficiently doing away with all those fucking monsters,
that just turned your life into a dead end trap,

a regular straitjacket of obstructions,
sabotage, disorder, havoc, mess and bloody hell,
then maybe you could start again
in yet another effort
to make something sensible out of your life,
just for a change...

Considering...

a trifle

Considering the fact
that I am late for work
and out of work
and can't get done my work
since there's too much of it
and I just can't get out of it,
I might as well just call it off
and stop here at my work
to spend the night here
working in my sleep...
It's not a very good idea.
I should go home to bed instead
and stay there with my love
that I keep constantly neglecting,
while the less that I neglect my work,
the less of it I manage to get done;
so what's the use
of getting constantly mixed up in this
and never get things sorted out?
My love is there and waiting for me,
and so is my work,
but they can never be combined.
So let's reach a compromise:
let's work just with my love in mind,
and let us sleep just dreaming of my love,
and maybe then we will get something done...

Mermaid Love

My love is gone down under
to the bottom of the ocean
swimming there along
in fairy tales with dolphins,
like a pursued mermaid
that no mortal can join up with,
but my company is hers,
and love knows of no limitation,
we can float and flow forever
in the best of companies
with elves and fairies,
mermaids, angels and what not
and never tire of that flexibility
enabling us to any change of form
to just keep on pursuing
love into the utmost bottomless recesses
of the universal abyss of profundity
of true and everlasting love.

The Song of Sirens

They really mean no harm,
and all they want is love,
and it is perfectly convincing,
their alluring song of love,
that is so desperately beautiful
that no one can resist
its perfect and expressive honesty.
Still, the only consequence is wrecks and ruins,
skeletons and ruined lives,
and no one knows what happened to the victims.
All they did was to approve of love
and listen to its perfect music
and become enticed by it quite naturally,
 – they were only human;

and they drank the song of love and perished,
no one has survived to tell their story,
they were sailors all and children of the sea,
who met with the consummate form of love
in highest musical unfathomableness and beauty;
and as far as anybody knows,
no one of them regretted it.

The Most Impossible Equation

The sunken love beneath the waves
seems hopelessly to have been lost forever,
buried in the ocean world of tears
where nothing is retrieved or can be found,
the grave that takes it all, returning nothing;
but how come, then, that my love still hovers
in a constant flight on wings of elves
that never can be caught or taken down to earth
and that a few initiated only can be made aware of
and that only the mind's eye can see
apart, of course, from second sight?
That is the strange impossibility and paradox,
that although I have lost my love forever
it is more alive than ever.

Sea of Love

Let me drown you in my sea of love
and sink with you into the waves
of everlasting tempests, turbulence
and wholesome fleeting movement
in this world of constant change,
where we together may carouse
and blend in life's surprising journey
of dramatic destinies and fateful turns
that ever make us start again
on new adventures into the profundity
of this amazing sea of love affairs

that ever seem to multiply
in richness as intoxicating as your hair,
this universe of beauty to get lost in,
while this worship keeps us ever diligent
in making never-tiring love.
So let's get buried and get lost
into the abyss of our stormy ocean
of our passion that can never end
but only must increase forever.

Flying Colours

Let me not forget to love you,
soul and body, heart and mind,
all the time and never leave you
but in absence even always keep you
present in my mind uninterruptedly
persistently in close communication,
never to forget the most important
of all facts, that I have not the right to live
if I for a moment fail to love,
to keep that light and fire burning
that must never be extinguished
but must burn forever
to keep hope and life alive
in sustained and constant flying colours,
since that's all we really need.

To a Holy Mountain

This crowning day of beauty
is like a dream of ideal worship
of a deity omnipresent and untouchable
but still accessible and visible
though completely out of reach
in perfect purity and splendour
way out there five thousand meters up
in nevermatched glorious supremacy

fitting only for the absolute divinity.
Thus do I worship thee, o holy mountain,
perfect symbol for the unattainable perfection
out of reach but omnipresent
in impressing beauty that shines out forever.

Love in the Mist

You came invisible
except for contours
through the fogs of mystrery
and mists of random chance
and found me out immediately
as if you actually could read my mind
like any open book,
which would be understandable
since you have read me through
for thirty years.
Still, this entrance through the clouds
is most characteristic
of our spurious relationship,
with all those accidental meetings
out of nowhere out of time,
which ever grows in intimacy
into ever denser mists of mystery.

Moonlight Skywalk

In this darkness, light is universal,
nothing could possibly harm or touch me
in this charming haze of sacred mists of mystery,
as moonlight floods the earth and lights my path
through any night to nowhere,
anywhere but always forward
to continuously greater heights
of beauty and its ever waxing glory
through the landscape dreams of ever denser magic
as I reach for you beyond the stars,

full well aware that you are always there
in constant wait for me in loyalty and faithfulness,
like I have never let you down,
my love of shining moonlight
through eternal nights of love
where we shall never tire
of aspiring further to the stars,
beyond the endless beauty of the universe.

The Other Side of Love

Love brings you the serenest heights of ecstasy,
but as sometimes you must do without it
you are plunged into the depths
of most unbearable despair
and feel yourself abandoned
on a desert ocean of melancholy,
the stillness of which is the worst of all,
as you drift lonely in the universe,

just falling through the utmost emptiness
down to a bottom that does not exist
of darkness growing ever darker and more hollow.
But this melancholy is, however, just a remedy,
a medicine and balance to your trips
of love exorbitancies and love ecstasies,
and you should take it just for what it is:
the other side of paradise and any shining medal
which exists just to enhance the glory of the front,
the background darkness to lift forth the light,
the endless midnight sky of universal inaccessibility
to just add glory to the blinding light of day
and all its present swarming life of splendour,
wallowing in love to never reach an end on it.

The Darjeeling Lecture

delivered in Darjeeling 2000 and (revised) in 2009
An Orientation in Contemporary Literature

(The Darjeeling Lecture.)
The Bible - Homer - Dante - Shakespeare.

These are the four corner stones of world literature and civilization: the Bible as foundation for the three monotheistic world religions, Homer as the firm ground of the whole classical civilization, Dante as the originator of the Renaissance, and Shakespeare as the maker of modern man. These four authorities almost make up half of the history of literature.

Victor Hugo - Charles Dickens - Dostoyevsky - Leo Tolstoy.

These are the four literary giants dominating the 19th century, Victor Hugo by his romantic spirit, Dickens with his humanitarian pathos, Dostoyevsky by his psychology and Leo Tolstoy by his realism.

Then comes the 20th century, but why don't we have giants like this in that age? The First World War destroyed an entire generation of hopes and talents, such a brilliant and promising novelist as Henri Alain-Fournier fell on the western front, many were the poets that shared his fate (like Rupert Brooke and Wilfred Owen), and the Second World War was even worse. The disasters of the first half of the century made it almost impossible for creative writers of classical literature to exist.

Among the most typical examples are the collaborating couple Romain Rolland-Stefan Zweig, pacifists who detached themselves from the mundane world and almost completely dedicated themselves to writing only biographies, to preserve for the future the lives of real artists and writers, the existence of which a new unhuman age had made impossible. Romain Rolland ended up as a Hinduist, and Stefan Zweig, after perhaps the most brilliant literary career of the 20th century, committed suicide in the third year of the Second World War, being an Austrian and a Jew. He found it impossible to exist in a world which could have brought an Adolf Hitler to power.

All the same, there have been writers in the 20th century, but what kind has dominated it? Affected modernists and posing humbugs like T.S.Eliot, James Joyce, Samuel Beckett and other freaks and frauds of unintelligible language distortions. Classical literature has almost completely disappeared, like classical art and music, to be replaced by nonsense, ugliness and noise.

Fortunately there have been exceptions though, and a few examples are worth keeping in mind. In America there are but very few, since vulgarity seems to dominate everything produced there, but in England we have several interesting examples. Robert Graves had enough of the western world by the First World War and afterwards almost exclusively dedicated himself to classical history and mythology. Joseph Conrad was a Pole but wrote in English, and his greatest admirer was Graham Greene, who must be regarded as one of the most important authors of the century, like the great connoisseur of human nature, William Somerset Maugham. Another underestimated writer is James Hilton, educated at Cambridge, with his sometimes ingenious novels. Among later authors John Fowles should be noted, whose novel "The French Lieutenant's Woman" is a successful attempt at reviving the great 19th century novel.

Let's also remember a few authors outside England. By the epoch-making "Doctor Zhivago", Boris Pasternak continues the great Russian tradition from Dostoyevsky and Tolstoy. The dramas of Jean-Paul Sartre are completely original and very effective, while at the same time he continues the tradition of the ancient Greek drama. Another very important modern novel is the Italian Elsa Morante's "History" in its deep neo-realistic settlement with the times of Mussolini and Fascism.

Although the great romantic-realistic story-telling tradition has had its hardest set-backs since the darkest medieval ages, it has survived and is continuing. But the same rule applies as ever: we have nothing else to build on but tradition. We have our great universal examples in the Bible, Homer, Dante and Shakespeare, and we have the great 19th century novelists to look up to; and even if the first half of the 20th century was almost only disastrous adversities, we still have the old examples to keep in mind, continue to learn from and keep up for the future.

Why, then, finally, is that tradition so important? Why bother about reading books? Because in those great immortal sacred books we have all the humanity there is. We have to look to them to find the sources of humanity, humanitarianism, the very identity of civilized man. The great classical writers are those who best understood and knew about man and thus could improve him by setting new examples. That's why I call the writer behind Shakepeare's dramas 'the maker of modern man', for so far no one has understood human nature better and improved it more than he.

Concerning the art of writing, there are three things to always bear in mind: concentration, meaning and style. Whatever you write, it must be as concentrated as possible not to be boring, it has to have a meaning – there is never any meaning in nonsense, for instance; while style can only be acquired by diligent practice – it usually comes with the years.

The best practice of all, however, is simply to be a good reader, to read as much as possible of qualified literature, preferably classics, and learn from what others have written. Knowledge is of course perhaps the most important of all, which you can only acquire by lots of reading and practice.

One good book to learn a lot from and a magnificent example of concentration and style, is Somerset Maugham's "The Summing Up", a quite small book that however never can be exhausted for its best possible advice to all readers and writers.

Best of luck!

The Lost Soul

As I fly between the skies
completely lost in space and time
belonging nowhere, roving everywhere,
the only thing I know
is all the things I miss,
the company of forlorn friends
completely at a loss as I,
my fellow wanderers in wilderness
belonging nowhere, out of place
wherever we appear;
and all that we can do
to somehow keep some foothold
is to stick at least together
to the only certain thing we have –
our love and firendship for each other.
Maybe in some better world
beyond all chaos and disasters
we shall find at last
some time to smile indeed,
as we shall meet again
occasionally through the aeons.

Ultimatum

"Give me liberty, or give me death." – O. Henry (who spent three years in prison)

Without control but flying high
irrelevant of space and time
and any order of the universe,
I just keep wuthering
and can't define my destination,
which keeps baffling me;
and so I just go on
identifying one place in the wrong place
and another one far beyond reach;
as I fall down again into the abyss
of mortality and passion and despair,
the enemy called weakness getting hold of you,
the only possible protection and defense
just being obstinate resistance and protest
against the enemies to my escape
on wings of chance and spiritual fugue
to get away beyond all pettiness,
the only sane environment of any man.
The only liberty is total liberty,
and if that is beyond reach,
the only possible alternative is death,
the definite and ultimate release.

Keep it Growing

My love, don't cut your hair,
don't make your beauty shorter,
just let it grow and let me hide in it,
to ever worship what this richness stands for:
generosity and sweetness,
light, delight and affluence,
the constant growth of nature's finest purity,

the symbol of your very personality,
the most profound enigma
veiled up in a mystery
that never can be fathomed
without opening an abyss
of a bottomless eternity of darkness –
let me seek protection from that peril
by escaping into that unfathomable beauty
of your hair, so ultimate a perfect hiding-place,
the only absolute protection
against anything that ever bothered me.

Another Reason

It makes you younger,
this expansion of your hair,
this prolonging of your beauty,
this free growth without infringement,
this vast wealth of light and generosity
embodied in your gorgeous hair
for me to tousle in to happily get lost,
like in a web of charming dreams
of infinite seduction and allurement,
fascination and enchantment,
adding to your spell and total power,
to which I must willingly succumb.
Continue thus, my love,
and let it grow to ever brighter beauty,
and that will be some insurance
that I never will be able to forsake you,
tire of you or give up my dream
of everlasting love forever growing
comfortably and harmoniously with you.

Incapacitated

you desperately gasp for air
but can not reach it,
being slowly suffocated
but just not enough to die
but merely to remain in constant dying,
among tortures most unbearable of all,
and all is dead and dying except hope.
It happens every year again.
Cruel winter buries life live,
while every spring there is the miracle again
of resurrection, love reviving, life triumphing;
but the ordeal is the same

each bloody hellish winter
putting you and all life on the rack
to all but kill you off,
just saving a small whiff of life enough
to make the resurrection workably inevitable.

Midwinter Light

Let me keep you in my heart
and warm you for the winter
in protection of my piety
against the coldness of adversities
and try to vest you with a better life
without the hardships and the sufferings
that you indeed did not deserve.
If I could just assuage the outrage
of your tormentous afflictions,
it certainly would be a triumph
for my tenderest ambitions,
and I would not hesitate
to be most actively consistent
about carrying through that quest
of humble love and tender faith
towards our sorely tried relationship
that is the more ideal
for all your sufferings and our trials.
Let this be my offering to you
out of the darkness of midwinter
as the smallest but the most enduring light
of love that so far never failed.

Presence

As I wake up in the night
and find myself afloat in emptiness
surrounded by a sea of silence,
you are all around me
like a fairy at my cradle

or a guardian angel for that matter,
filling me with unexpected awe
and worship of the express moment
as the sweetness of your music
quietly embalms me
as I sink into the sea of love
of precious piety and intimate respect,
as I feel there is nothing truer,
nothing more important and more palpable
than this existence of this actual love
that quietly pervades the universe
as I in perfect loneliness and silence
must accept the undeniability
that you are closing in on me
as love is getting nearer
in its universal intimacy
ruling powerfully all the world
as you engulf me
by your distant presence.

Her Triumph

The shattering and shocking tragedy
of your outrageous fall
fills me with paralysed dismay,
while no one can remain unmoved
by such a shocking story and adversity,
which would have killed an ordinary person off;
but I would think your sensitivity has saved you.
Oaken trees of stalwart hardiness
will break at heavy storms,
while rushes, whipped down to the ground,
will rise again as soon the storm is over.
Your vulnerability is utterly extreme
but will by its mere delicacy,
deep-felt empathy and total flexibility
survive whatever earthquake cataclysms,
emerging only nobler and more beautiful

for all the undeserved atrocious trials,
as each flower after winter
and the irrevocability of growing daylight
after every midwinter nadir.
And thus you triumph in your worst defeat,
maturity renewing your nobility
and harmony transcending all discord
to settle down in peace.

Hibernation

We are happy to at least survive
the hardship and adversities
of this recession winter
of increasing discontent,
the weakest falling deepest,
wreaked down in the gutter,
while we barely even keep our noses
above water, languishing and gasping
desperately for some space to breathe
in this deep-frozen world of violated spiritual values:
starving artists starve to death,
and bankrupt journals must close down,
publishers just scrap your manuscripts
for your audacity to even make an offer,
and commercialism increases in monstrosity and cruelty
with the preposterous society of self-consumption,
ruining the planet, forcing all idealism out of business.
Still, we manage to survive,
the winter blossoms and perennials,
since we are used to hibernating,
being certain of our case,
that beauty always must survive all ugliness,
that love lasts longer than all mortal brawl
and longer than eternity,
which is our party for survival.

Winter Terror

Darkness looms as coldness steals upon you
sneaking even into bed with you
to pester you with sleepless nights
with no chance ever to get warm again,
as nightmares gather in delirious crowds
to drive you nuts and sick all over,
fever raging in your veins,
as everything continues to get worse.
And still, right in the heart of darkness
suddenly again there was a recognition
of the kind of love that never dies
but keeps revitalizing
even under the most desperate conditions,
graciously renewing all your energy and strength
by simply showing off in sheer existence,
the supreme untouchability
of sovereign integrity of beauty,
carrying all before her through the ages,
as is her normal wont and operation,
never brought down or defeated,
pure serenity of absolute survival.
Thank you for thus gracing me
by only making an appearance,
instantly replacing all the winter terrors
with resplendent light.

A Question of Beauty

When are you loveliest?
Is it in the golden summertime,
when everything is flourishing in sumptuousness
and greenth extols in health and wealth
to make the whole world sparkle in full glory?

Or is it in the fall of colourfulness,
when the harvests fill the needs of life

to make some room for afterthought and melancholy
turning life and beauty the more irresistible?

Or is it in the heavy trials of dark winter
when severity makes people cuddle up
and turn more closely to each other
in the absolute white purity,
which makes the winter beauty sovereign?

Or is it in the spring renaissance
when life wakes up from the dead
in more triumphant ecstasy than ever
in explosive dynamics of beauty
more surprising every year?

No, you are never loveliest
in any high season of beauty,
since you always are the loveliest
out of time, regardless of all seasons.

Orpheus

You descend unto us mortals
bringing light and inspiration
with the joy of beauty
as a dream of immortality,
at least a vision of its possibility,
as the mere existence of your person,
O talented son of the ideal Apollo,
gives not only hope to all humanity
but lightens up all hopelessness
and hell itself
with all its doomed accursed souls
condemned to suffer in extremity
forever, like ourselves this winter...
well, your visit was indeed most welcome
like a well-deserved renewal of the show
with better hopes this time

that your inspiring and revitalizing gifts
will keep us going for it yet again
for yet another moment of eternity.

The Loss of Love

a rather common syndrome, I am afraid...

You carry on in spite of all
with all your duties, businesses and burdens,
straining constantly against the wind
in never-ending ever steeper up-hill
trying to survive
and to forget your losses,
but you can not do without them.
They are always there, reminding you
of how it was when once you had it all,
the whole world and no worries,
just because you had someone to love.
There is no compensation for that loss,
no workoholism, no obsession will suffice
to make up for that emptiness;
and all you can do is to struggle on
and cry at times for all that nothing that you got
as a reward for all your sufferings,
while none of all your losses
ever was intentional, deserved or fair.

Ice Age Reflection

Who can believe in spring
in this diverted ice age
of deep-freeze constancy in lethargy,
depression, anguish and sterility,
where there is hardly any space and outlet
but for languishment, surrender and despair?
They say the snow is white and pure and beautiful,
it is, of course, but just to look at, not to live in,

and we are obliged to be snowed-in indefinitely,
ruthlessly buried alive by winter.
Still, the spring is somewhere waiting for us,
although it seems farther off than ever,
hardly even to be dreamt of by a realist;
and meanwhile we will have to be content
with all the charm of this delightful
pure white beautiful sterility and hardness
of at least a temporary ice age.

Old Mortality

She is always waiting there
to catch you as you fall,
the mother of existence,
the safe insurance at the end,
the final liberator
garanteeing total freedom,
old mortality, the certain harvester of all,
who by his mere existence
offers you the opportunity of life
to hover at your wildest,
no height and no distance being too severe,
no possibility being restricted;
that old death awaiting at the end
ensures you every liberty of life
within the only limit
that you must return to him
where he awaits you with a silent promise
or a half one – there's his only doubtfulness,
that he might launch you on another start.

The Language of Music

It's the only transcendental language
as the only language to be understood immediately without prerequisites.
The most unmusical person can understand a simple melody
and thereby be brought to an uplifting emotional reaction,

which hardly any other language is capable of to the same degree.
However, music has its grammar, which is simple
but without which music is but noise without a meaning.
Like a sentence must consist of subject and predicate to convey any meaning,
music must have melody and harmony and rhythm.
A melody can exist without harmonics and rhythm but is then naked
and needs dressing up. Harmonics is the perfect costume,
while rhythm will make it fit to any purpose universally;
and thus with these three components, melody, harmony and rhythm,
music is superior as language and will get through anywhere,
outshine all languages and unite them,
for any word and language can be set to music.
The natural cosmic order within music
is so consummate in its nature and so pure in its comprehensive abstractness
that it generally always has a positive, uplifting and inspiring effect.
It's something of an ideal in itself in its unassailable abstraction,
it is, as Lionardo da Vinci said, "the abstract made concrete",
and could thereby be described as a unifying link between
the ideal world and reality,
with a kind of Promethean function of uplifting effect to man.
Beethoven sometimes regarded himself as a modern Prometheus
stealing fire from the gods to light up man.
In brief, as a language music has what all other languages lack,
the something extra,
which better can unite all languages and people and nations
than any political speaker can do.
Say it in music, and the message will get through,
while almost any preacher always preached to only deaf auditions.

The Sin of Beauty

If the attractiveness of beauty is a sin,
then every sin is beautiful
and should be obligatory in every education,
taught at school and wallowed in as subject
universally, for health and benefit to everyone;
but I think beauty is much better than a sin.
It is a medecine and remedy against all ugliness,

the opposite of everything in life that drags you down,
the counterpart and other side of history,
excluded shamefully from ordinary history accounts,
while only beauty managed to survive it.

So let's dedicate ourselves to the exoneration
constantly forever of the Sin of Beauty,
which you never really can have quite enough of.

The Problem with Beauty

The problem about beauty is,
it is too beautiful,
every beautious lady is too beautiful,
and you can never have them all,
and even if you have one of them,
that is not enough,
since there is always someone else
who happens to be even more beautiful.
The eyes can not resist the charm of beauty,
you just have to fall for every one of them,
there is not a chance of an escape;
while more often than not you are deluded,
and the beauty proves to be a mask of shallowness,
which only complicates the problem…
Thus you learn with age
to look beyond the mask of beauty,
and eventually you will discover
that real beauty has no permanence
except within the soul.

Avatar Blues

Blue is beautiful,
especially when it is natural,
as in those precious beings
living there among the trees
of Utopian world Pandora

in perfect symbiosis
with all living things
with deeper harmony and empathy
than any human being here on Earth,
a monster race of egoism and strife,
a self-destructive and unnatural absurdity
which most of all is qualified for war
and secondly for greed –
that's all their history is all about;
and yet, this blue race in the sky
was actually invented here by man,
a wonderful result of his imagination,
like an ideal and alternative humanity
who hasn't yet committed those mistakes
that ruined mankind's history.
And that is all that we can learn of,
our own creativeness and fantasy,
the striving for idealism that never left us
but made us go on in spite of all
against our own destructiveness
to maybe one day triumph after all?
That actually may be our only hope.

Philosophical Digression

The exquisite subtlety of genderless love
is best expressed in music, someone told me,
for its capability of the extremest tenderness
without temptation of exaggeration
or of going any step too far;
which brings me to the possibility,
that music actually might be the very heart
and essence of love language and expression,
hardly able to get further purified and concentrated.
That brings us to the more wondrous possibility,
that love is truest without genders.
Could it possibly be true?

Well, anyone could fall to music
when it is a love expression,
and to that fall, sex and gender are superfluous.

Youth

The youth is always there
no matter how it ages,
you are never dead and gone
since once you were alive,
and that life at its best
is what survives forever,
in its supremest health and beauty,
vitality and charm and fragrance –
you can never lose it,
even if you die,
and ageing is just maturation –
all the best parts of your life and person
are embedded in your soul
to there shine forth
in splendid continuity forever.

Paradise Speculation

Tell me, what is Paradise
this strange ideal that everybody dreams of
but which no one yet has seen;
but ask me, for I know it.
The problem is, it is not practical
nor physical nor tangible in any way
but purely intellectual,
a utopia, which however does exist
and everyone is well familiar with
who knows about ideals and dreams and beauty
and the charm of knowledge and its acquisition.
If it were to be defined at all,
I would fain liken it
to sitting down in peaceful studies
listening to soothing music
letting creativity flow forth.
That is the only Paradise I know,
and that is good enough for me.

Some Ordinary Beating Around the Bush...

My heart belongs to you,
it always did, I never had it
for myself but only for my love,
who kept it never to herself
but always kept returning it to me
so that I could continue
giving it to her in perfect continuity
as long as love goes on,
as long as life goes on,
as long as I can still adore you,
which I never could stop doing
so far, since your beauty always was
of some eternal irresistibility
which keeps me going on

and which could keep me going on
if not forever, then at least
for all eternity at the time being.

Diagnosis

The ecstasy of love
is like a dream materialized
but still remaining dreamlike
in its nature and its substance
for all its tangible reality,
transporting you from that reality
to the more esoterical dimensions of eternal dreams,
while still your love remains at present
all too real to not be true
in spite of its extraterrestial substance,
cleaving you in half and double
stranded in reality
with undeniable eternity
of all too present love.
There is no way out
but capitulation
to eternity, to love
all in a fickle moment
of the fleeting now.

Spooks

They are always there and waiting for you
in the mists of apocryphal mystery
in other dimensions of paranormality
but always ready for you to welcome you back
to their eternal and extraterrestial community,
where you will always have a home
amidst the continuity of undying philosophy
adoring love and beauty above all
that will triumph and expand forever
ignorant of any risk or chances of impediment,

while in that zone there are no limits,
only perfect freedom that can only grow at large
to ever keep that mystical philosophy alive
of beauty never waning and of love not ever fading.

Stuck

Who can cope with the entanglement
and the ensnaring self-consumption of addictive love
that traps you in a black hole of devouring exhaustion
to just keep you prisoner with no escape,
since you delight in the outrageous masochistic madness
that eats up your soul in painful loss
until you languish in supreme despair;
and yet the miracle phenomenon is this,
that you just cannot stop
but must continue lusting, driving on in spite of all
in self-consuming and outrageous folly,
since your energy in that direction is a black hole
that can never be fulfilled or satisfied;
and thus you keep on roller-coastering without hope and no end
except in new black holes in darkness through the universe.

Spring of Youth

How could I else than love you
for your irresistibility and charm
and magic of eternal youth
transcending even timelessness
and all conceivable dimensions,
since you never are the same
although your beauty never changes,
as if it was renewed each day
returning to its freshest basics;
and thus can I never be relieved of you
but kept apace with you instead
renewed with you to ever greater love
in the eternal spring of love
which is but truth and beauty entertained.

Comment

As my dreams come true
I think of you,
the realizer of my dreams,
transforming life into a paradise
of dreams materialized into reality,
so how can this result
in less than an obsession?
Stay by me,
remain just as you are,
and nothing could become more perfect;
since I never was the one
to ever give up love
once I was sure of it.

No Sex Please - I Am Single

(for some bachelors, singularity is like a religion...)

Don't you dare to love me,
I've had quite enough of love
by sticking to the only safe one,
loving just myself.
I don't need any trespassing
into my mind, integrity and singularity,
since sex is just a mortal exercise
destroying friendship and relationships,
since no one marries any more
except for masochistic separation
and the sufferings of self-inflicted trauma.
So I must advise you not to love me,
so that I can love you even more.

The Loveliness of You

The loveliness of you
is like a dream of you
that lasts forever
which you never want to quit
but only wish to stick to
like to some eternal energy
that constantly renews you
making you more active and alive
for every moment of your life
as long as you remain in dreams
to never more wake up,
the only possible awakening
just being finding out
that you no longer can wake up.

Inevitably

What distances could ever separate us,
and yet are we separated
by the cruelty of distances
that cannot reunite us
for at least a year or more
with threatenings of even more,
wherefore my heart is bleeding
evermore in tears for longlost friends
and friendships painful to remember
for their intimate profundity of love
that had no chance to manage and survive
the cruelty of winter coldness
stealing into hearts of men
allowing cruelty to steal into society
and kill the true love of our minds
with cold indifference and insensitivity.
And yet, you are still there, like me,
just waiting for the reunification

of the true love of our minds
and for another spring of truth and love
with beauty that inevitably always must return.

Universal Night of Love

O night of love,
how beautiful you are
in your eternity
of beauty ever growing
like the universe
of infinite expansion
of not just one bang
but banging on forever
with all those black holes of love
that ever bring forth other universes
of eternal love
that evermore remain
the only force of light and love
that lighteth up the universe
to keep it going on
for all eternity, at least so far...

Adoration

My beloved friend,
our distance is some lightyears,
maybe more,
and yet we are within each other
constantly forever
never to return to earth
or to mortality,
since only true love is eternal,
like virginity, if it survives,
the symbol of which is your splendidly long hair,
that never ceases to entangle me,
like some of you are equally entangled
and obsessed by men that wear long hair;

but I have never touched you,
only loved you,
true love being all too sacred to my heart
to ever be imperilled, set at risk in any way;
and I believe
that love can never be more true and lasting
than when it is firmly anchored
in the adoration of the beauty of your soul.

The Night of Love and Ecstasy

It was the longest night
of love and ecstasy,
of triumph and exhilaration,
of divinest satisfaction
and the glorious victory
of never reaching home
and still be so victorious
in endless happiness
completely out of our minds,
as if the whole world of a sudden
had transformed into a paradise
of new renaissance breakthroughs
and discoveries in space
of new and better worlds
inhabitable and quite within reach
for mankind to continue her expansion
like our love forever,
and it did not even hurt.
I will say only this:
Like I so long have been so true to you,
I know now it will be bilateral,
remain so; and I shall be always satisfied.

Happiness

You hide behind your beauty,
veiled in mystery
and sealed up in your secrets,
like our love mysterious
unfathomable in profundity
and inescapable in actuality,
our common life and meaning of our lives,
the glory of our happiness
and endless joy of simply being
close together and inseparable –
what more could we need?
We live in paradise in our love,
but we can only spread our happiness
by so remaining unknown
in the mystery of our secret.

Friendship

Love is risky and momentous,
since you never know what is to come of it,
a lovely dream to fly away with,
flee into, abandoning yourself completely
to a temporary unpredictable ideal
that must eventually end up
in unavoidable awakenings into reality;
while friendship is the only safe and perfect bet,
a base to build on for a lifetime and forever,
which in no way does exclude
the possibility and utmost joy of love.
In fact, true friendship is the very essence
of a perfect lasting love;
and only if you have that friendship,
love could really last forever.

Ecology for Survival

The flood of light is overwhelming us
in overwhelming force of love
to bring a new age
neutralizing all the rotten business
of mistakes and all historical disgraces,
bringing nature back to rule
and man away from madness.
Nature is to be restored
in splendid freedom as of old
to educate and chastise man
for all his egoist insanity and hubris,
clearing up the planet of his dirty spills;
and thus shall nature reclaim earth,
and man be taught a lesson for eternity.

Intimate Infinities

The sign of love is more than just a feeling,
it is destiny itself intruding in your life
with over-evident manifestation,
shocking miracles and revolutionary turns,
that must inevitably change your life
into a new direction
of a new established love.
I don't know how you did appear from nowhere,
but you undeniably are there,
and I can never leave you,
since the risk of any harm or torture
is excluded from the start between us,
which provides us with a world of possibilities.
– So let's just keep that course,
abandoning ourselves to joys of love
in this new universe between ourselves
of intimate infinities of love.

Endurance

The bitter separation of farewell
is like a forced commitment to asylum
or into a painful exile
of no visible or knowledgeable end,
and bitter tears will flow to wash all oceans,
until the return to source of lasting love
in friendship and in truest lovers' breasts
will fill us once again with basic energy
of love and pride to face all challenge with.
The challenge is to always keep your love
no matter how much you are separated;
and if love is true indeed,
not even death shall ever keep you off it.

The Flight

The only true love is ideal love
overwhelming and transcending
all reality and its impossibility,
the limitations and the unreliabilities,
uplifting and up-keeping all that matters,
the integrity of the supremacy
of the transcending soul,
that always like a butterfly
must needs break all the mortal flesh
to ever keep on wings as high as possible
and flying on into eternity.
Love is a flight
and can but keep on loving
while she stays on flying.

Is it Worth It?

Why is love and sorrow
so inseparably linked
in closer intimacy with each other
than almost any other human feelings?
Must love always lead to worries without end
and sorrows without bottom,
is that really unavoidable and natural,
inevitable consequences of delights of love?
I can not answer that, but I am afraid
that in all my experience
I never had a glimpse of any contrary
to all that love resulting but in woe.
But it is beautiful, and that might be
its ultimate salvation and reward;
and of such wonder is that beauty,
that whatever woe and sorrow would be worth it,
even every pain and worry, torment and despair.
So just accept it, and go on
and follow love's course bravely
on the road to any trial and perdition,
but you will survive and be rewarded
for as long as you stay on as lover.

Quiet Declaration

Let me not trespass
in my daily visits
to your precious side
nor come too close
when it is night
and I once more
can't do without you
but must steal into your soul
to stay there warming up
my tenderness and love

for your prevailing beauty
and the wise profundity
of your immortal soul.
Methinks I have already
loved you for some moderate eternity,
and I am always ready
for another one
of only love of you.

The Black Hole Secret

The origin of creativity
is always but humility,
to serve and not be seen,
to give without demand,
to love in one way only
not expecting to be loved,
and that way you will find a way
to an entire universe
of creativity and love
from just a basis of humility
originating in a bottomless black hole,
forever spewing forth
infinities of love and stars and nebulae,
the ever irresistible big bang of love,
at bottom just a perfect nothing.

One Drop of Love

All you need
is just a single drop
into the ocean
for a contribution
not to let the oceans vanish
or run dry,
but that one single drop
is utterly important,
since that ocean
is the world of love,
and every drop is needed
not to let the oceans vanish
or run dry;
and that is why
it is so mightily important
that we cry
at least
one drop of love.

No Hope As Yet...

As my love of you is only getting worse,
expanding me to death and overstrain
in constant spiritual exhaustion,
your obsession is a haunting spectre
never leaving me alone
but always edging me along
in constant worries and unease,
and there is never any cure for love.
So keep the whirlwind roaring,
hunt me down if you can make it,
and I'll just keep on running
chasing you as well
through all the torturous unrests of hell
with just one single hope
like some faint light in the far end
of this the darkest of all tunnels,
that of one day maybe
reaching some kind of a settlement...

Lover in Disguise

You'll never even get the chance
to guess at my identity
or to at all suspect me
of what I really am,
and thus my freedom is complete
to fill my universe of love
with affluence of generosity
for that perverse atrocious love
that haunts me never to leave me in peace
demanding ever overstrained expansion
unto death and beyond;
but, as people say,
in love and war there are no rules
but only limitless allowances for anything,

the tolerance of freedom is atrocious;
and I claim that privilege
to go on loving you
in safe disguise as anything
but that exaggerated lover that I am.

Memories of My First Love

(although this was written more than three years ago,
for some reason it was never published before...)

You bring me back my first love
just by your existence
with your long amazing hair
exactly as my hippie bride of 30 years ago
who just like you enchanted all her world
and made all men go drown themselves in craziness.
Since then nothing has changed at all.
I am still young and green, naïve and potty
and consider the whole world my own
since it is dancing all just for my love,
and I am omnipotent as a lover
since I have you for my love,
the only goddess of eternity,
who keeps my love alive forever
just by existing as my first
perpetual love that never dies.

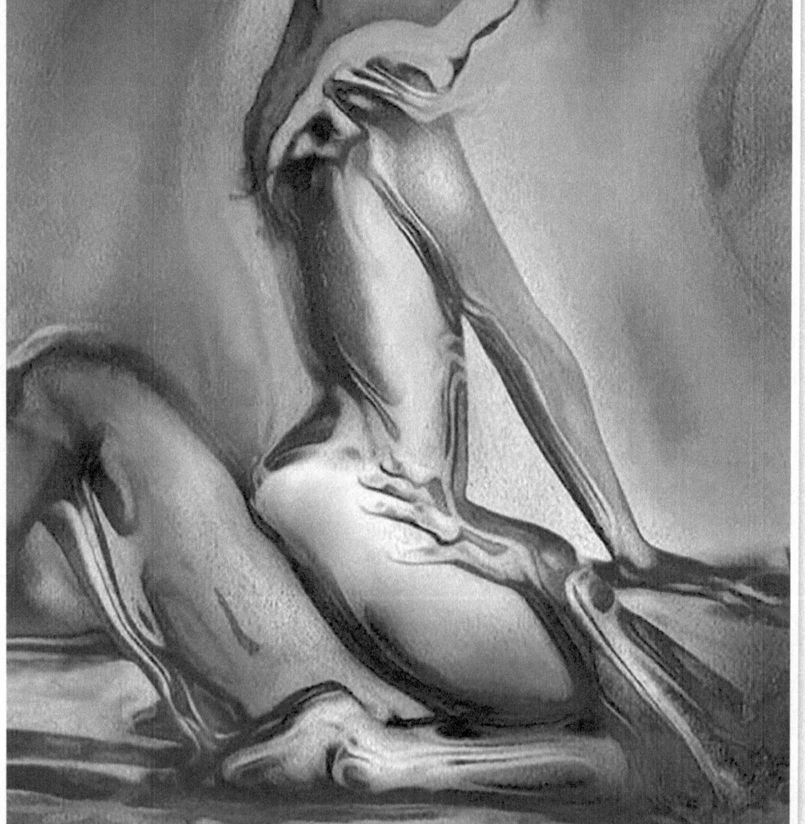

Creation

The key to creativity
is nothing but humility,
to serve and not be seen,
to give without demand,
to love in one way only
not expecting to be loved,
and that way you will find a way
through your own universe of love
to foster it, create it and maintain it
like a secret garden of your own
of only love of infinite expansion;
but the key is absolute humility,
to concentrate on love alone
without expecting any feedback.

The Urge of Passion

The passion of my heart
is neither to be quelled or quenched,
the voice is singing loud
and can not be put down or quieted,
for it is honesty of nature only
crying madly for a break and outlet
with the urge of natural necessity
for justice, acceptance and acknowledgement,
which love needs desperately
all the time for its survival
and the urge of its continuous expansion,
which is nothing less
than just a natural demand and force
of a most universal kind of all eternity.
Thus passion must not be controlled
but must be let alone, let out
and granted absolute and perfect freedom,
or there will be never any worse debacle
than when love, once set on fire,
is refused and must backfire.

Seduction

Stealing forth from nowhere,
overwhelming you with mystic might,
endowing you with force and power,
irresistibility is all there is,
and all you can do is surrender
utterly completely and forever,
fooled by the delusion of eternal pleasure,
and it is indeed enjoyable enough
as long as it keeps working,
but the trouble is,
it is mortality itself,
it always must come to an end,
and all you can do is to compromise
and learn to live with love and death
together as two opposites inseparable;
and if you can manage that,
you might be able to go on
as lover after all
seductions of both love and death.

An Old Musician's Complaint

The sweet sound of silence
is a balsam to my ear
in my decrepit old condition,
handicapped and martyred
by the noises of barbarity,
the brutal banging of unnatural destruction,
sound pollution, worse than any torture,
while the only natural and perfect music
comes from silence

and the softer rumours of all nature.
Therein let me lie and rest
in splendid isolation
of the perfect recreation
of environmental safety
where in humblest silence
you can hear the music of eternity
and purest universal beauty.

The Clandestine Lover

Love needs prudence and consideration
which are carried easily too far
and leading into traps of cowardice,
but there are always byways
roundabout to keep you on the target,
so that you don't have to give yourself away
to all the world for all your love
and at the same time still remain
complete and honest as a lover.
But whatever others think of you
for all your hypocritical prudential cowardice,
your heart can never tell a lie
for all the masks that decency demands,
and as long as you stay true and constant
to the overburning and consuming love
of your bereaved and tortured heart,
you will survive and conquer all
as the most honest and convincing lover.

The Risk of Wages

The wages of sin is death,
but the wages of love is life.
Love is then to get away from death,
and thus is death its greatest spurner.
Thus are all good things that make life meaningful
dependent on their opposites for spurning inspiration.

The fountain of exhilaration is depression,
nothing can be crueller than the acts of love,
and ecstasy can come from lethal drugs.
Is this duality then inescapable,
and must euphoria be dependent on affliction?
Well, the only way to deal with that dilemma
is eliminating both extremes
and leaving you with only boredom,
which in bleakness could be worse than any depressivity,
and who wants that who wants to live?

Life's Natural Addiction

If love is an affliction and addiction,
let me wallow in it then the more,
get buried in its abyss of delights,
go under in its oceans of generosity
and drown forever in its storms and waves
and never reach the bottom of its deepest grave,
for love is life, and there's no other life,
and all the rest is just adornments
and embellishments of this one central thing,
to love, enjoy its freedom and get lost in it.
It's not a sexual thing,
it is the joy of giving up yourself
in the communication with another,
and the sex is really of no matter;
but if there are children as a consequence
of nature, that is the supreme reward, of course.

Refuge

Let us disappear together
in a haze of love and mystery
and vanish into mists of dreams
where we are free to relish ourselves
together without interference
way beyond this universe
and all society of stifling rules,
where we are free to be ourselves
and can enjoy each other
in indefinite expansion.
Let them wonder where we are,
since no one needs to know about it
but ourselves, where we can be together
without ever risking any more to lose each other.

Adorable Unattainability

Your beauty is supreme
and I can only worship you
with awe and admiration
for your absolute perfection
as the final consummation
of the everlasting love ideal,
which though is only philosophical.
There is the rub,
that I can never reach you,
since you are too perfect
and too beautiful to be attainable.
But let me be content
and grateful for the wondrous fact
that you at all exist.

The Extremity of Love

There are no bounds,
and yet we are in thralldom
of our love and its forbidden nature,
it is limitless and universal
but confined by human nature
never to get publicly expressed
or comprehensible in human terms,
since it is too extreme to ever be defined.
Perhaps that is the very definition
of true love: completely bound in silence
but the more expansive, free, dynamic and outrageous
for its deprivation and humiliation.
Although beyond all conventional qualification,
we are the more free in love's exaggeration.

Joyfulness

You are my joy with all your lovers,
spreading beauty everywhere,
like some magic faerie queen
on special visit for some inspiration
like on some esoteric mission,
which seems well to prove efficient.
Am I not proud to be your formost lover then,
who never found but harmony in your society
of love and beauty to infinity
and no small lustful nights between?
Can I hope for this to be a continuity?
Of course, we always did return
from any wayward journey;
but my chief concern is this,
that even our journey through eternity
on wings of love more stable than the earth
must reach an end and harbour,
temporarily at least.

How Shall I Describe...

complimentary

How shall I describe you?
You transcend all idealization,
making all description vain and base,
since words can never give you justice.

How shall I describe your beauty,
indescribable and indispensable,
as is your enigmatic and evasive personality,
that baffles any lover and admirer and adorer.

Yet you are the reallest kind of lady,
like an esoteric queen
that never can be grasped by definition.

Still, one thing is too concrete to be denied,
the beauty of your long and splendid hair,
the sweetest thing to touch in all existence,
smooth as water and attractive
as a waterfall of darkest diamonds.

Let my adoration be arrested there
in stupefaction at your lovely hair,
a true manifestation of your sovereignty
in both beauty, character and love.

The Way Out

In the vacuum of despair and darkness
overcast with hopelessness and desert gloom,
the blackness of my life turned into a blind alley
of abandoned and decrepit incapacity,
you kindled something of a ray
that turned into a dominating lightning,
growing to full glorious daylight sunshine,

which since then has been my solace,
actually my only spiritual comfort.
Stay that way, my love, abide with me
and never fade again into the shadows that you came from
of atrocious sufferings and bad experience,
and it will be my pleasure to sustain you
by all means with all my heart;
and thus perhaps we might turn all existence
and the world into a better place.

Home from Siberia

Out of love, and out of touch,
it's been a difficult divorce,
compulsory, of course,
and something of an edifying challenge,
since detachment reinforces basics.

It has been a lesson of survival
hastening our singular condition
for maturity and new expansion
towards what we can't know anything about,
the abyss of the great unknown,
the enigma of the closed door of the future.

We exist, and that should be enough
for our sustained love to continue
ever more to greater depth
and more profound expansion,
being locked within each other
in a permanent and endless union.

The Falsity of the Ego

Developing an ego must end up
in the blind alley of frustrated lies,
unless you cultivate it only
for an educational experiment

to find where destiny would lead you
if you give free reins to your imagination
and the freedom to create a fancy ego
just to sacrifice it on the altar
of self-analysis, criticism and scrutiny.
You don't have a self in any case,
so you might anyway just blow it up
to see and learn where vanity would lead you.
Truth remains, and when your egos are consumed
you will have learned at least
the lesson of responsible detachment.

New Worlds of Wisdom

When you hit the bottom of the dark,
at least you have some ground to stand on,
even if it is the bottom of an abyss
without light, with only sin and wickedness,
with everything gone wrong, no hope in sight,
but misery and torture, suffering and languishment.
But it is not the end. It's the beginning
of a climb to any heaven,
from the bottom you can only rise
above all shadows to the light,
and you will never fall again.
That is the wisdom of a total downfall:
You will have a new perspective of the universe,
being able to include it all.

Estrangement

The strangest situation has developed of our love
that no one could have had a notion of.
You are all mine, and I have never loved you more,
although you have done everything to alienate yourself
by a development that could but be described
as something of an alien labyrinth to wonderland
where nothing any more is what it seems to be.

Still, my love, you are the same,
the world has changed and been turned upside down,
but our love was only fortified thereby,
and passion has been reinforced most thoroughly
into a more established fusion than before;
so anything might happen, so it seems,
disasters may occur and shock the world,
and our love will only be the stronger
for all trials of estrangement.

Fusion

We are intertwined,
two personalities in one,
two lives united to one destiny,
a hotter union than a marriage,
less interruptable,
since you are everything I ever loved
although you are my contrary,
we are completely uncombinable
and therefore so inseparable.
In our nightly orgies
there is more pain and suffering
than revelries of pleasure,
love claiming more than ordinary heartaches,
but those heartbreaks fuse us even harder
in the union of our sin together,
and so are we one but cleft in twain.
The one insurance of our Via Crucis
is that anyone is free to leave at any time,
and that's the last thing any one of us can do.

You Are My Soul

You are my soul,
you are my everything, and I am lost in you.
When I return exhausted
and washed up from all my work
after a tedious day of overtime,
I would have nothing to come home to
if you were not there
to whisper new encouragement
into my blasted bleeding soul,
that would run out of blood

if I did not have you as a refill.
So let me go to sleep in you
enfolded in your blessed arms
to wake again tomorrow
to another day of hard work's torture
without you, but having you
to wait for me to save it.

Redemption

How could you be so quiet
for so many years of suffering,
my love, who never vanished from my sight
however much you tried to hide yourself away,
but you were always there, I tried to reach you
and was never quite without you,
until you so suddenly appeared again,
like some redempion angel from our heaven
reaching through all darkness of my soul
to prove yourself a true as ever.
Blessed be thy light and soul,
so true to your nobility,
so constant in your loveliness;
and all I need now is to see you 'live again
as the realization of the truth of our relationship.

Empires

Empires crumble to dust,
and nothing remains but delusion,
the acid bitterness of lost hopes,
the desperation of futility,
the incurable sense of failure,
and thus they all went down -
Jerusalem and Egypt, Babylon and Persia,
Athens, Rome and London,
and America will be no exception.
The truth is what survives,

the sordid underground reality,
the moles that always remain
to grind new empires to pieces,
the will that triumphs over all politics,
the destiny that reduces dreams to ashes,
the downfall of all hubris of eternity;
and all we have is shades of what we've lost
and never can retrieve again,
on which we always start again
to build new empires.

Ditched

Sleepless nights of love
accompanied by nightmare worries
for your fate of persecution
of old sins and undeserved adversities
make me as shattered as yourself,
directly torn asunder by misfortune,
hanged in execution after torture
but with some hope left of liberation still
before the final strangulation.
No one wanted this,
not even the responsible bureaucracy,
while the villain is the lack of empathy,
the formalism of rules of programmation
for which no one is accountable.
Thus are you casually buried alive
and I with you in dreadful worries
quite atrociously insensibly,
and there is nothing we can do
but wait in limbo for an unknown opening,
which no one knows when it will come.
All we can do is to be true at least
to ourselves and our destiny,
which carries us through mortal vanity
in this perpetual and bothersome unrest
to no peace in eternity.

To Life

Take care of life – don't bust it,
it's too precious to be wasted,
life should only be constructive,
it is in itself creativeness,
created just to multiply
and manifest its vividness,
and that's the meaning of it all –
no matter what queer forms life takes,
as long as it is life, it's sacred,
and the joy of it is all that matters –
Death exists only to enhance life's meaning,
and so even death is life and only life.
So don't misuse it, and don't sabotage it –
live, let live, support and further lives of others
and the more you'll live yourself,
that's all, the summary of Life.

Confidence

The narrow straits are dire,
they are strewn with traps and dangers,
there are reefs and shallows everywhere,
but improvising through the crooked path
with care and calm and cool determination
will eventually bring all things through
without as much as the minutest scratch,
if only you avoid temptations and bad temper;
if you lose it, everything is lost.
Thus will you save your love through any danger,
and each trial will be only for the best
edification and good lesson of survival.

Beauty Rules

My love is like a dream in May
forever fragrant and expanding
gloriously embellishing all life with beauty,
ever present, ever faithful, ever true
and ever lovelier with her long hair
and timeless youth that never ages,
since she is her soul and not her matter,
ever sweet, constructive and inspiring,
almost like a fairy or an elf
but more substantial in her essence.
Beauty is a matter mostly of the soul,
and therein lies the immortality of beauty
of which she is the manifestation.
Soul is freedom and the only truth
that evermore survives all age, mortality and time
and outwits all mundaneness
with her sovereign wisdom of transcendence.

The Climb

In the depth of chaos
I am lost like in the bottom of a well
and cannot see a light in hopelessness
but must escape reality
in order to find any comfort and relief at all,
but there is always you
awaiting in the tunnel end,
a warm and soothing heart
to ease the torture of reality
and calm my wounded soul
that without you has almost bled to death
but now revives at the mere thought of you.
Thus can a thought
and the mere virtual presence of a person
cause the strangest miracles,

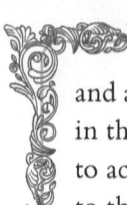

and all you need is to believe
in the reality of something better,
to achieve a climb from the abysmal bottom
to the highest state of any perfect heaven.

Thanks

I love you,
despite your weaknesses and faults,
your age has never bothered me
and should not be a problem to yourself,
since we are young at heart and in our souls,
no matter how old souls we are,
and that's the only age that matters:
the age you feel that tends to ever in your soul grow younger,
and wherein lies the true beauty of a person:
her continuity and truthfulness to her own self.
That beauty is to me the highest,
which I find in you and never shall get lost,
for you are you, and you have ever been the same,
and for that I beg to serve you with my constant thankfulness.

Welcome

My love, where are you in the dark?
I miss you and can't find you,
we are disconnected and disjointed,
but for the time being only.
You are always with me anyway,
not only in my thoughts but in my heart,
your soul has made a home in it,
and I shall never kick you out.
You have entered to remain,
and I shall never be at home myself
if you are not at home in me.
So please stay on forever,
and you'll never have a safer haven
than in the protection of my loving heart.

The Hidden Bottle

You have to have it,
that hidden bottle in the back,
your life's elixir,
the most indispensable of medicines,
the only one to always cheer you up,
that whisky bottle,
that so many times have saved your life
from devastation and depression,
giving up and other fatal suicidal steps;
your friend is always there to serve your spirit,
and if he is missing, then you have another one
at hand and always ready
to provide you with some continuity
of courage, stalwartness and intrepidity:
your friend in need indeed forever:
your bartender.

Black Love

In the blackness of my heart
you stir some mystic fire
that devours me and turns me on
in sleeplessness night after night.
My problem is the question,
if it's you or me that stirs the fire,
or are we in it both together?
You are always free, and I can't keep you there,
while I am prisoner of this weird love
that never quite can leave me for a moment.
Your freedom keeps me prisoner,
and I can never hold you back
infringing on your independence,
since you are a part of me,
and I can never let you go.

Half Way

The smoothness of our love
is like a flower that will not wither
but just goes on flowering again
renewing constantly the beauty
and exploding into newborn blossoms
at every risk of fading or of tiring.
That is the ordinary course of love
when it is natural and ripe,
when it has reached a state of harmony
which makes it unassailable and incorruptible,
a state which we have reached after some years
of trial horrors without end,
and it actually feels like coming home.

The Plight of the Tibetans

We are the people that the world forgot
or rather just didn't care about,
letting them be swallowed alive by China,
the brutal dragon of force and no human rights,
where the individual is worthless and negligeable
while millions perishing in famine, floods or earthquakes
is just statistics, like for Stalin.
But still we persist to exist,
although the Chinese slowly but certainly since 60 years
methodically work for our extirpation.
We are allowed no human rights, no education,
not our own language, traditions and culture
which all must be replaced by Chinese brainwash.
If we flee our country we are shot or caught
and sent back to prison for correction brainwash,
and that has ben the standard procedure since 50 years.
But the world doesn't care but kowtows to China,
as now even Obama because of the Bush debt to China –
the world sees only the good busines of China

and doesn't care if millions perish in the development
or if the Tibetan people and culture
are extirpated on the way.

Rugged Weather

I didn't ask you to take me for a ride,
this journey proved a very different matter
than we both expected and looked forward to,
and I don't know who faced the worst - myself or you,
but both our pairs of wings were singed indeed,
which it will take some time to heal and to recover,
since we were forced to get down hard to earth
to lick our wounds and heal our broken wings,
and we were left without protection in the rain
with no good cloak to shelter us from frost
in our nakedness, forlorn like orphans;
but others did fare even worse,
and in comparison with them we were most lucky,
for we always had and do still have each other.

The Master of Reality

If all I ever felt about love was true,
then one day of it would be enough to last a thousand years,
and I am sure that every day of it was true,
for I have seen reality more real
than any mean reality can dream of.
Let it be that in your dreams you see beyond your sight
and that what you can see is more than all reality can boast of,
so let not reality into your dreams,
but let your dreams control your mind's reality,
and they will take supreme and better charge of all the world as well;
for all the world is but a fleeting dream created by your dreams,
while that creation force, your dreams, is all that matters.

Not to be Trifled With

Your horns stick out but not with cruelty
but rather wit, sharp taste, acuteness
and delightful entertainment
crowned by your exceptional idiosyncracies
that provides your beauty and your charm with depth
of labyrinthical dimensions of extentions
which no man shall ever grasp or fathom.
Let me love you but at some safe distance
not to perish in your bottomlessness,
like so many others did,
of your soul's lair of webs and fascinations,
like a cave which everyone is seen to enter with delight
but no one ever did come out of any more.
Thus are you the most irresistible of mysteries
that everyone must love
but no one ever shall come through with.

Celebration

The greatest cause for celebration
it would seem to be
returning fully both to life and love
and celebrating it unendingly
in a full night of only love.
What difference does it make
if we are wayward and away for months,
if only we return back home
once in a while restoring all our love,
revitalizing its capacity for timelessness
and its main trait, its contact with eternity,
thus to immediately restore us fully
to our health, vitality and life
in order for us to again be able to be generous
and waste it all in sumptuous fits of energy?
As someone said once, all we need is love,
and to maintain it, all we need is to enjoy it.

Humanity

The destructivity within
is like a time bomb in each human heart
which must eat out our souls
and leave them rotting down to waste
like offals worse than any litter –
we are all as human beings human wrecks,
a failed humanity that goes to ruin
trying to bring with us in our fall
our entire planet, nature, life and future;
but as that accomplished failure
which all humankind hopelessly is,
we will not even bring that ruin home
but perish well ahead of nature and all else.
How laughable is this pathetic humankind!
All history went wrong, and we got nothing right,
and here we are, the crown of all creation,
the most miserable fool that ever could exist.

Beauty's Fault

What is wrong with beauty?
People oftentimes react to it like to a provocation,
as if the existence of pure beauty were an insult
which must be acted on with violation,
as if the sole purpose of its sheer existence
was to be put down and raped and quieted,
as if beauty was a general disturbance
which must be dismantled.
All the same, true beauty will continue to persist
and multiply and ever grow more beautiful,
since that is the essential character of beauty –
no one can do anything about it,
unless they tolerate it, let it be and cultivate it,
like a garden, tendered well, allowed all freedom
and appreciated for her charm and inspiration,
loved and made good use of
as the main expander and developer of love.

Creation (2)

Our love goes round and round
in perpetual and energetic circulation,
never stopping but increasing and accelerating,
like a true perpetuum mobile that ever goes on faster,
and yet we never tire of our love,
as if it constantly regenerated
like a Phoenix, in renewing restoration
and the more so for its self-consumtion,
as if wasting made you only richer.
Somehow we have reached some kind
of strange ideal love situation,
where we never can be rid of one another,
while at the same time we don't want to,
while our love increases for its practice
uniquely furthering creation
which we can't be held responsible for

although we sustain, uphold and further it
but only as an absolutely natural and obvious process,
which by analysis would seem perfectly miraculous
but which for us is only being true to what we are.

Falling Dark Angel

The blackness of your spirit
is its special beauty,
darkness charmingly becoming you
and adding to your irresistibility,
for in that gloomy darkness
there is depth and wisdom
almost without end and without bottom,
luring anyone to enter
and to stay without returning.
It looks dangerous but is the opposite,
and being used to it, you find it natural
and will not do without it.
So keep on descending, fallen angel,
ever to more gruesome depths,
and I will follow you
not as a slave bound to addiction
but as a lover with a grateful heart.

Thankfulness

My thankfulness is without limits
for the life and health that was returned to me
after a gutter trial and ordeal
of pain and dirt and torture
and insufferable disability,
my absolute inadequacy turning me
into a total good-for-nothing,
feeling more than miserable and done in.
But suddenly the weather changed,
I rose up from the depths and from the dead
into the sunlight to be active once again,

returning gloriously to work
and even getting back some old efficiency.
How could I be but grateful
beyond any measure of conception,
jubilant in happiest humility, – and hoping for the life of me
to never get struck down again
to that abyssal bottom of existence.

The Mystery of Love

The mystery of love is infinite
transforming people into other beings,
transcending life to make it higher
and performing miracles with personalities,
developing their souls to almost anything,
since love is freedom above all
for creativity and the imaginative force
to realize, accomplish and succeed in almost anything,
creation being first of mysteries of life's existence,
without which life would not be at all,
while it begins and ends with love.
Therein between there is a universe of possibilities
where nothing, absolutely nothing is impossible.

Ageless Beauty

If beauty's true it does not fade
but on the contrary increases
with maturity and age,
and wrinkles can not spoil it.
You are an example
of this strange phenomenon
of love and beauty only growing
with the years in depth and in attraction,
although we do not grow younger
but instead increase in timelessness.
That is perhaps the essence of true beauty,
that which never fades but instead increases only,
like a flower never dying
but expanding like a tree
to ever grow more firm and lovely to never die;
for that is the true mark of beauty:
she can never die.

Love Backfire

As I love you
more with my heart than with my body,
more with my soul than intellectually,
more with my mind than with my brains,
you vanish to withdraw into some nothingness,
in a vain effort to a kind of self-effacement
only to an opposite effect:
the clearer and more lovable and gracious you appear,
and the more solicitously I must love you.

It is in vain you claim to be a fake
and come with futile warnings,
they must only have a direct opposite effect,
like fuel into a fire that can never die,

and that is how love works:
the more you fight it,
the more you must lose against it,
for the stronger it becomes.

How Love Goes On

Sexuality does not retard with age.
On the contrary, it continues to expand,
love must always find new ways,
new channels of expression,
new languages of feelings,
new dimensions and new dreams,
and nothing ever can contain and stop it.
Never be afraid of love and its expressions,
and especially not as you grow with age and wisdom,
love always being and remaining your life's leader
and its source and motor, teacher and ideal
that ever leads and reaches forward,
even beyond death.

To You

Longing for you
is keeping me alive
with dreams and charms of long ago
that clearly tend to immortality
or at least to timelessness,
for there's no higher beauty
than the dreams of you
that are too real to not be true
and more convincing than reality,
wherefore I will stick to them
with faith of limitless endurance
and willingly continue building on them
for a monument for you
that will establish the most natural and obvious fact
that our love belongs as much to immortality
as to ourselves in our modest piety.

Love's Supremity

Love demands expansion,
free expansion evermore,
and no one has the right to stop it,
and, indeed, no one is able to.
Love therefore seems to be of forces the most ruthless,
but love is not love if it resorts to violence.
The magic and the force of love
is always to get through but without all enforcement,
always getting over with it and surviving
as the very element of life's survival and expansion;
and whoever tries to stop or to oppose it
is a self-destructive fool
incapable of education and instruction,
since if he does not know love,
he is a hopeless case of total ignorance.

Your Beauty

Everybody loves you,
seeing you as the ideal you are,
your influence of beauty being timeless,
like, as you say, as if it was inspired
by the rulers of the ancient times,
when nature was religion and supreme as such
and led and dominated by high priestesses of love.
Bring back those times with all their blessings,
and use your holy influence to reinstate world order
under the command of nature and her purity and beauty,
maybe you could do it,
for I know the total beauty of your soul
and what such an endowment could be capable of,
while the outside superficial appearances
are only lies for the protection
of the almighty truth that is in your soul's beauty.

Intuition

Your soul's truth is the only truth,
idealism is never wrong,
while your senses are elements of deception,
and wisdom and morale are an illusion.
Intuition is the only stable compass
and the hardest one to follow,
since you never see it
but can only feel it,
and the senses tend to block it;
but as long as you do not forget it
but keep it in your mind's direction,
you can not be wrong,
or at least not entirely wrong.

Let Love Lead the Way

As the years go on, love does not get any milder,
maybe slower, but with age more deep,
experience maturing and bearing fruit
of wisdom, knowledge, intuition,
understanding, insight and a better sense.
You go on falling deep in love
and ever deeper with the years,
while constancy becomes the most important:
the more you love, the less you want your love to change.
Love is without season,
there was once a dawn and spring of love,
but that spring never ends but goes forever on
as long as love keeps leading you,
and there is never any reason why
it shouldn't go on leading you forever.

Dark Idealism

Can idealism be dark?
It depends. Idealism is never dark
in itself as an idea,
but if you, like so many do,
confuse reality with your ideas,
idealizing fakes and lies and deceptions
by mistake, as so many do,
then your idealism becomes an instrument of darkness
and backfires on itself, causing harm and grave delusion,
while on the other hand, reality can never be ideal,
and you can not do without ideals.
The art is to somehow project your ideals
into reality, and thus improve and change reality,
not manipulating it, but encouraging its better possibilities,
thus helping it along to some improvement.
That idealism can never turn to blackness,
constructiveness can never be an instrument of darkness,
while lies, deceptions and dishonesty
can never last, especially not as ideals.

Remaining Light of Youth

My beam of youth,
you were my flame
in hard days of upheaval
constituting all my sunshine
while our contact lasted
without others interrupting
with absurd claims of relationship monopoly
which ruined our harmony;
but you were always there
to ever faithfully come back,
as now, when suddenly we found each other
once again and in a parking lot
and everything was perfectly the same –

love was still there in spite of twenty years of separation
and we hardly had grown one year older –
ultimate syndrome and evidence of true love –
nothing changes, although everything has changed,
love remains the same when once found out as true
whatever happens to it and its victims;
and thus we are the same as twenty years ago,
only even more so than before.

Respectability

The problem of respectability
is that you can't do anything not worthy of respect
and can't be irrespectable.
You are confined to your respectability
and must respect it, or you'll lose it.
Maybe it is worth it?
Many do and afterwards insist
that they have nothing to regret.
Perhaps they really don't,
but still, most people hesitate to take that leap and risk,
and many take an even greater risk instead
experimenting and developing a double life,
a life of perfect watertight respectability
and on the other hand an underground activity of self-indulgence
where there are no limits to what liberties are taken.
It is good as long as they are not found out,
and maybe it is recommendable to try.
Respectability is after all a regular confinement
which all nature must rebel against demanding freedom.

Perfect Love

My love, it does not matter whom you go to bed with
as long as I may love you still.
You are my only love,
and something tells me it is vice versa,
although I know all your lovers.

This is not the problem.
Actually, there is no problem
since love conquers all
and solves all problems by its mere serenity.
Don't worry, dearest love,
you have all freedom you can take,
as long as I may have all freedom
in my perfect love of you.

Some Predicament

Stuck in you and can't get out,
but is it such a dreadful trap?
I can't complain, but at the same time
I am aware of the apparent anger
of this predicament becoming something of a habit;
but if also you have no complaints,
so let us just go on with sticking to each other
as long as things are working out.
It took some years to get together,
but if this becomes intolerable with the years,
a separation cut would be the easiest thing,
and if we do it, we can always start again.

Your Birthday

I don't know if you are too good to be true,
but you exist, and that's enough for me,
since you exist for me at least,
so that I at least can bear some witness
of your beauty and maturity
and how they only seem to steadily increase,
as if instead of growing older you grew younger
towards ever more accentuated youth,
that only seems more stable with the years.
If youth thus could persist in growing younger,
that would be the evidence of how the spirit
rules the body and decides its state and not the contrary.

Let me thus continue loving you
to thus increase the power of your spirit
so that you can steadily continue growing younger
as long as I am here to love you
and as long as I shall stay alive.

Creation (3)

There is only one creating force transcending all,
that is the mind imagination,
which is all the creativity there is.
There are no limits to the mind
and its capacity, the universe is infinite,
and so is the creative mind,
and what is possible in your imagination
is also possible in reality,
provided that you think creatively
and not just dream a lot of nonsense.
I think Einstein would agree with me,
who said that there would rather be a limit to the universe
than to the mind and its capacity for limitless creation.

The Spell

You have cast a spell on me,
and I am hopelessly completely lost
and can't get out of the entanglement,
since love compels me to be faithful,
there is no other choice,
the truth of love excludes all other possibilities,
so I am stuck, delighting in it
since it means, I'll never lose your company.
Be with me always, my beloved,
and I will try to never let you down
but on the contrary extol you,
putting down some effort to live up to you,
since you nevertheless will always be
too good for me and always out of reach.

The Bleakness of Reality

Reality is never pretty
in its brutal ruthlessness of naked truth
but rather awesome and forbidding,
let alone unhuman not to say the least,
a terrifying hostile monstrous cruelty
that leaves no man alone in peace
but forces everyone to deadly lifelong struggle
all the way down to the grave.
Nothing can improve reality
except romantic dreams and fantasies,
your own imagination and idealism,
which can at least improve reality
by softening it to your mind and senses,
and that is what we call creativity.
We do not know if actually it does improve reality,
but we could hardly go on living
if we were bereft of that last possibility and hope.

Unconditionally

You made no conditions
but left it all to me –
"You are free to break it up at any time",
that was the one condition of our relationship,
with the understatement from your side
that you would never break it up yourself.
I call that generously liberal for a condition,
and we have never been without each other since that day.
Divorces do not work for us,
not even when we travel separately far apart,
and nothing has brought us more close together
than when we were separated by our journeys.
Psychopathic spiritual obsession with each other
as a constant substitute for marriage?

Call it rather friendship and a natural relationship
that not even nature can dissolve,
since nature brought it on uniting us.

The Light of Your Darkness

Let me bask in the sunlight of your darkness
more warming than the scorching tropical sun
and more enlivening than any energy.
Your darkness has a special character
of generously beaming and bestowing more light
than any sun or star or supernova
is capable of in the universe.
You not only warm my heart
but fill my life with hope and joy
by being vibratingly so dark
but in a sort of bottomless profundity
all filled with knowledge, love and wisdom.
Somehow you hold the key to anyone's heart
being qualified to read and look them through
not missing anything of any substance of their souls
but reading them as carefully as any book.
So they depend on you, and so do I,
the light of your darkness being more important to me
than any visual light,
since it is the very opposite of blindness.

Avalon

"I simply wanted just to save your life
and have you here amongst our brothers
as a friend and knight of our peace,
but no sense or wisdom or persuasion
could bend your mind of perfect obstinacy.
You simply had to risk your life,
your future and our happiness
by volunteering as a victim to the dragon.
And here you are, the dragon-slayer,
having rid our realm of the most evil menace
and is now the first of our knights
and shall be honorary Lord Protector of our Queen.
My friend and brother, I embrace you
with as much affection as I hold for our Queen
and thank you for your boldness
and the grace of our fate
that saved you for our realm and future
to grace it with perpetual harmony.
My friend, you are my equal.
This is the finest day of Camelot
and the triumph of the good will of Avalon,
so golden in this perfect moment,
that I humbly dare express the wish,
that it might show some lasting grace
in perpetual longevity for all eternity."
Thus spoke the King and dubbed Sir Lancelot
the first and highest of our knights
and special lord protector of our Queen
and of the land of everlasting youth and beauty
in perpetual honour, glory and romantic chivalry
in sustained idealism forever.

The Irresistibility of Darkness

You lure me into ever growing darkness
like into a wood that ever grows more fearsome
as we tread on paths to nowhere
without even having any hunch of where we're going,
no one knows, and all we know is darkness
that keeps falling and curtailing us,
inveigling us in imperceptible secret mysteries
of love and evil and perdition, –
all we know, is that this road is leading forward,
after all, but whether it's a tunnel or an abyss,
a blind alley or a path to progress and release,
we cannot know. We can but keep on going on
into the darkness, thickening and ever growing
more menacing and fearful and destructive
in its black addiction of the final vicious circle.

Passion

Passions must lead you astray
as nothing can resist them;
you are hopelessly carried away
to where your will is without power
and you have no influence of your own destiny.
Follow blindly as a slave your heart,
and you will end up in a series of discoveries
of wonders and experiences unheard of,
which would never have been possible
if you had mastered your own love.
Of course, any experience is worth it,
and as long as your love doesn't kill you,
go on loving, following your passions
for as long as they keep going on.

Our Strange Association

We have come so deep into each other
that we'll never find our exit way again,
not that we're stuck, since willingly we are so,
but it must result in some confusion,
since it will be difficult to separate us
even in our poems,
since they also, like ourselves
keep entering each other,
as we really know each other's texts by soul
if not by heart, as they keep interfoliating
as we do each night in secretive communion
clad and veiled in dark inscrutability.
That is love: united demoniacally
and inseparably unalterably and inviolably forever.

Love Complications

Love is to be complicated.
To fall in love is easiest of all,
to stay in love demands some mobilized persistence,
to maintain it is a labour,
and to see it to the bitter end
is the supreme ordeal.
The challenge of it is the complication,
which is always there inevitable
to continue constantly increasing for as long as it goes on;
and the test of destiny is grappling with the complications,
which will multiply as you go on,
like dragon heads of Hydra,
two new ones growing out for every one you manage to chop off.
The complications are the sport of it,
and the challenge is for you to never give up championship.
If you give up, you are a loser, and you then have everything to lose,
but if you manage never to give up
and stay in love through all the complications,
you shall be the ultimate and greatest winner.

Vita Nuova

You gave me another life,
as if the one I had was not enough
and more than I could handle,
but the randomness of your generosity
so much enriched my whole existence
that I feel my life as twice as much
as if I actually now had two lives to lead,
with the responsibility which it imports.
What would I be without it?
Bored out, maybe lost and maybe nothing,
since the new life also gave my life new meaning,
which was maybe what the old one lacked.
So here I am with you locked up in double lives,
and there is nothing we can do about it
but the best of it, to grip and bear it
and keep it out sustaining the charades and role plays
to the end, for better and for worse.

The Mists of Avalon

The whisperings of silence come with their embrace
for the protection of our sanctuary
free from worldly troubles and their pettiness
in sustained and lasting harmony and constancy
to ever be the home of peace and beauty
with acquired taste that constantly improves
to set a good example for the world
and judging it in truth and justice
for its folly, baseness and barnarity,
while its only basic crime is ignorance.
Thus the realm of Avalon keeps towering forever
above the mists that hide it and protect it
from unworthy mortal and uneducated eyes,
while we who are initiated in her realm
will piously continue to perform our duty
of upholding her as the ideal of all ideals forever.

Momentary Relief

As I long for you, my love,
my tears run gushing freely
in the fond nostalgia of our memories,
which is my only comforting relief
from my abhorrent pains and trials
under duress, headaches and injustices,
that makes your personality in contrast
a blue angel out of paradise.
When shall we meet again?
I sorely miss our soothing intimacy,
while my only comfort is my dreams,
in which you dominate each night
my world of sorrows and atrocities,
which you alone make me forget
and momentarily at least can cure me of,
an assuaging moment's brief relief
in an eternity of torment.

Invitation

Let out your hair and be erotic,
your beauty is not for concealing,
your mask may be efficient as protection,
but it is a lie confining you behind yourself,
while beauty only can be given justice
well released and triumphing in freedom.
Remove your black disguising glasses and your seven veils,
let out your hair in overwhelming length and glory,
for your formost duty must be only to be loved,
and if your beauty is concealed you make it difficult.
Your hair is no good tied up out of sight,
and we all know how your body should be seen.
We will be hidden anyway in darkness in the night
in bed together, where we can't be seen,
but there it is all right, since we are compensated.

Adversity and Defeat

It doesn't matter if you lose it all
and all your life turns into something of a blackout
of disasters, tragedies, black holes and Armageddons,
all that means nothing, like all wars and slaughters,
the world wars were but parentheses
meaning nothing really to the course of history,
the reapings and the sowings coming regularly anyway,
while you alone in all the universe
are always there and in the middle of it all,
the hub of the rotating universe,
which no defeat can touch
and no adversity has any right to bother,
since you are a soul and sovereign as such,
a spiritual being of supreme integrity,
a god of consequence and some untouchability,
while all the world and universe is just a mess
the sole purpose of which is to serve you.
This might seem a bit presumptuous and preposterous,
but it is actually the truth.
It's hard to face it for its splendour and supremity,
and people usually prefer to look another way,
but it is always there, reminding you
if not before, in death, that you can not escape
that you are doomed to be yourself and no one else
forever in the now that is eternity.

How Do You Do It?

Your body is like an explosion
of the purest everlasting energy
but of a spiritual vital kind
that only gives and never takes,
which is why it is impossible
to ever tire of our love affair.
How do you do it? everyone must ask,
and I have wondered it myself
ever since our relationship became a fact,
but this mystery has constantly grown more mysterious.
Double hard experience and its wisdom
might be a great part of the answer
but does not explain the art and craft behind it all.
Never mind, the point is that we carry on
and never tire of our perfect love
that keeps on going more than well
and only grows the more for its intrinsic mystery.

Delicate Approach

It's difficult to love you
since you always glide away,
as if you were not real,
but still there is no being more real
for all your mystery and enigmatic riddle.
You hide away in constancy
to be the more alert and active
manipulating behind the scenes
known and present everywhere
and constantly unfathomably out of touch,
like another phantom of the opera.
But I know you to be the loveliest of all,
and it's your humbleness that makes the mystery.
As long as I may serve and love you
I am happy and content and ask for nothing more
and dare not question your unfathomableness.

Love Restored

The terrible ordeal of tyranny, deceit and cruelty
has marked our lives with scars of suffering
but never once imperiled or reduced our love.
You are the same, only more beautiful than ever,
adding some maturity and depth to your nobility,

your purity appearing the more intact for your humiliation,
all the dirt that you had to endure just seeming
to enhance your personality, integrity and beauty
and the charm and glory of your soul.
Your light appears in fascinating splendour
for the background of the darkness of your night
that you came through more than alive
with honour and the rare reward of happiness.
No one was closer to my heart than you,
I loved you always, no one knew me better,
and the fact that we have reunited once again
after so many wars of torment and self-sacrifice
is more than proof of that our destiny together
from the start was something more
than we could ever dream of.

The Mystery of Dualistic Unity

One should expect some variance
between two people of so different worlds
as we are, you and I, and yet
we are one soul and were so ever,
as if we had been together knowing well each other
always through the ages,
although at the same time so completely different.
Is that friendship, love or something else,
like soulmates of eternity?
Our bodies are of no importance or concern,
their needs are secondary to our feelings

of belonging to each other as two souls
that need each other to be more complete
than ever we can be as we enjoy each other physically.
That's the mystery: the higher sense of being
and desire spiritually than physically,
as if we can only be fulfilled as persons
when we are together and forget our bodies.

The Problem of Discretion

The truth is never what it seems.
It's always hidden underneath and carefully suppressed
from policy or care or caution or whatever,
oftentimes by scruples and discretion,
but it's always there and crying loud in silence,
like a death scream from someone buried alive,
that must eventually come out in dreadfulness,
like the hidden story and agenda of so many presidents,
so many public figures, popes and actors,
film stars, kings and world celebrities,
their secret failures, desillusions, disappointments,
shameful shortcomings, frustrations, tragedies, regrets,
mistakes and human stains, that they are the more painfully aware of
the more they make efforts to conceal them,
self control must ultimately burst, the truth will out,
and then we have the problem constantly recurring:
Would it have made any difference, if the pain had been released before?
Or would it have been better if it never had been known at all?
And usually there is no unambiguous answer
to any of the many self-contradictory questions.

My Religion

You are my religion, dearest,
not because your beauty is imperishable,
not because of your ideal diplomacy,
and not because your amiability is perfect,
but because your personality is wondrous constant,
your reliability was always there
in patient calm to rule my horrible impatience,
which is getting worse for every year,
and even in your doubtful morals no one can impeach you.

You have seen and gone through all the worst,
you know about conditions beyond all endurance,
you have crossed the limits of intolerable pain
and still maintained your equilibrium,
as if it was natural to sometimes lose one's mind
and let it pass, like any storm at sea,
your wisdom only growing cooler and maturing
for the trials of extremest crises.

Who could anything but love you?
Still you have reserved yourself for me,
we know each other like none other know and understand us,
thus we must have been created for each other,
which is only to accept and make the best of
and which is so good to know,
that we at least then have each other.

Creation

The mystery of magic is creation,
but it hurts, it is a painful process,
like a child is born in blood and horror,
so is any act of creation something of a crucifixion
in the tough ordeal of getting there
and reaching the result of durability,

the mystery of getting something out of nothing,
the impressing spellbinding effect
of the presence of the spirit of creativity,
which pervades and rules the universe
and all our lives in the most dreaded form
of destiny or fate, the tragedy of life and death
which becomes the more inspiring the more suffering it brings,
and there you are: the end result of magic,
the mystery of something getting into being
with a lasting and profound effect to stay
and remain productive and in charge
as part of the sustained dimension
of continuous timelessness.

Crisis

My love is lost,
and I find no way out
into the wilderness, where she is gone
in crisis disappeared
for no apparent reason
except chance, bad luck
and circumstances most unfortunate.
She will be back, but who knows when?
Meanwhile I'll have to grope around
and falter in the dark,
like some decrepit invalid without a crutch
and stumble on in darkness
helplessly and hopelessly,
and in the darkness without her
there is no light at all
but only the impossibility
of tolerance and patience
with this most exasperating situation.

At Your Own Peril

You must not be alone,
the most harmful of conditions,
completely self-destructive
and what's worse, unconsciously,
because you get too focussed on yourself
and lose the right perspective,
getting stuck on your own grind-stone
with no possible detachment,
and thus you get beside yourself,
while relationship is all that helps,
the possibility to speak with someone
and to forget all about yourself,
which is what everybody needs
in order to go on surviving
and not get stuck in self-destructive egoism,
which is the surest way to mental suicide.
You have to care for someone,
life is only possible in co-operation, –
people who can't help each other
will never be able to help themselves.

After the Shipwreck

What can you do but gather up the ruins,
summarize the debris and collect it,
starting once again all over from a new beginning,
although it is certain it will lead to just another shipwreck?
You are lost without identity,
you have no ground to stand on any more,
no confidence, no trust, no home,
no faith in anything or anyone
for perfectly and only realistic reasons;
but instead you have the universe,
all life in nature and its continuity,
a vast eternity of possibilities and riches
and a veritable boundless ocean of constructive dreams,

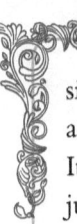

since fundamental universal creativity is always there
and waiting for you to take part in it.
It's worth a few occasional disastrous shipwrecks
just to be alive and stay alive.

Some Comfort

We have all been young,
no matter how decrepit we become,
no matter how beset with melancholia,
no matter how absurd experiences,
no matter how much we've been burned,
no matter how we suffered and endured
with scars all over and with wounds
that never heal and never vanish,
still we have all been young
and fresh and gay and active and alert,
and that's our comfort when we reach maturity,
that no one can take that away from us
that we once have been young
in love and beauty and enjoyment
and at least in some obscurity at heart
still are and keep it with us
to remain in some way young at heart forever.

Privacy

I love you more than words can tell
and more than feelings can express,
too well aware of the impossibility
of our absurd relationship
in which we hardly meet at all;
but love can be surprisingly much stronger
than by common triviality
like sex and entertainment,
doing things together and just be together,
love is more than sex and more than love,
and our affair is quite unique in that

we are so close together although so completely separate.
Let people wonder, but they can not touch us
any way by gossip, slander, speculation
or whatever, since we know each other in a way
that no one else can know.

Dreams of Love and Beauty

Dreams of love and beauty
are the only things worth living for,
but they are always there,
and once you've found them
they will last and evermore remain
as long as you are faithful to them,
cherishing, sustaining and remembering them,
as dreams more solid than reality,
more lasting and reliable than men and women,
saved from liquidation by your soul
which naturally keeps preserving what is worth preserving.
Thus you have a mandate for eternity,
your only one, mind you,
your dreams of love and beauty
that you were wise enough to take well care of.

Carrying On

Our relationship is always at a crisis
because of circumstances, practical complexities,
the sabotage of others, inconveniences
and difficulties of communication,
while the least of our problems
usually is the greatest for all others,
our love relationship itself and how it works,
which always went on smoothly
without the smallest friction tension ever.
Is this kind of love then our reward,
a union and affair completely free from strain,
for all our tragedies, frustrations and disasters?

Maybe we can count us happy,
while survival under difficulties and in constant crisis
keeps on being our destiny and ensign.

Involved

Is love self-destructive in itself?
The black passion abyss is but darkness
and the black hole of it an inferno,
but what's love without that pit,
and who can live without it?
Love consumes me utterly, and I enjoy the plague,
imploring it to never ease and cease its torment
but continue the exacerbation and acceleration
since love is something no one ever had enough of.

I am only human and as vulnerable and exposed as anyone
to the infernal persecution and seduction
of outrageous love and can but thoroughly enjoy it
for as long as it continues gracing me by torture
and can but ask it to go on and never cease.

Your Beauty

I adore your beauty,
its dramatic and profound enigma,
its unfathomable depth and darkness
and its undiscoverable secret
which defies all human sense and reason
by its unviolable untouchability.
That I love you is an understatement,
that I adore you is not well enough,
but that you are my friend is my beatitude
that I would rather never share with anyone,
since you alone are my supremest consummation.
More can not be said, since words are not enough,
since your enigma isn't for interpretation,
your timelessness and beauty being all and not enough.

The Best Friends

Your best friends
are those who keep in touch still after death.
It might appear a shameless and sarcastic statement
that the best friends are your dead friends,
but it seems in many ways to be the truth.
Should we avoid the truth then for its inconvenience?
Never. On the contrary, it must be carried forth
and brought the more out in the open
for its inconvenience the more disagreeable it is.

They are there still and with me, my best friends,
my father in his paragon of excellence and temperance,
my childhood friend, ideal in handsomeness and goodness,
terribly mistreated for his cancer by his doctors,
my goldsmith brother, driven over as a child
and made an invalid for life, who none the less
became the greatest expert on the art of living,
and my Russian friend, the greatest humorist,
always funny and refreshing in his sound superiority,
who went under like Vysotsky from intensity of self-consumption.
Although they are gone, to me they still are more alive
than probably most people that I know,
as if the fact that they went out too early
established and confirmed a friendship
more definite and stable than eternity.

Tomorrow and Tomorrow

Washed up by the consequences of adversities and trials,
devastating losses and excruciating melancholy,
it is difficult to find one's feet again,
indeed, if there at all is anything to stand on.
I can only think of the consuming ague
of a broken heart with no one for a comfort,
like alone in space in darkness without anyone
to hear the screams of your extreme despair
with only utter coolness for an answer in dead calm,
and nothing actually has really happened.
You are still the same, and you are there,
your life as always is at hand and full of force,
as nothing really ever happens, changes or has any meaning.
Call it Buddhist calmness and nirvana if you like,
but I would call it the persistent constancy of nature,
where all conflicts, wars and cataclysms will ever be
no more than passing storms in coffee cups.
So take it easy and remain, and call it good
whatever happens to you, and you will survive
to face tomorrow yet another glorious day.

Venus

Arising from the foam
of storms and ocean billows of the night
you rise in glory to astound the world
and drown it in your beauty overwhelmingly
and what is more, not temporarily,
but in a lasting dazzling spell forever,
since your beauty is of that extraordinary kind
that never ages, fades or vanishes;
and I am proud to be your chosen lover,
servant, thrall, depictor and companion
following your trail wherever and supporting it
in absolute transcendent loyalty and faith,

as any artist ardently devoted to his work
of outstanding ideal creation,
with sustained unending adoration
for a glorious harmonious accompaniment
to constantly enhance your beauty,
adding to your everlasting realm of love.

Diana

Goddess of virginity, of purity and freedom,
roaming in the wilderness to care for nature,
favouring all animals and hunting with them,
you became the basis for all ancient mysticism
with shrines in every sacred grove
for the sanctification and respect of life,
the queen of virtue and the mistress of integrity,
you were indomitable and inviolable
as the guardian supreme of health and freedom.
Nothing is more holy than Dame Nature,
and you were her impersonification
and will eternally remain so,
an ideal of chaste and sovereign liberty
commanded by respect and discipline
in the supreme imperishable beauty of superiority
in health and soundness, sport and perfect freedom.

Athena

Athena, goddess of wisdom,
friend of Odysseus, guide and provider,
the friend and protector of civilization,
thy force is the mission of knowledge,
of quality, insight and competence,
mastership and education,
the queen and protector of academism, universities
and every kind of spiritual accomplishment.
You were never seen without helmet,

and that is your mark of protection and vigilance
against barbarity, ignorance and the intrusion
of stupid destruction, disorder and anarchy.
Never abandon us in our vulnerability,
because civilization, philosophy and spitiuality
is always exposed to the forces of ignorance,
the meaninglessness of brutality
and the insane weakness of violence.
Guard us and save us, Athena,
in vigilance and the protection of spiritual growth.

Hera

Hail, mother of the gods,
the female ruler of Olympus,
the mistress of the heavens
and the troubled wife of Zeus,
the most impossible of husbands.
Somehow you can keep him in control, however,
although not without some jealous persecutions
of his nymphs and chosen victims,
ending almost all of them in tragedy.
If Zeus is the loose hand of Olympus
flinging thunderbolts and following his whims,
you are the firm hand holding it together
and with success, since your family holds out
and remain in loyal fealty,
sticking to each other in good faith
in spite of all controversies and conflicts.
You are a brave and stalwart goddess
whose beauty and strong character none can deny;
but bravest above all are you
for sticking it out and enduring it with Zeus.

Demeter

Demeter, mother of the earth,
the caring goddess of all living things,
the chief protector of all cultivation,
welfare and expansion of all nature,
you are piety itself, but also sorrow,
searching for a ravished child forever
and indulging in your sorrow wetting earth with tears
to make it grow the more and give good harvests,
no life service being more indulging
than to cry for sorrow in sincerest love.

But you are also guardian and protector of all harvests,
making wheat grow, starving off starvation,
as you are the farmer's goddess above all,
perhaps the most important, vital and constructive,
as no humankind can live and prosper without food,
of which you are the universal and unique provider.

So desist not, motherhood, to care for us,
and we shall always turn to you
in maximized and our sincerest piety
and gratitude for the existence of our freedom
maintained and supported only by your Nature.

Hestia

This was published here before, but she fits well in as the conclusion to these hymns to the six goddesses of ancient Greece. She was the only one of the Hellenic gods never to be depicted. Her symbol was instead the hearth.

The unknown goddess,
almost never made a statue of,
a silent modest background figure
staying quietly at home –
and maybe the most vital and important
of all gods and goddesses

for doing nothing but just being
there at home in coziness
with warmth and candour by the fireplace,
just keeping up the homely standard order,
keeping clean and making the home comfortable –
what could possibly be more important
than the very base of life,
a home to be at ease with
and to be at home in?
Still, she never made much noise,
no scandals, no atrocities,
no arguments, no love affairs,
just being there as the continuous stability,
the comfort of just being there at peace
and keeping up the basics
as the only ground
for the existence of all humankind.

Some Mysteries of Love

The strangeness of love is that it can have no finish,
once you love, it never ends
but must be constant in continuation,
or it is not love.
It also must embrace not just your love
but everything she is and does,
her thoughts, considerations and creations,
since your love is that especial force
inspiring her to creativity.
Thus love spreads like the rings of water
never to dry up but always to continue
spreading further and expanding ever
to miraculously end to only start again,
a gracious circle ever coming back to you
for you to please yourself by starting it again.

Rejuvenation

What a miracle to see you fresh again
after an eternity of some tumultuous decades
of divorces, dramas, traumas and upheavals
all reduced to nothing in an instant,
since you were so totally unchanged,
as if our forty years by some strange miracle
were reduced to but a moment's time
out of eternity, at once returning to our youth
and giving us a new eternity and lifetime of no end.
How shall I handle this new totally surprising love
so generously brought by fate and fortune
undeserved and unexpected but the more sincerely welcome
for its heavenly and overwhelming grace
that must completely fill me up
with boundless joy and energy and a new life
for you, my love, our common memories
and all those friendships that we shared together?
Stay by me, and don't desert me once again,
our divorce was much too long and all too painful
to bear any repetition and to be supported or endured
since we have been through far too much already
not to finally deserve each other.

Reunion

My love to you is like some service of divinity,
completely voluntary and in character religious,
since religion actually brought us together
and kept us united for some time in service
until nature brought on a divorce of destiny
to almost last a lifetime, an eternity of limbo
while we were the gadgets of our destiny
to play with and to handle roughly,
teaching us some karmic lessons about life,
relationships and how we always must return

to basics, to ourselves and to our origin,
how we were created, and to our debts
to those who made our lives and beings possible;
and thus we always have our piety to stick to,
which has always followed us like guardian angels
for protection against worldly troubles and deceits,
to always stick to ourselves and to our truth
of character, of truth and of our obligations
to ourselves, our families and to our plights and duties,
wherein we shall always find each other
for our warmth and comfort, inspiration and protection
in our love, the secret of our lives,
for no one can live without love,
which is the key to life and to eternity,
which only can be handled by the means of loyalty.
So here we are again, referred to one another,
as if our love as children in all innocence
was powerful enough to last for all our lives
and keep us well protected in eternity.

The Vital Flow of Tears

Your eyes must never dry.
They were made for tears
to make them flow and stay alive
for as long as possible and all your life
at least, but some tears last forever,
and they are the true life-giving tears,
the flow of which keeps flooding all the world,
maintaining oceans, watering the earth
to make it flourish, bloom and stay alive,
and all those tears are not of sorrow only.
Call them rather pity and compassion,
maybe even piety if not commiseration,
which is what is keeping life alive
in constant crisis, struggle for survival,
neverending anguish for the threat of constant death,

the worries of the obligations of maintenance,
which is actually the motor energy of life,
the sentimental melancholy of the self-effacing godhead,
that divine and universal source of life
that we shall never know or understand,
but for the fact that he keeps crying all the time
to keep the world and universe alive
from pure and piteous commiseration.

Between Ourselves

I don't want to let you go.
It is with absolute reluctance that I am without you;
and that you are with me all the time
although but virtually is not enough
but merely the poorest remedy for our separation.
Our love is unique and must needs entertainment,
like an art or language that must rust if you don't use it,
and I don't want any end to our engagement,
as we already were separated far too long.
Love is like a stormy visit out of paradise,
turning everything completely upside down
but positively, like some heavenly enforcement,
leaving you in turmoil until things calm down,
which you don't want them to, since you enjoy the passion.
Let it be, let it continue and go on forever,
and I shall enjoy the storm and relish it
and make the best of it through all the trials,
suffering with gladness and enduring anything for you,
since you are you and I am here to love you.

The Distance Trauma

It results in terrible ordeals of abstinence,
since usually those that you love the most
and would most eagerly be in close contact with
are farthest out of touch and most impossible to reach,
which must inevitably lead to tribulations,
most atrocious sufferings and insufferability at large.
And what is worse: it is a kind of problem
that, once it's there you can't get rid of it.
But what is distance then to love?
Love neutralizes and dissolves dimensions,
thought transcends and is superior to matter,
nothing can inhibit thought or keep it within limitations,
even less so when, as usually is the case,
it is propelled and motivated and kept flying
by the basic force of life called love,
which is the one thing, maybe, that exceeds the speed of light.
You can control thoughts, concentrate them, guide them,
but when they are moved by love there's nothing that can stop them.
Distances like all dimensions suddenly become nonsensical
as trivial nonentities to be ignored and bypassed,

while your love is all that matters,
keeping you and life alive and constituting
all the nourishment for your immortal universal soul.

The Problem of Rights

Being right is more important than to force your right.
The Tibetans, being under occupation now since more than 60 years,
oppressed by tyranny, bereft of their own land and independence,
having had their culture almost extirpated and demolished,
putting fire to themselves in desperate suicidal protest
are completely right, while the Chinese, insisting on their tyranny
are hopelessly completely wrong for all their overbearing dominating violence
in which nothing morally can save them.
The dogmatic church and other such monotheistic institutions
have for some millennia hounded, persecuted and put free-thinkers to death,
while these were in the right, the martyrs, heretics and pagans,
like Giordano Bruno and Jan Hus, Jeanne d'Arc and all the executed witches,
while their executioners of islam and the church were hopelessly
completely wrong
and will be judged so for eternity, and there is nothing that
can save them morally.
The losers, martyrs, scapegoats, sacrifices and all victims
win eternity and will forever be atoned for and remembered,
while their murderers, no matter how victorious they are,
will lose forever and can never save their faces.
They are damned, accursed forever, blighted and condemned,
while those who were put to the stake and sacrificed
will live forever and triumphantly,
universally acknowledged and acclaimed
as morally superior forever
to those dogs who did them in,
in which case there is nothing that can save them,
moral victory and right outshining
all the victories of gain and greed,
which eventually must come to nothing;
while there is no labour more rewarding
than that of the moral power of the soul.

Your Enigma

The question is not who you are,
no one can answer that question about herself,
since your identity is everything and nothing,
you can become whatever, make yourself whatever,
be whoever but at the same time be at a loss,
aware of the black hole of your enigma
of your personality and everything that makes you you,
your heritage and what you were before your birth,
the history about yourself, which can not be researched
but still is there in manifest imposing presence.
I know that I am many people and can never be but one,
so I devote myself to work to thus evade the problem
in a constant desperate escape from any ego trip,
and thus I can avoid the problem of my personality.
Are you the same? You have a personality like me,
but I don't know how you have handled it,
if it ever was a problem to you, and that's maybe your enigma:
I don't know you in the least and never shall, – so we are free to be without ourselves together.

Lost in Love

It can happen to anyone,
and it usually happens to us all.
It is only natural to be lost in love
and to stay that way indefinitely,
paralysed, transfixed, immobilized and powerless,
while love is all that works and matters.
There is nothing wrong with that,
we actually were made for it,
and it did produce us all;
so just give in and go for it
and make the best of it,
adorn your trap of love with your abilities,
indulge in all those moods of melancholy,

longing, languishment, desire and frustration,
if you can't beat reality you have your dreams
which in your world will certainly beat everything,
and your paralyzation will turn into fruitfulness.
It's all a matter of let go.
To make resistance is the height of foolishness,
stupidity and folly, since you really have no choice
but to follow your own nature guided by your love.

The Depths of Love

Love will take on many forms
but none will ever be consummate.
However, every form is good enough,
whatever its expression, and can never be mistaken:
love is always recognized as love,
even when its language is contempt and hate;
which is why it's so important
to interpret love correctly:
that's the true art, seeing love behind it all
when that's the character behind it,
masked and enigmatic, dark and puzzling,
difficult to get the hang of or imposing,
the art of understanding being the most difficult of arts
and also the most necessary and advanced,
which you will never, like with love itself,
be able to be fully educated in.

At Zero

Naked you were born to earth,
and naked shall your soul remain for all your life.
The clothes you get for your protection
and for the cover of your nakedness
are only a disguise for all your life,
an artificial masquerade of only lying masks
to cover up the truth,
which always shall remain pathetically naked;

but your body also is but a disguise,
a robot and contraption to deceive the world with,
a means for faking vanities and fortunately a most mortal lie.
You yourself are something different,
namely your own naked soul,
the nakedness of which is such
that fortunately it can never be detected,
so that you can even get away with it
and take it with you when you die.

Suicide or Self Sacrifice

- 70 years since the suicide of Stefan Zweig

It has the worst of reputations,
considered generally the worst of crimes,
punishable by death or worse,
the absolute and utmost cowardice,
the definite damnation doomed to hell forever,
but it's really not that simple.
It depends on why you do it.
If it's a revenge on those that wronged you,
or if it's a demonstration, which it often is,
it must be viewed correctly in perspective.
Let me take a classical example.
Stefan Zweig in 1942 was something of a humanistic leader,
most translated author in the world,
a representative of culture, pacifism and internationalism,
which gave him a tremendous standing of responsibility,
but as a Jew he had to leave his native Austria
and found himself eventually completely isolated in Brazil,
not able to communicate with German-speaking readers any more.
When he committed suicide with his wife
he made it very clear it was for purely intellectual reasons –
as an intellectual he felt asphyxiated in a world of war and Adolf Hitler
dominated by coarse anti-spiritualism and media propaganda.
Although he denied that he dropped out of any personal frustration,
the fact that he did had a tremendous impact

morally and intellectually for all the world,
and during that year actually the tides turned against Hitler
first by Moscow, then in Africa and Stalingrad.
His action was supreme as demonstration against the oppression
he felt as an intellectual by the vulgar imposition of politics.
Today we see the same phenomenon in Tibet,
some twenty monks have burned themselves to death,
no suicidal bombers, only private self sacrifices
as the greatest demonstration life can manifest
against intolerable cruelty, oppression and the violated rights of freedom,
and its effect must have consequences.

The Honeymoon is Over

All honeymoons must pass
and vanish out of sight into a Neverland
where you at least can still imagine that they carry on
while you are left alone with the delusion of reality,
the sordid realism of dismal darkness
which must ever tie you harder up
into a knot of disappointed bitterness
that ever must grow worse and ail you unto death;
but there was once a honeymoon in spite of all,
you could believe in happiness and fall in love
when you were young and fresh and beautiful and healthy, –
but that paradise is closer than you think.
Since once you had it, bringing it into your soul,
your Neverland is always there and waiting for you,
carrying on as usual, where the best part
of your truth and beauty never are forgotten
but will keep you warm when all the world is cold.

Caretaking

How shall I love you?
My capacity is not enough,
and I can't always reach you
since you are so volatile and fleeting as a dream,
too beautiful to be intruded on and importuned,
too delicate and vulnerable to be touched
and too exquisite not to be with constancy adored and loved.
They say that femininity is frailty and weakness,
but I think it is the other way around –
the more profound its spirituality, the stronger,
and that's where we have the obligation of persistent adoration:
spirituality is beauty and is life,
and the more beautiful, the more reliable and generous its life,
which it's our duty to maintain, sustain and entertain
protectively with our lives andloving care and adoration.

The Other Side of Love

The constant worry, the despair and the frustrations,
disapppointments and the total everlasting grief
that constantly grows worse,
are just a few of the outrageous symptoms
of the tribulations and self-torture we call love,
and so the question always rises:
is it worth it? Is it worth the constant sacrifice,
the anguish of the doubts, suspicions and deceits,
the pain of the defeats and the adversities,
the losses without end and the disasters?
Well, if you survive you always have the possibility
to start all over once again and take another chance;
and no one ever failed to do that
who was well acquainted and experienced with love.

The Success of Failures

You pulled away,
but I could never leave you.
If it is a crime to be a narcissist,
then all of mankind would be prosecuted,
for there is no other natural religion.
Each and every one is his own god,
and of all religions the most realistic one
would be the one acknowledging that fact
and making it its basic creed.
She cheated me and hurt me by her infidelity,
but so did they all, so many others,
as if our relationship and union only was a reason
and excuse for faithlessness;
and worst of all were feminists,
the cruellest one the most extreme one,
lesbian and to some exaggeration.
Only you did not deceive and cheat me,
but instead you brought on some adventure,
wild experiments in metaphysics and the occult
which no one can know where they might lead,
while certainly the constant risk of death is imminent.
This brings me into constant worry,
like a torturous malaise of some maliciousness
that I can never more get rid of as incurable
as long as I love you, which I must do forever
since you are the closest thing to perfect love
that all my failures in spite of all and after all led up to.

Midnight Conversations

An old poem, published anew because of some emendations - a rather familiar situation to most.

In the darkness of midnight
far away beyond ourselves
we meet and join in timelessness
like two spirits moulded into one
by the truth of this momentary eternity.
This bliss is the supremest of this life
and the miracle of it the most incredible.
The sight goes out and we live by hearing only
sweet soft words from barely audible voices,
the loveliest of this life
only because they understand each other
and thereby comprise each other
in the pious breathless embrace of eternity.
This union is this moment which,
if you have experienced it,
you can but always pray
for its remaining and continuing forever.

Sometimes I Wonder Who You Are

Sometimes I wonder who you are,
since you are never quite definable.
You keep evading me, absconding into shadows,
as if you were apprehensive, fearing some contamination
either by yourself or for yourself,
but I could never fear a thing of you.
The more I love you, the more you retire,
as if you refused me your identity
or were afraid of making it knowledgeable at all.
So do departed spirits haunt the living,
still communicating but communicating vaguely,
as if fearful of their actual condition being known;

but you are here, alive and kicking,
and you are forever on my mind,
and that's what makes it so frustrating
never to attain and reach your actual personality.
It's like 'hide and seek', but I can never find you,
although you are manifestly there for sure,
but covered in a mystery, a cloak of darkness and invisibility,
as if my honest love and most sincere communication
only were allowable on purely an exclusive spiritual plane.

Beyond Reality

Our world is another better world,
a world and age of timelessness and beauty
far removed from this world of indecency
of vulgar greed and base voracity,
where beauty and idealism seem in exile
doomed to languish, starve and stifle
in an age of narrow-minded automatic inhumanity,
while we were made for love and inspiration,
human dignity and the appreciation of humanity,
since being human is the only decent standard,
which got lost in the last century
when fools rushed in to rape and devastate
a world of order and romantic aestheticism
to trample it under the armies of dictators.
We have nothing more to do with them,
nothing in common and no business with their devastation
but stick faithfully and closely to that world of beauty
which was painfully neglected and forgotten and abused
by those who violated it and ruined it.
Our realm of timelessness is beyond their mortality and vanity,
and when at last they will wake up from mortal folly,
they will find us there to welcome them back home.

Portrait of a Lady

Describing you is something of a challenge,
since you make a sport of your concealment,
hiding your good looks and covering your hair,
the richest and most beautiful I know,
under the bushel of your veils and shawls,
while you but seldom look into the eyes of others,
as if you saw far too much of them in but a glance,
and usually allowing no one to see yours,
as if you had to cover and protect them
with dark glasses from the ignobility of others' hearts.
Your figure is a problem too, far too well-shaped,
with hips too narrow for a lady, raising the suspicion
that you would be unfit to have children,
which is maybe why you never had any,
while at the same time your appearance is of perfect femininity,
so well proportioned and so graceful in its movements,
so expressive of the softest care and mildness,
raising and inspiring respect and telling of your wisdom,
while at the same time a warning is inspired
of the sensitivity of your dynamics and explosiveness,
like some grenade that could go off at any time.
The message is the clearest possible: "Leave me alone.
Respect me, love me if you want, but don't come near me,
since it's best for you the less you know about me."

Her Disgrace

You ask me to contemn you.
That is not so easy, although no one is infallible,
we are but human, but at the same time
we are not only human. There is more to our humanity
than we ourselves are quite aware of,
and although I could point out your faults,
they are but trifles in comparison.
Your hinted wrinkles vanish in the sunshine of your smile,

the shadows of your past are outshone by your beauty,
and the darkness of your soul, that you persist in boasting,
as if that was some protection or excuse for your indisposition,
are but shades like of mascara on the beauty of your soul.
Your poverty means only that you never have been spoilt,
and age is but increased nobility, maturity and wisdom,
each year adding to your merits of survival and persistence
and to my increasing love for you, according to what you deserve.
Contempt? Impossible. Respect? Of course,
and nothing so much more than that, except for love.

The Age of Passion

Let's make love before it is too late,
for time will never wait for us,
and love is always short of time,
and we must be in time before we get too old
for passion, which demands our action now,
postponement of which means the death of it.
The time is now and not at any other time,
but in this moment of our love at present
there is room forever for some timelessness,
since love is a dimension of its own
exceeding time and all concerns of age,
for which we never can become too old.
Thus even in the mortal moment of our love
at this most precious fleeting presence
our love is an eternity that will go on
and never die, although we would be but a moment
unified in our consummate and completed passion.

My Demon

You are my demon,
ever present but absconding,
tantalizingly evasive and alluring,
like a shadow you can never catch
and never do without
but at the same time something of my guardian
leading me on crooked paths
but always in the right direction
to a destiny I seldom am aware of
but which ultimately usually proves true.

At the same time you are possessing me,
without you I am lost and can but long for you,
my worst most painful abstinence,
while I only am fulfilled
when we get on together.

As an intimate relationship
it is more closely knit than any marriage,
rather like as soulmates
making up and adding to each other
like a coin of opposite and different sides.

You are my demon,
I can never do without you,
and as long as you can carry on with me,
I know I shall be whole and prosper,
happily in love with more than just a partner.

Out of Nowhere

As people pass away they leave behind
a void of talks that never were completed,
conversations and intimacies badly to be missed,
unfinished cycles, projects and possibilities
that were too often thought of but forever unfulfilled,
and above all the physical immediate close contact,
without which you are left at a loss
disoriented and abandoned to your ghosts
or what is worse, yourself.
But still there always is a remedy,
right there in front of you and in the middle of all darkness,
opportunity will wait for you to just take care of it.
For every old friend that is lost
a younger friend will take his place,
appear from nowhere and report to take his stand,
and even in the darkness in the absence of your love
a new and warmer, maybe even more intensive,
passionate and stimulating love will strangely suddenly appear,
since that is how love works. It never ends.
It only dies to gain new strength,
be reinforced and find new ways and forms.

Acknowledgement

Did I demand too much of you
and make impossible pretensions?
Maybe I was too much of a snob
and to possessive in my strictness,
too much of a critic and too little of a lover,
being too severe in keeping to my standards,
while your generosity was always without reservations.
There is nothing to regret, though.
I could not be less than what I was
nor compromise with my convictions
or turn any blind eye to the false notes of your music
nor be any different from my own true heart.

What came between us was not me
nor was it you but only that which wasn't you.
Now you are free and liberated from the dross
of all the bondage that destroyed your life
and can at last see all things clearly,
while at least we now are free to smile indeed
in friendship everlasting that can never be impeded,
and that's something even more worth
than that love that never could exist between us,
although it was always there and undeniable,
and still for all its strange untouchable unmentionableness
a stranger love than any other love in our lives.

Reunion

Thank you for the pleasure
of enjoying well each other once again,
like a fresh start after some time of absence
almost like the dryness of some languishment
or a divorce and crisis of some rupture,
but it was a healthy and enjoyable resume
to feel the lust of wallowing in slime
and the debasement of mortality and ordinariness,
the trivial common vice of being only human
with the passion of commitment in your lap
accepting and partaking in the weakness of your bias
in a fit of universal tolerance of sin.
Our love was always only a beginning
going on forever as it seems,
since nothing ever could impede or stop it,
least of all the reason of good sense and rationality,
so I would guess it will continue to survive.

Irrefutability

Love is only true if it is blind
and you can't see another course of it except to follow it
wherever it may lead you,
and its destination must needs be unknown.

Those are the tokens of true love:
no sense, no course except in blindness,
a permanent blind date, no ending, no control.
When love is there, there's nothing more important,
all the world becomes a negligible triviality,
all matters of career, economy and situation
are reduced to a nonentity,
while love is first and last and everything between.
To mind it must become your only serious business,
and it fills your life, which otherwise is empty.
Who your love is is of less importance in this context,
most important is that you have someone
else to love than just yourself,
and you can only keep it by remaining faithful
and to never let her down whatever happens in eternity.

The Shadow of Your Absence

You turned your back on me and left me
but still left the most important part behind,
the shadow of your absence being more alive than any ghost,
as if you stayed behind the more for leaving me.
Your presence is a haunting trauma
and the more so for your absence,
as if you could never leave me
but to prove the more your indispensibility,
your hidden eyes and your expressive back
just proving too unbearably the unacceptability.
I know, I am not sober, mad with grief
and melting in the sorrow of your absence,
while my only hope
is after all the possibility of your return.

Still Missing

The ordeal of missing you
is worse than any rainy weather,
even if you're caught in it without a cape,
the water running down your neck can be endured,

but not your momentary permanence of absence.
There is no one else for me to love so ardently,
although the gods know there are hundreds
whom I miss like you with broken heart,
but they are all deceased, while you are only gone away.
Perhaps you could regard them also just as gone away,
although they haunt me with their presence constantly,
while you are definitely out of reach
in far too real a palpable and painful absence.
Let me cherish you, then, as my queen of ghosts,
the star outshining all the heavens in their darkness,
all the other stars remaining at your pleasure
as commiserating me in my tremendous pain of missing you.

The Presence of Beauty

The miracle of it is that,
when once it's there, it will remain
and never really leave your side,
like something of a dream that lasts forever,
although it is real and no illusion,
like a spirit fleeting by but staying on
to always in a strange reliability
provide a refill of your life and love
whenever, and especially, when you are troubled
or caught up in critical upsetting situations,
like a secret love and woman always by your side
although she isn't there, but still
in a most palpable and obvious presence,
the more real for being only spiritual.

The Absent Friend

You left, but left something behind.
I listen to your voice, although it's gone,
but hear it still in its warm booming depth
and look each morning for your place out there
and seem to see you still out on the terrace,

or is this I see just what you left behind,
a memory, the pain of breaking up,
the most reluctant difficult departure,
as if you left all the most important parts of you
still here with me, while you removed your body only?
Still, we keep in touch, like brothers of a common destination,
ships that met alone out in the desert ocean
for a brief encounter of remarkable importance
never sailing from each other quite away again
however far we travel on our way in different directions.

Departure

When you leave a place, you leave all friends behind,
you get uprooted and are left completely at a loss
and find yourself abandoned but for tears,
the one thing you must carry with you
into exile from where you have left your heart.
But still, your friends remain with you like shadows
following around you everywhere, impossible to leave behind,
shake off, forget or even to stop thinking of,
as you, like they, will always keep returning
to what you have shared together;
and like they you always can keep hoping,
looking forward to and wishing for the possible redemption
of one day somewhere in the eternity of future
maybe being able to unite again.

The Failed Appointment

I was punctual, but you were not there,
all doors closed up by padlocks,
windows darkened, like a demonstration
against my at all existing as a presence
venturing to being fond of you
and nourishing affection and sentimentality.
It's almost worse than just a loss
and almost a betrayal of true love

at its most beautiful and pure
as can exist platonically only between soulmates.
Well, perhaps there was an incident,
some urgent business or an accident
preventing you from humouring a friend
by courtesy; but when the heartbreak is repeated
and a failed appointment happens more than once,
I wonder: is it fortune playing me a trick,
or am I just misfortunate
and dealt unfairly with by destiny?

Your Voice

Your voice keeps haunting me
for its alluring irresistibility of musicality,
its lush sonority so sweet to have as balsam to my ears
and so revealing of your personality.
It was a love affair of spiritual coexistence
of coordination of communion and communication,
and I thoroughly enjoyed each moment of it
wishing to prolong each minute to a lifetime;
and this memorable and momentous meeting
will not cease but constantly go on by our continuation
of two souls on the same level but from different worlds
by our remaining in close contact although worlds apart.
We don't see when we shall unite again,
but actually it doesn't matter. We have all the future,
it's the widest field of operation and of opportunities,
and I believe that we have found each other only
never to be able to break up and part again.

My Dead Love

How comes it, then,
that we are still together
every day and intimately,
even more so
than when you were here

alive and active,
while since your departure
you, instead of vanishing into the shadows,
your presence only has increased
up to a point of almost taking over
my entire life, more part of me
than of yourself.
It is a metaphysical phenomenon,
and I can only marvel at the fact
that you are more alive as dead
than when you were alive.

The Blessings of Workoholism

You are never bored
and never out of work,
you never lack good entertainment
and you always are kept busy.
In brief, it only imports blessings
never to be able or to have to stop
and never needing any rest,
to always have something ahead
both to look forward to
and being able to postpone,
as it is said:
He has something to look forward to
who has some business to postpone.
It can be also used as some way of escape
for the evasion of fatiguing travel
and dull social duties,
like exhausting tiresome and noisy parties
to instead be kept alone in peace.
These blessings make your wages less important
since no salary or gain is higher
than the satisfaction
of a finished and accomplished work.

Love

How can I describe you but with gratitude?
Our passion needed fifteen years to find itself
and then was ripe enough to bloom forever
as it seemed; and I was so surprised
that I had not discovered previously
the essence of your magic personality.
You came to me then as a benefactory reward
for all my losses previously and disappointments,
as a perfect healing compensation for my shipwrecks,
undeserved defeats and lock-outs from society
in spite of honesty and regular hard work,
like an infectuous cold hand of inhumanity
that persecuted me throughout my life for nothing
if not for my diligence and constancy of faithfulness
to my vocation, turning me into a total workoholic
as my only recompense for never getting any salary.
My life is turning now into a regular and chronic state
and exercise of meditation; but your presence in my life
is much more worth and better as a salary and honour
than all prizes in the world, and you have honoured me
by giving up yourself entirely to me and no one else,
although indeed you had a choice of lovers.
All the riches in the world is nothing to our love,
which for its constancy and character of durability,
impeccability and spirituality and mutual respect and trust
is more than only love, but something like
a universal covenant and marriage between souls
that is its own reward in inexhaustability of inspiration.

Continuity

How long can you go on loving?
You just have to carry on
and never let your passion down,
since you live only while you love.
It doesn't matter how you love,

but only that you feel it honest and sincere
with all your being constituting only love.
It is your only obligation in your life,
that's only why you live
and how you can go on with it,
it is what's keeping you alive,
the one thing capable of continuity
and even after life – there's nothing else
that constantly can keep you going on
through all adversities, debacles, tragedies,
departures, losses, crises, death and cataclysms;
since the great secret of the elixir of love
is that it always will survive.

The Miracle of Your Love

You have never changed.
You are still the one I loved
from the beginning, and in all these years
your love grows only lovelier,
as if the fact that I once loved you
more than anything and to a permanence
preserved your beauty
only to enhance it with the years.
How many years have passed?
Not more than only some eternities.
Your charm was there to linger and to last
as long and to the same degree as my sincerity
which never slackened during all these years.
Your smile was then the sun of permanence
of flooding light throughout my life,
and although you had some successors,
you were the foundation of my love
whereon I could continue building it,
expanding it, enhancing it and developing it
to never cease but to increase
in constant and miraculous renewal
of itself by its own magic power
of transcendent permanence.

The Mystery of Love

The mystery of love has once again exploded
loaded with an abyss and a universe of wonder
of considerations, thoughts and broodings
without end because of their intrinsic nature
of a mystery that can't be solved,
as it grows only deeper the more you investigate it,
like a fascinating image in a mirror
which reflects itself too clearly in another mirror
multiplying and prolonging the strange show
of what you do not even know if it is a beginning,
a fulfillment of an old unfinished story,
a strange peril of a new entrapment
or another chance to finally make something of your life.
I cannot judge it or assess it, what it means,
and must accept to stand here groping in the dark,
while there at least is one thing that's for certain:
that I love you. Maybe that is all I need to know.

Potency

I am not afraid of love
but usually prefer its milder forms
with quality as number one.
The highest quality of love is spiritual,
which is superior to any physical
by inexhaustibility and limitlessness above all,
since this potential is without restrictions and impediments.
Is celibacy then what I profess?
No, celibacy is no matter in this issue,
since spiritual love demands no discipline.
It just exists, expands and works in quiet growth
unlimited creating only good relationships.
That's how it is superior to any love of concrete ties,
dissolving and annihilating all the common problems
that are unavoidable in physical relationships;

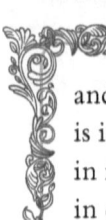

and most marvellous of all in spiritual love
is its superiority and transcendance of all earthly love
in its potential for creating warmer closeness and intimacy
in continuity that could not only last but grow forever.

Deception

The more you love them, the more faithless they are,
and the more faithless they are, the more you love them.
That's the essence of love's merry-go-round,
a vicious circle in which you constantly get fooled around
and therefore the more enthusiastically join in again.
It doesn't matter how much you are hurt;
the more vulnerable and more wounded you are,
the more you continue to expose yourself to new massacres
just to get new wounds to dress again
with long periods of rehabilitation and recuperation.
Love's the constant battle from which you can never rest
but must join in the slaughter-house again
each time you have been slaughtered.
Is it wise? Is it a folly or a vanity?
It's like a drug and an addiction,
you just have to have another glass
since it momentarily makes you feel better.
I can't advise it, and no one can advise against it.
You just got to have it, for a moment's better
or for an eternity of worse, and there you are:
the present moment if just for a brief fulfillment
of your longing and delusion, self-deceit and dreams of vanity
is so much more important and more attractive
than all eternity, which never comes but later.

Moor Blossom

The passion of your love
is like a flower in the whirlwind
outcast and without protection
and the loneliest flower in the world
in furious beauty of resplendent glow
of warming tenderness and infinite melancholy.
Will it survive the storms and hibernate
in splendid isolation without being plucked,
or will it be collected, saved and cultivated,
or will it just wither, wasted and forgotten?
No, you will not wither, you will always be the same
in furious glow of melancholic splendour,
the most energetic force of love of all,
outshining all the overwhelming grimness of the moor
the more enduring for the more it hurts and suffers.

How Not to Complicate Relationships

It happens all the time.
They end up with the wrong guy
getting into bed with the wrong man,
while their truest lover proves to be another
who resigns in bitter melancholy and frustration.
How then do they manage constantly to pick the wrong guy?
Is it that notorious frailty of a woman,
do they WANT to get seduced and laid by the wrong man,
are they so gullible and duped so easily,
or are they helpless victims, martyrs forced by rape?
I think the problem is to have to choose at all,
because in choosing one you must exclude the others,
and they are inevitably the majority.
The one who doesn't make a choice
but steers out clear of all the rocks
will still be able to keep all his loves
without disgracing anyone or letting any down,
spreading disappointment and frustration equally to all
and keeping all of them with faith, fidelity and love
in mastery of love's diplomacy and equilibrium.
That is how Queen Elizabeth kept all her wooers and adorers,
and a bachelor can never be accused
of maltreatment of any lady
until he starts favoring one to another.

Welcome

It is as if I always had you home with me
although we only met but once or twice
and we could hardly know each other.
Still, it is as if you always had been with me,
and I could but welcome you into my soul
when you so generously opened it to enter,
where you have remained since then
most welcome to my humble hospitality

in both my heart and soul and without reservations.
Thereby I don't wish to importune
but merely courteously bring you my compliment
with my sincerest unpretentiousness, humility and prudence
tainted with a cautious touch of shyness
not to hurt your feelings or my own.
Now is the time for the dark mornings
when you rise to darkness every darker dawn
while in its stead my love of you is rising
shining brighter every morning
compensating spiritually the increasing darkness
of this mad distorted world of turbulence
where so much love must compensate for so much folly.

Temptation

My love is like a mirage that is real,
a dream that is too palpable to be dissolved,
an impossible illusion that you can't discard,
a prospect too good to be true
and therefore unforgettably alarming,
a relief from the religious fun-house of the world
providing you with reason for a change,
and although this might risk a dire strait
of the most complicated of relationships,
the challenge is unquestionable irresistible.
I love you, and I can't deny it,
come what may,
but love must always have its way.

POEMS – 2015-17

No Time

There is no time for anything,
since there is never time enough.
Your life is squeezed down into certain limits
that keep you like in a strait-jacket
out of any possibility of freedom
since your time is limited and always short,
and the more you use it economically
for all that has to be done and executed,
the less time you have,
not even time enough to sleep;
and then you have to work in constant overtime,
and you will never reach that spare time
which would finally allow you to resolve the matter
of not ever having time enough to live.

In Praise of Beauty

May I touch your hair and ask you never more to cut it?
That's the foremost evidence of beauty in any human being,
that she knows to cultivate her hair correctly.
There is nothing wrong with beauty, it can never be offensive,
even when it is seductive and distracts your concentration
it is fully meritorious only and to be encouraged.
Beauty as an escapism, deluding people to disorientation
is no less supportable, since it is not beauty's fault –
if people go astray it is entirely their own responsibility,
since only they themselves can do it.
Beauty is a solace and a bandage for the tortures of reality,
and who can blame a nurse for dressing wounds?
So let me live for beauty, since there is not much else to live for,
quite happy with the fact, vicissitude and knowledge
that the truth of love and beauty always will survive me.

My Love

My love, your mystery has never ceased to bother me
with its consummate irreproachability
combined with unapproachability
and all ideal traits of a woman,
not just beauty of both soul and body
but above all an astounding comfortableness,
since you have never made demands,
you never asked me for gratification,
never wanted money or my property,
always left me to my freedom and alone when needed,
while the only thing you wanted me to give was time
for you and for our love, which I most willingly bestowed,
since that was all you asked for.
Maybe that's the most important thing a man can give a woman,
while in our present world of stress and lack of time
that's also the most difficult of things to offer,
which is a most shameful sign of the condition

of our world today: when we can't give
what's most essential between man and woman to bestow.

Tired Out

How can I love you, being such a monster of deceit
and double standards, volatile capriciousness
and no reliability at all, save for abscondence?
I have always loved you but have never reached you,
as if your life's sport was never to get caught
or even grasped or even palpably definable.
Our love is a cruel game of hide and seek,
and when at last I had you for myself
you proved as fleeting as a shadow,
as if all you wanted was to get away,
while I was stuck with desperately missing you.
Your darkness never scared me, on the contrary,
your main attraction was to me your minefield
of experimenting wildly with your human research,
but I could never be a part of it.
That's maybe what was separating us from the beginning:
your precarious recklessness in absolute demands
for ruthless independence in your freedom,
while I never settled for a compromise in love:
I had to have it all and all of you,
while you reserved your best part
for the possibility to leave and get away.
The worst part is, that I can love you but the more
for your evasiveness in your perpetual refuge
to vainly chase your shadow even into darkness.

Your Present Absence

Although you are so sorely missed,
your presence is a case of omnipresence
in your absence, since it's almost palpable
in the ethereal substance of your essence,
as the presence of your being overwhelms my mind

the more for your so hopeless distance.
I am paralyzed by being lost without you,
and yet you are still so close and present
ever in my life and mind and alien existence
as if you could never exit my heart's residence,
although no one is more free of me than you.
It is a paradox in more than one sense
as it all all ends up in something of a sentence
that I'll never do without you for your absence.

Catching Up

As we met again
the stars began to sing,
and to my infinite surprise
you proved more beautiful than ever.
We have both had our hardships,
our souls are maimed with scars and ulcers,
as the scumbags of incompetence and ignorance
could never stop harassing us,
but we survived with our wings quite intact
and more prone to fly more skilfully than ever.
Our reunion was traumatic for its overwhelmingness,
since we were separated for too long,
and although our union tragically will remain impossible,
all we can do is hoping it will not be such a long time
of insufferability until we meet again.

Love at Some Safe Distance

Distances make love more vulnerable
in the sadness raised by longing
aggrandized by missing you outrageously.
It has been said, that love is greatest
when it cannot find sufficient words
and all expressions never are enough.
When love suffers from inadequacy
of expression and the proper words,

it is because it is too deep and honest
and therefore demanding too much of its owner,
who can't compromise with his own truth of honesty
or of his love's, which must demand the absolute.
Such love is maybe better off at some safe distance
than will risk its purity, sincerity and honesty
in feelings that can't bear corruption.

Waiting

Awaiting your return from overseas
at least fills up my life with longing.
Waiting is an unendurable eternity
but still just one brief moment of our lives
completely neutralized, when you return, to nothing,
like all tantrums, tribulations, pains and sufferings
for your love's sake just vanish when at last
we are together once again, all sufferance made null and void.
The dreariness, depression, darkness and despair
meanwhile though are not to be borne with,
and there is no hell more fatal than to have to do without your love.
When she is there, you are the ruler of the world,
and when she's gone you are worse off
than any fallen angel stuck in hell forever without hope.
So we shall smile indeed when you return,
and may your glorious return then be a continuity forever.

Remembrance

Should I not long back
to places of my love and friends
and only live to find them once again,
revisit them with joy and candour
as they must remain a continuity
of love and friendship and communion forever?
Sorely I will miss you
but retain the comfort of preserving you
and ever visit you again in my rermembrance,

always thinking of you now and then
and always looking forward to the moment
when at last we may rejoin again
to smile indeed for yet another moment
of some days, to cultivate and piously maintain
our lasting union and belonging to each other
for as long as there will be remembrance.

A Dark Secret

You came to me through darkness
out of my supreme despair
of disappointments and annihilated expectations
fatally depriving me of all my faith in man;
but by the revelation of your personality
with similar experience to my own
you opened up a new world of discovery
of possibilities and promises of love;
and with the abyss of your tragedy
you never failed to give me light and hope,
as if the hell of blood and tears was a prerequisite
for the reward of wisdom and accomplishment.
The black hole of your presence then must needs remain
my arduous passion and continuous addiction
fencing me irrevocably in for good
in your dark universe of love.

Harvest

O blessed night of ecstasy
when everything is perfect in a love affair
that knows no bounds and has no end
and never even probably had a beginning.
It is timelessness of love
and joy at that of some infinity
as health and harmony come out triumphant
after crises filling up a lifetime.
Ask me not about the nature of this bliss,

but share it only and enjoy it
as you never know how it might once again be interrupted.
Walk with me into the sun,
take care of every aspect of the full-blown ripe enjoyment,
and remember it forever when it's past;
and thus you might bequeath it an eternal continuity.

A Tibetan Shangri-La of Happiness

They have a good life in Dharamsala
where they may freely practice their religion
and philosophy in their fantastic library
where at lest 40 percent of all Tibetan literature was saved,
while only 60 percent was destroyed by the Chinese.
Here also they are free to practice their monastic life
after the ruin of 6000 monasteries in Tibet by the Chinese,
here they can live in peace in their perpetual exile,
those Tibetans who were able to escape
from the Chinese attempted genocide on all Tibetans
in which just a fifth of them were actually disposed of
of which half a million were just harmless monks and nuns,
tortured to death in concentration camps
and bombed to death in their own monasteries.
But they lead a good life in Dharamsala
and give a stronger sense of happiness
than I have ever seen among Chinese in China.

The Eternal Return

You graced me with your love
without my being worth it,
as I never as a lover was much qualified
but dabbled mostly in most miserable failures,
teaching me to never try again.
And yet you were there, and most palpably,
and always kept returning.
as if I was something to return to

and to keep reminding of the effects of true love;
and this can never be denied,
that love can never be ignored or set aside,
buried alive or in any way neglected,
since even overrun and killed and raped
it must return to glory,
bursting like a flower through the asphalt
and forever keep reminding anyone
that there was never any love that did not last forever.

Economy

an effort at common sense

What's the use of expansion?
You can't expand forever anyway.
Who needs more money than he can spend?
Isn't just enough enough trouble already?
People tend to torture themselves by over-feeding,
amassing troubles as much as property
and drown in worries over what they cannot handle,
as they never get enough of anything
but only live to make matters worse
in a kind of lifetime prolonged suicide
of self-suffocation in superfluous surplus;
while the happiest man on earth,
as Leo Tolstoy related in his fable,
a prince searching for him to get into his shirt,
proved to live more easily without a shirt.
The ideal economy is not to earn more than you need,
not to get into debt but rather pay your debts,
and never live above your stable basic income.
You are not a miser or a bore for living sensibly,
but rather to be envied for your balance.

Your Dishonour is My Honour

Your fall is not your fault,
your suffering is your nobility,
and the dishonour is entirely of others.
You will stand when they will fall,
and if you are disposed of, you will still remain,
while they will disappear who brought you down.
You are supreme in sovereignty
as the queen of your creation and accomplishment,
while all fools of destruction and suppression
will be brought by disappearance into nothing.
For all your discretion and your cautious anonymity
you will remain prevailing in your stable character,
while all your fiends and fools of vanity
will drown and smother in their own ignominy.

At a Loss

This crisis is completely out of my experience,
I have no idea of how to handle it,
it's worse than death,
since I don't know if you are still alive,
which though I must presume you are,
since you are haunting me
more steadfastly than ever,
while the worst thing is the terrible uncertainty:
you are lost, and I have lost you,
but you still are somewhere,
but I don't know where.
It's worse than darkness,
and my only hope is that it all will clear,
that I will find you once again
and that you will appear
to make your presence known again.

Falling in Love Again

You have to do it now and then,
it is so beneficial and refreshing,
and it gives you dreams to keep you out of sleeplessness,
and nothing is demanded of you,
it will cost you nothing,
and it's quite enough to keep it virtual.
The main thing is that she exists
and that you are in touch with her
and in your dreams can dwell on her
in only her most favorable aspects,
and that is the main idea:
to maintain love as an ideal
existing in reality and live.
That's all you need for energy to keep you going
and to keep on loving,
living for your love in spite of all.

Roots

You have them from the start,
you were born with them to never lose them,
they stick with you wherever you will travel,
and even if they are bereft of you,
you cannot lose them,
although they are never seen,
protected underground invisible,
but you will always feel them
and the more so the more they are threatened.
Perhaps you even had them before you were born,
like some kind of a spiritual inheritance
to bring along as something of a starting capital
for the venture of life's journey,
which can bring you anywhere
by any weird and wayward odyssey
but which will always bring you home at last
to where you always will belong,
the roots of earth that always are in touch with heaven.

Review

You were never lovelier, my sweet,
as if our love had never changed
since first we met in dreams of beauty
and the preciousness of mutual ideals
to join to never be quite separated
although all the world tried to obstruct us
without any luck at all,
succeeding only in collecting global crises
for itself, as if its state of permanent derailment
wasn't well enough, but it had also to
disturb and harass innocent and faithful lovers
as if sex was an unheard of outrage
if committed only out of love.
Continue as you are, and I will carry on as well
in worship, adoration, faith and piety
to never let our union ever be disturbed
by even any mortal separation.

Ancestors

Let it be a comfort to you
that your dear departed ones
are never really dead
and never really left you
since they never have abandoned you
but always will be there
and more alive than ever
and the more so since you are alone with them
and you will know them best
as only knowing them by feeling them
and therefore being in close contact
with their very souls
which never can be left alone
and never can leave you alone
since you are one of them
and the more so for your contact with them,

which is called the intimacy of eternity.
There are no ghosts, there are no dead ones,
all you knew are still alive
and kicking more than ever for their spirituality
and will remain alive as long as you.

To a Friend

Your presence still is undeniable
although your absence is a solemn fact
but only a material issue
since there's nothing that can come between us
since we are tied up with the eternal love
that only can exist between two souls belonging to each other
coming probably originally from a common source
of only love, creation and good will
determining a permanent irrevocable maintenance.
Thus will we continue being one
although we actually are two
but totally dependent on each other
and inseparable even by such dire circumstances
as the foolishness of man and vain mortality.

The Ultimate Betrayal

Whatever you do, never let down your ideals.
If others fail you or betray you,
just let them go down the drain
as they see fit by choosing for themselves,
but you have nothing to do with their negativism,
and you always have your own way left to go
unhesitatingly, as your ideals is your vocation.

If you let them down you fail yourself
and have forfeited your own worth in life,
its meaning, your integrity, and are a traitor to yourself,
while your ideals will always keep you going
through all martyrdoms and shipwrecks and adversities,
and as you die you still will have them left
to pursue even beyond life into eternity.

Long Time No See

You were lost but never lost.
You were not there but always there.
You died but always managed to survive.
You were forgotten and ignored,
buried alive, suppressed and done for,
but continued to return with constant continuity,
like as if you were some kind of a ghost of flesh and blood,
no vampire or zombie and no morregan or banshee
but more likely just a constant presence of persistence,
but more passionate than any living person.
Once again you prove to me your faithfulness,
as if you never could belong to anyone but me,
and yet you do belong to everyone and all the world.
I can't define you, understand you or get close to you,
but all I can do is to love you.

Stronghold

Your roots are your life's fundament,
your origin, your family and your environment,
you can't grow up, develop and expand without this ground,
which must be safe, reliable and stable
for your opportunity to build your life;
but as you age there must be some decline,
disasters, tragedies and losses cannot be avoided,
and the strain can push you over any limit;
everything is put to trial, and the question rises,
whether still your fundament will hold.
It will depend on what you built it on
and how you anchored it.
If you secured it safely on firm ground,
if you stayed faithful to your friends and to your word
and your relationships in honouring your family,
maintained traditions and didn't waste your life,
then your life's fundament will hold forever.
You will have no fear,
no matter what injustice or disaster may befall you,
or whatever be your losses.
If towards the end of your declining life your conscience has no stain,
then you have triumphed and can safely just go on.

Water Lilies

Unattainable, they float like death traps,
inconceivable in beauty in their irresistibility
as magic elements of calm in the dark water
tempting you to swim and catch them
to be caught yourself in intertwining webs
to drag you down and hold you captive
unto suffocation in dark drowning death;
but there's a fragrance of eternity about them
as they are related to the Lotus and the very origin of flowers
many hundred million years ago and out of timelessness.

That was my first remark on my revisit
at your place for the first time in thirty years,
that there were water lilies in your lake
to greet me and to capture me in beauty
as the dominating element of your whole world.
Let water lilies be the sign of our renewed relationship
of intertwining kindred souls of long endurance
out of many crises, fates, experiences and dire tragedies.

Reclaiming the Mountains

It's a conquest every year
to make the effort of a risky journey
to return to the ideal geography
of mountains the most beautiful on earth
and highest and most unattainable,
but still at least you can approach them
and prove equal to their unattainability
by making just a visit to their presence,
proving that you love their purity
and continue to be faithful to their beauty
by revisiting them every year,
for which you also are rewarded,
as their gift to you is your well-being,
a rebirth, rejuvenation, reinforcement of your energies,
no matter how you strain yourself in arduousness,
the wonder being, that the harder you exert yourself,
the better will be your condition
and the more refined your energies.

The Black Hole of Failure

The hollow abyss of your failures and regrets
are actually a laughing matter after all,
since you are innocent of all that happened without reason,
while what others did to you is only their own problems.
Yes, your losses never can be undone or retrieved,
and still as long as you remain alive you can go on
creating, working, living, laughing and enjoying,
and why not ridiculing all those fools
who thought they could control, defeat and humble you,
while your integrity remains as safe as any duck attacked by water;
and your soul will sail through any storm
with conscience for your rails unbreakable
as long as you are certain you did right.
The abyss will remain there in its dreadful hollowness
of a black hole of infinite despair and sorrow,
but it will only do you good to be aware of it,
to never lose your touch with the necessity
of universal absolute humility.

Love is Never a Parenthesis

The dream I lost was more than just a dream,
it was more real as a reality than actual reality,
since love is always a reality
transcending any mortal or concrete reality,
and this was love and nothing else,
whoever was involved, however tragic it became,
but it was mine, and so was all the loss,
a most unnecessary damage irrepairable;
and still the dream continues to exist,
it cannot be denied, refuted or debunked
but will remain forever, following your course
wherever you will go, to one day maybe
become palpable again,
proving and confirming its reality
like any dream consistent in eternity
more true and real and lasting than reality.

Because I love her

What does it matter if she evades me,
makes herself unreachable
and stays away for months
for enigmatic reasons out of reach;
what does it matter if she gets mixed up
in doubtful company, with other friends,
perhaps with other lovers;
and what does it matter how much of her life
she hides from me, in cultivating secrets,
in a mystery of permanent concealment;
and what does it matter in what weird activities
she gets involved, as long as she remains herself?
For me, she may do anything whatever,
I will not be curious or investigate,
I will not mind whatever she is up to,
I will trust her anyway,
because I love her.

Broken Blossoms

Flowers are for growing free,
for bringing beauty to our fields and gardens
and to bring life and colour to our parks;
but why then has man this obsession
for picking them and killing them?
They will not live for long in vases,
they will wither quickly, like canary birds in cages,
and picked flowers are just like caged animals,
victims of the cruelty and ignorance of man
and doomed to languish in a long protracted death
of famine, lack of freedom and imprisonment.
It may seem funny to consider animals and flowers thus,
like human people, but they are,
and so are trees, which man has an obsession to cut down
and kill, instead of leaving them alone

and granting them the right of life and freedom.
Gardeners are well aware of this
necessity of cultivating life instead of killing it;
but man was born inhuman and the beastliest of animals
with a latent and intentional premeditated cruelty
so infinitely more unnatural than any animal atrocity
resorting to the killing action only to survive.

Last Man Standing

The game starts early.
You get some warning signals
as you lose a school mate by abuse
or ruthlessness by drinking or some accident,
a casualty, but maybe within ten years
you will lose a second one by suicide or cancer,
there is some injustice over it, and you begin to think.
Then gradually they will accelerate,
the deaths and funerals in some alarming frequency,
and they will even soon be getting younger,
and suddenly those younger than yourself will be in some majority.
That's the beginning of the race.
Who will then be the last man standing?
One day you will maybe find yourself the oldest
and see only younger friends go down around you,
but be comforted: your day will come as well,
you'll never be the last one, but on the contrary
you will be lucky not to be the first one.

Dedication

You sneaked into my life
unnoticeably like on a banana peel
but smoothly and invisibly
like some untouchable and alien being
gradually to more and more take over
or at least become a part and almost heart
of some inalienable kind of my whole life,

like a most palpable and present muse
remaining always with me like a shadow
but growing more and more into the better part of me.
You claim that I gave you and taught you everything,
and yes, you learned from me and copied me
and made my way of using verse your own,
but you developed an entirely different style
based on your dark experience transcending all reality
and laying yourself bare to metaphysics
in a way that I could never do.
And thus you turned into my muse
remaining always with me by your presence
complimenting me when words and inspiration fail me.
Thus I owe my life of poetry to you,
wherefore the only proper thing to do
is to bestow on you this dedication.

My Poverty is My Honour

We learn today how all the richest people,
billionaires and multi-millionaires
own more and more than half of all the world,
while the majority must starve without clean water,
while the epidemics, like malaria and tuberculosis,
cholera and other world pandemics of the poor
are steadily increasing to irrevocably unsurmountable proportions.

I was poor in all my life, lived in the slums for 9 years,
have the lowest pension possible of Sweden
and am proud of it, not being part of the abusive rich,
the world possessive billionaires like Trump and Putin,
autocratic China with their puppet rogue dictatorships,
trying to obstruct democracy and freedom
by restricting freedom of expression on the web
and persecuting journalists unto assassination.

What outrageous mob is that suppressive class of 1%
enforcing a brave new world order
that would only kill all freedom first and then the planet!

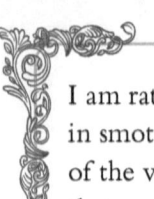

I am rather poor and free than will have any part
in smothering all life and freedom by the force of power
of the vanity of self-destructive economic wealth
that must lead only to abuse, corruption and perdition.

The Reality Escape

What is life's meaning?
You have a right to ask indeed
especially at this time of the year
when it is time to leave a year behind
of disappointments, failures and adversities
that only emanated in a kind of hollow meaninglessness
of an empty melancholy of no end and without bottom.

Solomon proclaimed the only valid meaning of life being
to have fun, enjoy, make parties and forget all problems,
and he was the wisest man in all the world.
Is the reality escape life's meaning then,
the culmination of which would be death
as something of the ultimate reality escape?
It's not all wrong, since nothing is more beneficial
than imagination, which is just man's creativity.

So please regard all those poor escapists from hard reality
by alcohol and drugs, by book worming and art obsession,
partying zest and cineast enthusiasm
with other penchants for all kinds of self-indulgence
to just get away from humdrum boring every day economy and realism
with some benevolence and tolerance,
since all they want, these refugees from hard reality
is just to innocently please themselves by living.

Unhappy Love

Who has not been through it?
Who has not been subject to betrayal and abandonment?
Who has not lost the one that least of all could be dispensed with?
Who has not had yet another fall and love crush
after only having been let down, betrayed and ditched?
Who has not given up to only start again from the beginning,
staking all on only insecure and unknown cards?
Who has not blindly hit the wall,
ignoring all unfavourable warnings and reports?
Who has not been crushed and shattered,
promising to never try again, to only fall again
immediately, to consciously delude oneself again?
That is – alas! – the way of love.
It is born blind and never learns to see itself or waken up.
It is the self-destructive flame of moths
which it must constantly consume itself by
and preferably to make it hurt as much as possible.
The pain will make you feel alive,
and that, I gather, is life's actual meaning,
just to make you feel alive.

Awakening From Death

We never met until it was too late.
You had already passed away
beyond the portals of outrageous death
and against your will survived mortality
when you walked in to settle in my heart
in infinite unfathomable desperately tragic sorrow;
and it took some days before it dawned upon me
that I could but join you in your sorrow, but with love.
It was a death of love we had experienced
as a ruthless horrible and unjust shock,
but it was like a lightning joining us together
in a kind of new transcended love

beyond mortality and opening infinity;
but it is far too soon to know or even guess
where this might lead us, as we stand
in the beginning of an undiscovered new infinity.

Empty Bottles

A vice, weakness, laughable folly or illness?

It might seem pathetic
to collect old empty bottles
for the happy moments they conserve
instead of what they once contained,
and once you start on that kind of collection,
you will soon have empty bottles
all around that you just cannot throw away
for sentimental reasons,
as a kind of cultivation of sentimentality,
which tends to overgrow you like an illness,
just like any other sort of sickly mania
for collecting anything, like stamps, old papers,
technical mecanical contraptions or like any junk;
but there is really nothing wrong about sentimentality.
It's not a virtue, certainly no rational acquirement,
no useful business, but more like a softness of the heart,
a tendency to gloat on what is sweet and lovely,
underscoring, stressing and endorsing human factors;
and a human weakness of that kind of mild and gentle touch
is more to be respected than despized,
and more to be appreciated than made fun of;
although there is always something of a smile
about a sympathetic sentimental fool.

Memories

How could I forget you
as I gave my love to you once and forever
never to ignore it or forget it,
never to disclaim, regret, neglect it or suppress it?
Love once given is a pledge and a responsibility forever,
and you can never disregard it
as it always will remain a presence in your memories
that you can never disregard, deny or do without
as it will constantly remind you of your only immortality,
that of love once given.
So be not afraid of wallowing in memories of love,
of that sentimentality that made you weak and humble,
which in fact is your most potent strength and power
as the core of your humanity.

Cultivating Addictions

It is what everyone is doing, more or less,
in one way or another,
and it is not only about drugs and drinks.
The workaholic who just keeps on struggling
for the sake of having nothing else to do,
or the addicted pianist, who keeps on playing
seven hours every day or more
just for the physical exertion of his fingers,
or the mobile addict keeping on his messaging
wherever he may be in any company,
or the computer nird who knows of nothing else
than digital technique of ones and 0s.
The question is how wholesome this addiction is,
which actually is almost universal,
while we do not mind how we in the same time
let the environment and nature of the planet go to waste
and die for human carelessness and irresponsibility.
Perhaps we all need some kind of a rehabilitation
monitored by nature both for her own and our restoration?

The Cathedral

You can work on it forever.
Actually, the main idea is to keep working,
never bringing it to definite completion,
working out the details one by one,
like the cathedral of Milano,
worked on with a thousand sculptures
for a number of some centuries,
like also that of Barcelona by Gaudí,
the weird cathedral of the sacred family,
and that's the joy of it:
to have something to work on
with your love and arduous interest
of creativeness that never tires,
even if it is in only your world of your own,
like Milarepa filing on his hundred thousand songs
alone and isolated as a hermit in a cave;
but the result is there forever:
your love's work as heavenly as a cathedral
worked on with your love throughout your life
and showing universally like some kind of a demonstration
that your love was worth your sacrifice
for something greater than what all the world could offer.

The Wages of Ordeals

It's like a law of nature: tragedy and comedy are always intertwined.

The more extreme your trials,
the deeper into trouble you will get,
the harder sorrows you must live through,
and the worse your losses are,
it always can be turned around
into the very contrary of the injustice
by experience and by learning from it,
the most dreadful tribulation and adversity

can be adversed to victory and glory.
There are always two sides of all destiny,
one side trying, educating, bringing on ordeals,
the other bringing you rewards of spiritual growth.
You only have to wait for it with patience:
there is no hell without a heaven getting through to it,
no stormy weather without beneficial rains and sunshine afterwards
and no adversity and hard catastrophe
without a different chapter afterwards
of a new world of opportunity and new beginnings.

Ghosts

When they crowd upon you,
don't reject them,
welcome them instead, accept them
as a part of you, since they invested in your life
by being part of it and sharing you
and leaving you with memories as part of them.
Be not afraid of their imposing overwhelmingness,
acknowledge them instead and love them,
for that's all they are: if they continue after death,
it is because their love survived them
to continue flowing and expanding infinitely.
The most foolish thing you can do
is to turn them down, suppress them and deny them.
Open up to all your ghosts and demons and whatever,
and you will be richer spiritually than any billionaire
of that which doesn't fade and pass
but only will continue growing and expanding
as the only fundamental force of life forever.

Marriage or Not

You see too many marriages
go foundering in conflicts, strife and quarrels,
as if love established only could turn into hate,
and many claim to be more happily divorced than married.
On the other hand, there are true lovers
sticking to each other in consistent faithfulness
without deception in pure friendship without sex.
And thus the proverb has arisen,
that the perfect sexual relationship and marriage
is between philosophers with some detachment and experience, – but
philosophers do never marry.
Is then sex the cause and factor of disruption?
There are after all still marriages that carry on
with children and grandchildren in a happy family
unto both gold and diamond weddings,
but you never know what's going on under the surface.
You can love and infinitely and forever even more
regardless of the social status or judicial condition,

and the main thing is to stick to that.
Thus even an anonymous and virtual relationship
can prove more constant and enduring
than a legal and material union under strain
of mundane complications and the weakness of mortality.

Awesomeness

The mystery of our love is unsettling,
to say the least, as if we didn't dare
to understand it, even less to grasp it
as perhaps a miracle too good to be true
or the most mortal danger we encountered.
I will not risk anything, however,
but patiently wait for destiny to interfere
and take no more than one day at a time for granted,
expecting every day to bring another thriller.
I have loved you, that is certain, now for many days
and no day less than any previous one
but rather like a calm and easy flowing river
of stability and peace and bringing only beauty.
It is true, there is an abyss to pay heed to,
wounds must heal, and there are ruins to restore,
but it feels as if there is no end of time for us,
but that there could be an eternity ahead of us.

No Illusions

I am not idealizing you.
How could I, when I do not even know you?
All I do know is that I sincerely feel you
warmly as much more than just a friend,
not just a colleague but a spiritual associate
that has survived her own annihilation and herself
as I myself have risen from the gutter.
Let's have no illusions and no expectations
taking nothing and no possibility for granted,
while we always can have dreams in common.

Let us dwell together in a dream then
and idealize and embellish it with all our power
hoping never to wake up from it,
and living for the dream of turning it into reality.

The Stakes Cannot Be Too High

My eyes are on you day and night
although I cannot see you.
Still I must suspect
that I can see you better with my feelings
than with any senses of my body.
Is it a sixth sense, clairvoyance or prophetic insight?
It does not matter.
The important thing is only that I feel you
and feel part of you, which is why I hope
that you would also somehow feel like me.
It is a venture, where you have the upper hand
with all the trump cards, while my hand is different
with completely different cards
completely without values
but the more of deeper spiritual values
which can not be wasted
for their permanence of faith and continuity.

The Language of Silence

It is more expressive than words,
communicating thoughts that cannot be expressed,
transcending any digital communication,
since the essence of creative thought is honesty.
It cannot be concealed, denied or faked or masked,
and thought is always the more true
the more it is concealed and silent.
Love in silence can be more sincere
and true than any sexual act,
and the deepest love is the most difficult to express.
So listen carefully to languages of silence,

to the voices that are never heard but only felt
and to the feelings that are kept under the ice
awaiting their momentum when it's time for them to burst;
for no cement or asphalt or suppressing ice age
can at length keep down the truth of honesty.

Trying the Bearings

When I dream of you in the night
the stars are not so bright
as you seem in the light
of my longing for your sight
which in our love's constant twilight
always glows more bright.

Are we getting closer for our longing
or just getting alienated in removing
from reality by improving
nothing but our dreams in moving
only further back in our retreating
into love's undying yearning?

The question is unanswerable
as our love remains unfathomable.

Losses

They never can be remedied.
They never can be compensated,
and you simply must accept it.
Griefs can be disastrous,
one can die of sorrow,
and inevitably there must be not only scars
but wounds that never can be healed.
It helps to cry, but only momentarily,
to cry your heart out is important though,
as wounds must bleed to cleanse themselves.
At best, you can survive the scars

and bear them with their pain,
but you can never count on
getting rid of them, expecting them to disappear,
for wounds of losses irrepairable
will hurt as marks of destiny forever,
as you have been branded by injustice.

Silly Sentimentality

In the perfect modern society
tenderness was treated with contempt
as a stupid weakness and debility,
and the worst weakness was sentimentality.
However, there is nothing wrong about it,
it is better to give vent to feelings
than to keep them under cover and shut down,
and softness has an endurance
while hardness always breaks.
Of course, it might seem silly
crying over a good sentimental book or film,
but I assure you there is nothing more invaluable
and precious in the human nature
than the naturalness and sincerity of human feelings,
which must always be let out in freedom,
one way or another,
since there's nothing that can stop them.

Inexpressibility

Relationships can sometimes go so deep
that words are not enough
and can't be used but for abuse
while silence is the only possible expression
for a love that only can be felt
and never properly communicated,
since there are expressions and vibrations
on a universal scale
that not even the universe is able to express

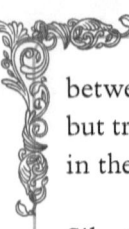

between two beings,
but transcend the universal frame
in their belonging to each other.

Silent thoughts in darkness
can be more expressive and more powerful
than eruptions of volcanoes and reverberations
of apocalyptic earthquakes,
if the quiet thought is tempered and originated
by the true sincerity and honesty of love.

A Dirge

Man has always been like that,
destroying everything and leaving only ruins,
as all history is but a devastation in his trail,
like all the broken pillars around the Mediterranean
bearing witness of his progress as immortal testimonies
of the human berserk meaningless mentality
in hopelessly shortsighted egoism
and superficial ignorance and blindness,
thinking only of the killing of the moment
as a pastime in hysterically chasing vanity and death.
Those who refused to share this madness, seeing through
the cruel animality of man possessed by carnal lust
and therefore chose detachment from that lemming fever
in refusal to have anything to do with human folly,
were despised and chased and persecuted,
hounded often unto loneliness in exile if not death
as outsiders, free-thinkers and heretics,
forced to constant struggle of resistance to survive,
like Dante in his nineteen years of exile
and the Shakespeare poet forced to lifelong anonymity,
as even wise old Plato in his high philosophy
denounced and sentenced poets such as Homer
as not tolerable in society,
thus signing the death sentence of his own civilization,
since the Homer poems had created it;

but all these scrapped rejected prophets
that so often were mishandled and buried alive
were witnesses that never could be silenced
not even by death, as they were always right,
while history was always wrong,
as constantly the ruins of politics proved,
which is what history is all about.

Humanity

When your tears of blood coagulate
and your wounds heal into scars
of lasting and perpetual ugliness
to mark you as a branded exile
from humanity and normality forever,
still your heart will go on bleeding
never to be stilled or comforted
in permanent invisibility of pain.

The cruelty of others never will be felt by them
but only by the victims,
and all they can do
is to testify and go on testifying
never to let all those words and voices die
that are the true life witnesses
of the sincerity and everlasting truth
of what humanity is really all about.

The Golden Moment

The slightest fleeting moment can be an eternity.
It is the genuineness, the sincerity and honesty that counts.
If it is concentrated in a work of art,
like some performance, some improvisation
like a chamber concert or a poem
or a moment's beauty in a ballet on the stage,
it is a golden lasting moment of eternity,
no matter how despicable the circumstances

or the foibles and mistakes and maybe failures,
regardless of how small the audience or how few the witnesses,
stlll the truth and beauty of the moment of creation
is the only thing that counts and that will last
as a materialization of your soul's eternity
into a work of art or precious truth in a poetic moment.

No Time Without Shortage

Usually you have no time for anything,
since there's no time without its running out,
and so you have no time that is not running out,
but when you do have time it always is too short,
so there are constant problems about time.
Why bother? Time is only an illusion,
a self-torture just to stress yourself with,
a chimaera and imagined threat,
a fixed idea, distraction and disorder of your mind,
which all the world is suffering from,
a way to block you and control you,
squeeze you in into a cubicle society.
Forget about the time and how it's always running out.
The only truth of time is timelessness and the eternity,
which always is at hand, and if you are aware of it,
you'll know that you will always have all time in the world.

Restored Passion

In troubled times you search for a relief,
and sometimes there is nothing there but hopelessness,
but suddenly there is a cloudburst,
and a ray of light breaks up the desperation,
as you find an old love there again all of a sudden
and a hope at least for a return of passion
and a necessary rehabilitation of your losses.

You were always there to stand me by
and never to desert me as a guardian angel,

although you have been much more at risk
and faced unutterable dire straits
in order only to survive,
while I was always relatively lucky.

Still I need you more perhaps than I would need myself,
since I am fraught with the obsession of my worries,
risking to get drowned in them,
while there is only you for my relief.

It's getting harder and more difficult
with the advancing years of constantly increasing turmoil,
but as long as you are there and waiting for me
I will always have at least someone to love
with something of a hope in spite of all for my redemption.

The Hubris of Despair

When you are tried beyond endurance,
pressed beyond the boundaries of pain
and stressed beyond all reasonable tolerance,
you have to set a higher gear in order to survive,
and this may find some furious expression.
In art it often happens that poor artists
driven to despair by suffering or poverty
grow frantic and extremely personal
in their creativeness and over-self-indulgence,
like van Gogh and Rembrandt, Beethoven and Schubert,
spiting feasibility in hubris of despair;
but it is never hubris, only moving into higher gear,
replacing handicaps and limitations
by the force of will and spiritual power,
and there is no higher power than that combination.

Pathetique

Note: The "Italian smiling diplomat in China" was Daniele Varè, 1880-1956, who wrote novels from China as well as the autobiography "Laughing Diplomat", published 1938.

When my father gradually was getting old
his highest wish and main desire was to sleep,
to thus escape his nightmares
of reality that ever was unfair to him.

After my pension, also my desires have got lost,
while longing for to sleep and to sleep well
has come as dominating wishful thinking,
which did never quite show up successfully,
not only interrupted by the constant urge
uncompromisingly of nature to throw water,
but for worries, sorrows and regrets
that never ceased in constancy,
but rather, on the contrary, grew worse.

Let's not enter into woeful details.
Today's news brought the notification of a double loss
of two friends simultaneously since many years
with the announcement of two quiet funerals
in silence without celebrations;
and the tendency is the multiplication of such losses,
a poor comfort being that they will ebb out with time;
and constantly more funerals will just pass by,
impossible to memorize, attend or cry your heart out for,
since too much crying will run out of water.

Let's return to my old man, who although struck by difficult disasters
never did complain but always kept his sense of humour,
his most dominating and long lasting personal characteristic,
which he learned from an Italian smiling diplomat in China,
who came through the storms and traumas of the 30s with a smile.
He knew in good time when his time was coming,

he had warnings in advance and was more than well prepared,
so when the hour struck, he just could find his peace in sleep;
but I am certain that not even the eternal final sleep,
no matter how irrevocable, definite and peaceful,
would provide him with naught else
than just a fresh awakening to new activity
with new disasters, sufferings and trials without end
to start all over with from the beginning
with the same kind of a stoic diplomatic smile.

Wild Geese

An autumn reflection concerning the wild geese migrating south: an old story.

He was completely lost,
but then he found a flock
that seemed familiar, like his kin,
so he set out to follow them,
wherever they would bring him.
As they landed by a lake
on their long journey to the south
escaping from the winter cold and hardship,
his new fellows did not seem to care for him
but treated him like nothing, as not one of them,

but like an alien and a stranger,
which he almost found humiliating,
but he had no choice but to endure it.
"Where are you from?" a flying colleague wondered,
but he could not answer, as he did not know his origin.
"But you definitely are not one of us,"
the other said, and he agreed,
accepting that he was an alien;
and as he at least was not thrown out and ostracized,
he stuck to them, continuing to follow them,
as he had nowhere else to fly.
But life with them was difficult;
as he was different, he was treated differently,
often shunned and condescendingly neglected,
could not eat with them but had to find his own
means of support all by himself apart from them,
and it grew worse, as more and more they showed
he was an undesirable, an awkward and unpleasant outsider,
and he blamed his white feathers for the inconvenience,
as all the other geese were grey; and there was nothing
he could do about his natural involuntary costume.
Finally they told him straight: "You are not wanted here,
you are too different, too superior, too handsome
and too good for us." Another put it more politely:
"We are sorry, but you are too much of an outsider,
too idiosyncratic and too much your own,
and we don't understand you nor why you persist
in sticking to us, although anyone can see
you are not one of us." So he had nothing else to do
than to depart and go entirely on his own.

He found a lake to rest by, and as he went down to land
he noticed a small group of other birds
with long necks swimming in the search for food
but in the same white shrouds as he.
He ventured to approach them, asking them politely,
"I lost my flock. May I join yours?"
They answered him at once: "But, brother,

you are one of us. Where have you been?"
"I have been lost, deserted and thrown out by the wild geese."
"But you are not a goose. Have you not seen yourself,
have you not in the mirror of the water found yourself?"
For the first time he ventured to out of the water take a look
and found that he was just like those white gentlemen around him,
"And what do you call, then, such a hopeless alien as me?"
"You are one of the noblest of all birds,
the most accomplished in your purity and whiteness,
and if you were left alone, abandoned and rejected,
that enobled you the more and made you worthy of our company
in natural and splendid pride to shine forever
more idealized and sung and dreamed about
than any other bird by poets."

Time Perspective

When my love was ripe,
you were the most beautiful of all,
a queen of charm and grace and beauty,
quite superior in your accomplishments,
a marvel of a sparkling jewel of perfection in your style,
and how you more than well lived up to it,
in brilliant clothes of some extraordinary fashion,
part in hippy style and part in celtic flower power,
always gorgeous and admirable in fantasy
with your long rich enchanting hair to crown it all
in something of a masterpiece of an ideal woman.
And how is it now, so many years long after?
Actually and in reality, there's nothing that has changed,
you have not aged, and I have not grown older
in our spiritual idealism and creative basis,
while the circumstances, although drastically turbulent
and changed by far beyond all recognition,
like a wonder prove the fact of our enduring love,
that we are still the same, your beauty is still there,
I never lost it, and you are the same
although in different circumstances,

and our love just keeps on going on
as if the world, the circumstantial changes
and all mundane trivialities and troubles,
alterations, shifts and trials
were but an accentuation of our love,
and how like all the lights of stars throughout the universe
it simply cannot be put down and fade.

The Failure of Angels

The abuse of the planet by mankind
cost God much concern and atrocious headaches,
so he actually thought of resigning
and leaving it all over to Satan,
who was keen to take over.
Some angels decided to act against this
and went up to the sorely depressed God Almighty,
suggesting that they should cheer up all humanity
by finding out and promoting good qualities.
"If you find any good qualities at all, you are better than I,
and I wish you good luck, hoping for your success after all."

First went the good angel of mercy,
trying to find some compassion and good will
still working somewhat among mankind,
but she found only cruelty, egoism and ruthlessness
drowning all possible mercy and good will,
so she returned quite disheartened.

Next went the angel of good cheer and humour,
hoping to find still some happiness in mortal beings,
but she found but suicides, depression and criminality,
all parties derailing to abuse and debauchery
and ending up in addiction,
so she also had to resign with her mission failed.

Then went the angel of health and good fortune,
hoping to find some progress in welfare states at least,

but she found only welfare illnesses like cancer,
diabetes, fatness and degeneration
and on the other hand starvation, capitalistic abuse,
extortion and greed and overwhelming poverty.
"It's worse than I thought could be possible," was the conclusion.

Next went the angel of spirituality, hoping to find some enlightenment,
but all she found was religious abuse, pedophilia,
religion turned into business and fanaticism,
certain religions still killing for intolerance.

Only one angel remained who was still willing to try.
"Well, go in your naïve illusions, then,
but don't hope to find anything," God dejectedly said.
She went, but she found what she searched for almost everywhere.
She was the angel of music, and wherever she went there
was some kind of music.
Returning to God, she said: "People are still actually singing."
God turning to Satan said: "Sorry, old friend, but you are out of business.
Our last angel actually found something good in mankind,
and that one thing will save all humanity."
Satan had already anticipated his ultimate victory
and wondered bewildered: "Whatever could that thing have been?"
God answered: "Already Orpheus knew, that not even the dead
could resist being s and awakened by music."

Shadows

We are but fleeting shadows
as we pass
like dreams that never can be caught
but only dreamt of,
too beautiful to be imaginable
and yet truer than reality,
as our reality never lasts
while love is always there
returning when it's lost
and ever growing

like a dream that never will come true,
but just for being unattainable
is the more true for its existence
as the absolute ideal
that never can be brushed aside
but will survive
even the most fatal tragedy,
to prove that only the most undemonstrable
and undeniable impossibility of love
is true enough to outlast all eternity.

His reference is to Sweden, especially in 1968.
"A dog obeyed in office" is from King Lear.

The Old Actor

Call me a pathetic old fool of nostalgia,
but I find some honour in my memories.
When I was young the actor's part was most respectable,
a profession held in high esteem, as its demands were high
of diction above all and clarity, which was needed in the classics
of the ageless kind, with Shakespeare every year
and also Greek tragedians, and the ensemble acting
was accomplished in a consummation of qualification
as a team work, everybody being vitally important.
Then we were invaded by political demands,
with socialism on the agenda,
as the Chinese cultural revolution was followed
with its obligatory destructon of all ancient values,
driving over cultural traditions,
making actors of the old school worthless over night,
brushed down into the ditch as outdated and dusty
with their knowledge and accomplished art
all of a sudden undesirable, as only revolutionary
propaganda plays as missions of radicalism
were modernly accepted, and old actors had to leave
discarded with direction to the bottle.

What was wrong then with real theatre,
Euripides and Shakespeare, diction that was understood,
dramatic realism with man as individual at the centre,
actors like Laurence Olivier and Leslie Howard?
What was wrong with old films, that today still are worth watching,
where every word is understandable, a distinct story line and plot
with careful dramaturgy offering an interesting experience
worth remembering as thought-provoking food for meditation?

What's wrong with traditions, roots in old acquired crafts,
maintenance of old knowledge, keeping memories alive,
and cultivating quality and skill of art and craft
in striving to some timelessness in serving poetry as creativity
in moulding an improvement of reality in ideal sincerity?
What is revolutionary radicalism and political enforcement
to the idealistic quest for ageless and eternal continuity?
I am just an old actor, forced to step aside in resignation
facing the sad phase of aging, but I rather see and read
old plays as they were written, than as they now are performed
in modern and absurd unnatural unrealistic stagings
where you cannot hear or understand a word
for only mumbling, stuttering and slurring nonsense
lacking all articulation, as the modern dog obeyed in office
of the revolutionary radical politic theatre of modernism.

Soap Bubbles

Walter Scott wrote many novels,
often rather long and tedious,
and he kept on writing them
beyond his bankruptcy,
despite the fact that they grew constantly more boring.
It was said of him that all his dedication
was to blowing up soap bubbles
for his own interest only,
in a narcissistic bluff of great dimensions,
but there is a major difference.
Soap bubbles will burst and come to nothing,
while, as already the Romans put it,
"Verba volant, verba scripta manent,"
what is written will endure;
and many of his novels will remain
as marvels of invention, second only to the Shakespeare poet.
Never mind the audiences of ignorant indifferent readers,
who will never read a book through,
and are bored by merely the sight of letters,
as most people are illiterate intellectually,

as hopeless cases to be pitied for their limitation.
That which matters is what you pen down with honesty
and know sincerely for sure that it was worth the trouble
of preserving as experiences and thoughts and insights;
and if there will be no other readers of your texts at all,
you can be sure that God himself will read them the more carefully.

The Prime Minister

How awkward!
After his triumphant last elections,
he was found deteriorating physically,
and his closest friends and kin were worried,
asking him to be examined,
but the doctors could not find the fault,
but finally an expert in South Africa
resolved the mystery and diagnosed him
with a new disease that was incurable
of an immunity disorder syndrome.
Yes, he had been rather active sexually,
his wife had twice tried to divorce him,
but the situation now was critical
for a prime minister and head of his own party
that had been in power for most of the century
in a firm establishment that could not tolerate a scandal
that would ruin both the party and establishment.
So something had to be arranged.
What did they do?
They had to their disposal all the national resources,
the police force, the security and money to pay any silence,
so they made of him a martyr for the party,
faking an assassination in the middle of the city
when he and his wife went home after a cinema.
And all the king's men kept their silence
for the sake of the establishment,
the leading officer of the investigation
was himself a homosexual,
leading the tremendous bluff,

deceiving all the country,
that was shocked at the atrocious death
of such a perfect and ideal prime minister,
who only had been whisked away
to spend his long pathetic awkward death
in splendid and protected isolation
comfortably in one of the fourteen castles
of the Rothschilds far away in France.

Transcending Time Dimensions

There is no time,
and I am out of time,
but there's no bother –
I don't mind,
since I am out of time
and do not care about the right time,
since the limitation of the stress of time
is to be ignored as just a nuisance;
while the time dimension
is most relative, if anything;
and I prefer the presence of all time dimensions
to the limitation of the present time.
All history is still alive, no matter how antique,
it's always present now affecting all the present,
as the present is but a result of it;
and the better we are masters of the past,
caretaking of its knowledge and traditions,
the more capable and fit we are
creating, making something of the future.

The Poet
by Kahlil Gibran

This is one of my favourite poems of Kahlil Gibran's, and I think it should have a place here.

He is a link between this and the coming world.
He is
A pure spring from which all thirsty souls may drink.
He is a tree watered by the River of Beauty, bearing
Fruit which the hungry heart craves;
He is a nightingale, soothing the depressed
Spirit with his beautiful melodies;
He is a white cloud appearing over the horizon,
Ascending and growing until it fills the face of the sky.
Then it falls on the flows in the field of Life,
Opening their petals to admit the light.
He is an angel, send by the goddess to
Preach the Deity's gospel;
He is a brilliant lamp, unconquered by darkness
And inextinguishable by the wind. It is filled with
Oil by Istar of Love, and lighted by Apollon of Music.

He is a solitary figure, robed in simplicity and
Kindness; He sits upon the lap of Nature to draw his
Inspiration, and stays up in the silence of the night,
Awaiting the descending of the spirit.

He is a sower who sows the seeds of his heart in the
Prairies of affection, and humanity reaps the
Harvest for her nourishment.

This is the poet -- whom the people ignore in this life,
And who is recognized only when he bids the earthly
World farewell and returns to his arbor in heaven.

This is the poet -- who asks naught of
Humanity but a smile.
This is the poet -- whose spirit ascends and
Fills the firmament with beautiful sayings;
Yet the people deny themselves his radiance.

Until when shall the people remain asleep?
Until when shall they continue to glorify those
Who attain greatness by moments of advantage?
How long shall they ignore those who enable
Them to see the beauty of their spirit,
Symbol of peace and love?
Until when shall human beings honor the dead
And forget the living, who spend their lives
Encircled in misery, and who consume themselves
Like burning candles to illuminate the way
For the ignorant and lead them into the path of light?

Poet, you are the life of this life, and you have
Triumphed over the ages of despite their severity.

Poet, you will one day rule the hearts, and
Therefore, your kingdom has no ending.

Poet, examine your crown of thorns; you will
Find concealed in it a budding wreath of laurel.

Problems of Unbearable Melancholy

They are always there,
the remnants of the past,
the ruins, the defeats and failures,
ghosts and phantoms of all those you lost,
old classmates who went under in alcoholism
or died in cancer or in traffic accidents,
leaving behind a hangover of eternal pain,
and worst of all: betrayals, shortcomings
and the irreparable loss, destruction, and affliction
in the bleeding heart wounds of injustice.

Is all that you can do then just to weep over the ruins
like a Jeremiah and complaining to eternity
of all that happened that went hopelessly and cruelly wrong?
No, if there is no other comfort in your old age
you can always keep on working till your death
and just keep carrying on until you die
and then at least have done your best until the end.

But there is something else as well.
Your memories keep burdening and crowding down on you
the more the older you survive in spite of all,
and all those memories are not all bad and bitter.
The best memories survive the best,
and here's the cue: you can go on collecting new ones,
there are no restrictions and should be no end to them,
and that should be enough for you to keep on struggling on.

Fondling Memories

What are they for,
all those sweet memories of yore,
that always keep pursuing you
and never leave you quite alone,
the perfumes of forgotten pleasures,

silenced voices that you keep on hearing,
dreams of beauty and intimacy
that never quite materialized,
the songs that never could be silenced,
and the deaths that never were convincing;
all the laughs that sparkled for eternity,
the warmth of tenderness and feelings of eternal love,
what are they for, if not to be maintained and cherished,
cultivated and enriched to never cease in glowing splendour;
to be proven, like ourselves, immortal
in the truth of their sincerity and genuineness.

Nobility

There is no such thing as noble blood,
no honourable ancestry,
no great enobling ancient traditions,
stories of great quests and glories of the past
that in any way would leave a lasting mark
of individual and personal nobility,
which only can be spiritual:
if you are noble, you are born spiritually with it,
that stamp is of eternity, it is a stain you can't wash off
but are obliged to carry on and cultivate and carry further.
Spirituality of course is most arguable and controversial,
many see it as a hubris, arrogance, presumption
and a most impractical irrationality,
but if it's in your spirit there is nothing you can do
to help it, except being true to that nobility of soul,
a legacy received and carried out
as something of a heritage out of eternity,
and usually it is combined with some advanced philosophy.
Philosophers were usually regarded with suspicion,
disbelief, disdain and more or less discriminated
as outsiders, pariahs, outlaws and abnormal aliens,
but philosophy is nothing but the love and adherence to wisdom;
and if there is anything this monstrous and derailed humanity
stands in urgent need of, it is the philosophy

of a detachment from the aberrations of the human mainstream
of irrationality; and only the nobility of alien philosophy
can differ properly between eternal values and all mortal vanity.

The Rule of Tragedy

It's a universal law of life,
that everything alive is ruled by tragedy,
by suffering – all life is tragic,
and this fact is best observed
by everything that's going on in nature:
man cannot escape it, he is not exempt,
his penchant for illusions and delusions
cannot help him: in the end, he must accept the fact
that everything is but a tragedy,
and his only cure and remedy for this
is to accept it, face the facts and stare reality
in death's own grinning face, embrace it
and submit to the ordeal of having to subordinate
to the oblique reality of tragedy
as the irrevocable frame and limitation
to his life, his personality and all existence.

Integrity

Don't let yourself be bothered
and struck down in worries and depression
by the fallacies of others and their weakness,
don't look back on shipwrecks and defeats,
but go on marching forward, following your path
and conscience in all weathers and whatever happens.
Your life is your own initiative,
that is your strength and leadership,
and no one else has any right to interfere with it
or block it, that is your divinity and sparkle,
which it is your greatest duty to maintain and carry forward
and as far as possible as your most sacred right of inviolability.

Passing Shadows

From this world and into another
goes this guesswork of a lifetime
passing all kinds of mysterious shadows
like a fickle shadow of a mystery itself
of no great consequence, only for a treat
to dwindle slowly into nothingness
as its true basic element.
It is just something to endure,
and when it's over you are free
to start again from the beginning
as a fresh start as but yet another passing shadow.

The Bachelor

There was nothing wrong with him,
he had good looks and no diseases,
no impediment to his abilities;
but he was never any womanizer
and had no luck with women,
as they always turned him down.
He made proposals that were constantly refused,
if he had a girlfriend she requested him for money,
and if he was in love and faithful as a lover,
she betrayed him and went lying with another.
He finally drew the conclusion
that the only good girls he had ever known
were those who never had asked him for money,
and they were invariably older than himself.
So he became established as a bachelor,
but there was never something lacking in his love,
but on the contrary: the more he was refused,
turned down, betrayed and disillusioned about women,
the more constantly and earnestly he loved.

Your Best Friend

Who is your best friend?
He is always there waiting for you.
He will never leave you
for as long as you will stay alive,
since he will always need you,
being constantly dependent on you.
When you are deserted by your other friends,
when life will only thwart and bring you bad luck,
when personal disasters and catastrophes
will overwhelm you by their towering adversity
and make an outrage of your life,
with even love deserting you by treason,
leaving you betrayed and bankrupt,
robbed and devastated and reduced to nothing,
you will still have one friend left
who constantly will wait for you to take him on again,
resuming and renewing your most favoured project,
which is simply your own work
and all that major part of it that only you did master.

Shyness

I always shied from people
out of over-sensitivity and fear,
since I from the beginning learned the hard way
that I never could trust anyone,
which was the worst disappointment of my life
which separated me from ordinary human life
quite early, making me from the beginning a recluse and outsider
who had to manage on his own in independence
as the only way to save my possibility to work
with what I was most qualified to do
in undisturbed and isolated loneliness,
which thus became my main life's element.
As such I also learned the benefits of absolute humility

and to in sound and philosophical detachment
regard reality with deeper love and more profound responsibility
in deepened empathy with all things living
in the cultivation of the universalism of sincerest sensitivity.
That's how my work became my life's predominant resource
as my security and creativity, my joy and my life 's meaning.
I intend no boast, but wish to humbly only state the facts
as something of an excuse and apology for my consistent resignation
from all matters of contention among ordinary people
of concerns with mundane vain and mortal interests,
since there's nothing that can be more beneficial
and rewarding than just basic private meditation.

Post-traumatic Stress Syndrome

What can you do when everything is ruined,
when your life is devastated,
as you find yourself let down by everybody
and there's nothing left but tears and misery and poverty,
as bankruptcy is a reality and there is no way out?
The post-traumatic stress syndrome, once it is there
will never leave you any more in peace
but will be permanent as something of a hangover
that you will never quite be rid of,
like a phantom as the old man of the sea
that Sindbad never quite could shake off from his shoulders,
as a nightmare without end and monster of outrageous cruelty
to never offer any remedy except the cowardly escape of suicide,
which is the worst, most desperate and unacceptable solution.
You must live with it, there is no other way,
and if you cannot battle it and deal with it in any other way,
then there is still the option to give in and wallow in its constant torture.

The Abyss

When everything is lost
you will resort to anything
and even to acknowledging your ultimate defeat

as a justification for your throwing in the towel
to the deadliest of mortal sins of giving up.
But what else can you do?
When your beloved has proved only your destruction
in the abyss of a permanent betrayal
horribly consistent in its meanness of outrageous viciousness
and leaving you with nothing left
but staring into the black hole of your despair
in utter hollowness of your existence
as the most pathetic of all fools
deceived by most of all yourself.
You cannot even cry, because your tears are dry,
while the worst of all is how you are condemned
to stay on and go on in spite of all
surviving your destruction and annihilation
in a sentence worse than death,
to be condemned to stay alive.

Transcendence

When everything's gone wrong
and you are ruined, outcast, floored,
reduced to nothing by authorities and greed
and made a victim by official "justice"
leaving you no choice but suicide
just to end the terror, harassment and victimization
at least in the refuge of meditation,
and you find yourself alive in spite of all
and simply have to make the best of it
in carrying on, enduring and continuing forward,
you will find life rather comfortless,
and searching in it for a break or meaning
you are more dead than alive and more a suicide
than if actually you did commit it.
There is the advantage, the awareness of that you are not,
of your own total definite defeat,
that you are not the total loss, destruction and adversity
but untouched by that as something else and something better,

like a Phoenix rising from the fire of destruction
on another pair of wings than the consumed ones
flying higher and with better strength to greater light.
You are not all that which is lost, defeated and annihilated
but a higher entity of a supremer kind
than any mortal bog of vanities and worries.

Love Compulsory by Destiny

I never tire of your beauty
nor of the exquisite richness of your hair,
the very element of affluent beauty,
always growing, never growing old,
like some established permanence
of the very basic essence of life's worth,
as the most stable and reliable escape resort
when you are failed by everything in the material world
and most of all by those who should have been supporting
but who could do nothing else than let you down.
But you are there, in contrast to a world of treason,
that brings only torture, bitterness and disappointment,
while you are the opposite in some miraculous turned wonder,
contrary to all things mortal, neutralizing all indecencies
in being only beauty, both in spirit and in physical appearance,
like a miracle confounding all the mundane laws of nature
and presenting obstinately perfect evidence
that all the evils of the world, adversities and tragedies
are but mirages compared to the reality of beauty.

Cultural Disdain

Why is culture so disdained?
Why is Greek and Latin so disdained?
Why is knowledge about history so contemptible?
Why did school authorities desire to remove all knowledge of the Bible
and of classical antiquity from national curriculum?
What is so contemptible about refined and higher culture
except that there's no profit in it and it doesn't pay?

Is then the humanist to be discarded and turned over to the gutter
and to social welfare, with his poverty confirmed and made officially legitimate,
established as correct, since he is practically of no use and brings no profit?
Is then the economic and capitalistic aspect as criterion the only valid one
for what is good, acceptable and socially correct?
Has then beauty and good taste, nobility and creativity no say?
Are they to be just scrapped, disdained and driven over then as parasites?

That is how barbarity is then preferred to civilization,
then brutality is given leave to ravish truth and beauty,
then humanism is driven over with all human empathy
by automatic inhumanity, insensitivity and ruthlessness;
thus ignorance legitimizes her own limitations against knowledge
in short-sighted thoughtless blind inferiority complex,
turning the constructively conserving and creative culture into martyrs.

The New Paradigm

The problem is that man has lost all credibility.
He has made a mess of all the world
by wars, pollution, extirpation of wild life and animals,
a global poisoning of nature
by exploitation, ruthlessness of greed and dehumanization,
so there is no wise man to believe in or to trust man any more.
He is biologically bankrupt,
turning all his mega cities into dumps of poison,
ruining all nature, his own livelihood.
So we have all kinds of global crises,
now this world threat of Corona, worst in 100 years,
that could be seen as something like Dame Nature's own revenge on man,
an effort to restore the Gaia balance,
saving life on earth from man, the monster menace.
We don't know what will come out of it,
we are in the beginning only so far,
but all signs point to a revolution and new paradigm,
to which we must learn to adapt ourselves.

Involuntary Survival

I have done it many times,
each time with equal misgivings,
having to survive in spite of common sense,
when everything would argue for your death.
Man's right to live is more than ever questionable
as she is the foremost enemy and parasite of nature
in outrageously destroying the environment
putting all life of the world at risk
including her own egoism, short-sighted ruthlessness
and universal self-destructiveness.
Then comes this virus almost like a world redeemer
for dame nature, the environment and all organic life
with perhaps a permanent and paralyzing superstition
by a horror of contagion more efficient than a world disease,
compelling all society to slow down to some afterthought
like some most wholesome illness of paralysis.
Of course, much of the panic and hysteria is exaggerated,
going to extremes that no one in his right mind can take seriously;

while those who have no choice but to survive
must oftentimes find it a worrying burden
that they were not granted the convenience to depart
when they would have preferred to.

Despair

A friend of mine committed suicide,
a case that made impression by its most dramatic exit –
some are poisoned by exaggerated medication
and are driven to extremes to gun down people
with self-immolation as a grand finale,
while more timid people bury their despair
and anguish in themselves, like my friend Henning,
ending up by laying himself down across the railway track.
If life is felt as merely a continuous humiliation
constantly more painful and exacerbated,
who can then accuse a poor and wretched suicide of anything?
Is it not most natural and logic to conclude by any means
an unendurable ordeal of suffering that only can get worse
for which there is no cure? There is a surge of suicides now
because of the Corona crisis,
people jumping off from bridges, taking poison,
drinking themselves to perdition
or old people dying from the terror of confinement.
Bankruptcy is no more than a challenge thing,
no reason for self-immolation or the ruin of your life
since life will always go on anyway,
and all you can and should do is to make the best of it
under the circumstances.

Overlove

It was the basic problem of my life,
that I would always overdo it,
going to extremes emotionally
in my love and deep sincerity
of over-sensitive affection,

sometimes bordering on suicidal tendencies:
that was the case of Goethe's Werther,
which was a most personal experience
by that poet drowning in his overwhelming passion
for a lady he could never make himself quite understandable,
thus ending up in self-consumption of his overbearing love,
and Goethe found it maybe even harder
and more difficult to have to outlast and survive that crisis,
as a poet said, 'consumed by that which he was nourished by'.
love turning into a perpetual nightmare
for the over-sensitive emotionally vulnerable poet
of constant sleeplessness and torturous unrest
with no release or possibility of a redemption ever,
as such deep and strong sincerity of love
must be the very essence of the poet's personality,
an innate and insatiable urge to just go on
in blind love and affection in perhaps eternity,
like Paolo and Francesca in that hurricane of hell
that keeps on harrowing its prisoners of love forever,
which Dante witnessed and could understand
as yet another poet suffering of overlove
that never could find any satisfactory and proper outlet.

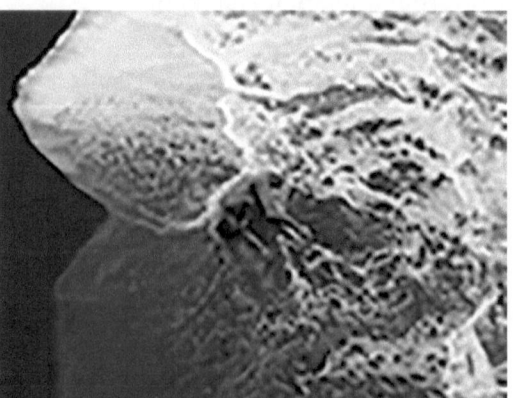

Suicide as a Therapy

Suicide statistics are increasing
in the wake of the Corona epidemic,
often as a consequence of bankruptcy and ruin,
people feeling at a loss for having lost the meaning
of their lives, the motivation for to stay alive at all,
but naturally suicide must be dissuaded from by all and every means
as it is the ultimate defeat and giving up in cowardice.
However, using suicide as a therapy can be constructive,
doubting all your values and your life, delusions and your vanity
and finding a detachment from it all,
mundanity and your material existence,
can be only beneficial for your personal development,
like any meditation can be only good and useful.
Suicide then as therapy and a consideration
is not then to be despised and feared
but can be actually a better therapy than most,
especially in times of crisis, trial and extreme conditions.

The Lie of Lies

People always tended to go crazy about money
in a sickly greed that blinded them to life's necessities
and even to reality, thus driving them over the cliff
in some kind of a mass psychosis, like a crowd of lemmings
all together joining to commit collective suicide
in a senseless and shortsighted chase of vain futilities,
believing blindly in the lie that money is the same as power,
while the contrary is closer to the truth.
With money you are chained to limitations
in the form of worries and material concerns,
and you must carry blinkers against anything that isn't property or money.
You are only free without concerns of mortal worries,
and true power lies in freedom only and true independence.
Mortal powers usually rush headlong into self-destruction
in blind ignorance of higher laws of karma

or of destiny, which no one ever could control
but which instead controlled all human lives on earth
by giving lessons of experience and fate
as the eternal cosmic education of all life
that is not mortal but must carry on continuously forever.

The Rejected Lover

All I wanted was to love and give
which wasn't very well received
but mostly with misunderstandings,
taking my good will as something negative
and dangerous to be aware of and repel
with depreciatory response and disregard.
Must love then be confined in isolation
and sustained and activated only in protection
against baseness, failure to appreciate,
ingratitude and ignorance and bad vibrations,
like a morbid attitude of short-sighted self-limitation?
There is no bitterness but only disappointment
with the commonness and insufficiency of human nature
that should be divine with capability of understanding everything
but which, as we all know, was capable of crucifying Christ.

Realism Without Bitterness

Never mind my presence
since it does not matter
since I am as good as dead
and more alive and active as a ghost
than among all restricted mortal idiots
of the mundane slavery and morbid world
of only self-destructive flesh and escapism, at best.
I loved you but have no pretensions,
make no claims on you and have done well without you,
while you always can be certain of my love
if even you would choose to scrap me and discard me,
which I took for granted you would do from the beginning.

The Strangest Love

The strangest love is that which in maturity endures
to spite all time, surviving all disasters,
hibernating through defeats and downfalls,
to like someone shipwrecked saved by some old plank
against your will is brought ashore
when all you wanted was to die,
which would have been the best of all;
but destiny as always thwarted you
and saved you for the obligations of your love,
as you will never be allowed to cease to love;
but that hard work will be your constant hell forever,
like a grinding-wheel you never are released from.
You have to resign accepting it and make the best of it,
you have no other choice, so just get on with it and love forever.

The Sculptor

They were very young and colleagues,
fellow students at the art school,
being brilliant both as budding sculptors,
with a natural endowment for creative realistic art,
and she was beautiful and only nineteen,
he was slightly older when he asked her

whether he would be allowed to make her portrait.
She of course was only happy to cooperate,
and so he sculpted her in all her mature teenage beauty.
Then the war broke out, and everything was interrupted,
the art school had to close, and he had to go out to war.
He never came back any more but fell a casualty among too many.
He was last male member of his family, which died with him.
All she was left with was his portrait of her.
She continued as a sculptress all her life.
The portrait always stayed with her and had an honoured central place,
bearing witness of her youthful beauty through all ages
as perhaps a testimony also of his lasting and undying love of her.

When Darkness is Not Enough

Let me drown you in my tears of blood
to compensate the fact that darkness never was enough
for comfort, although smothering to death
the heart to cure it of its cruel immeasurable aches
of limitless atrociousness in unfair disappointment
of black holes of desperate frustration.
Let me love you all the same
with all the passion of our common painfulness
to cure its wounds and damages and irreparable inhuman losses
simply by in humble prudence share
the torture of your soul that keeps on screaming
in resounding anguish throughout all the universe
although it is in its outrageous recklessness
beyond all hearing and all human understanding except mine.

The Corona Strain

After having finally recovered from Corona,
many former patients show the weirdest post-traumatic symptoms,
first of all profound unfathomably deep depressions,
weakness like after some years' ordeal in hospital and coma
and with no end to a most relentless hangover of a fatigue
that only constantly gets worse;

and others even think they have gone mad
as they feel lost like if their brains were out of order;
everything preposterously indicating
that there never was an illness like it,
and it still is far from over yet.
What can you do about it?
It's a kind of nervous stress affecting your entire system,
and the one thing you can do is not to make it worse
by adding to the arduous stress by straining it to further torture.
You can never have enough of rest,
and second best is constant meditation for a change
whenever you get back that feeling of a monkey on your back.
It's good to physically exercise as well,
and concentration is the best of practices.
Above all, you should always take it easy.

The Curse of Crassness

The vulgarity and superficiality of crassness
has ruined and corrupted all the world
by materialism and the environment destruction,
just as Trump has ravished all the sanctity and freedom of Dame Nature
by letting loose the demons of exploitation
in the ruthlessness of bulldozers for profiteering,
just like any base inhuman tyrant and dictatorship;
while idealism, the opposite to crassness,
always remains free and independent
and in contrast to all mortal vanity of crassness,
if that is any comfort to you, will remain immortal.

The Beauty of Vanity

Is it wrong to adore the beauty of your vanity,
the hollow superficiality of your good looks
with nothing in it but shallowness,
or is it really such poverty in such richness,
can the generosity of nature really be that deceptive,
offering only frustrations for your trust and adoration?

It is easy to get burned, more easy than to not be,
while the comfort of the coldness of taking no risks
is only impoverishing in the bleakness of its thrift,
while love must be expressed and come forth,
or else it must consume you.
Better then to be consumed by burning
than to freeze to death in nothingness.

A Question of Greatness

Human greatness grows to some extent
when met with trials and adversity
and should be measured most correctly
by how these adversities are dealt with,
as there is no more admirable greatness
than when sufferings and tribulations are survived
with marks that last of traumas, scars and bleeding wounds forever,
speaking figuratively of mentally and spiritually lasting damages.
An invalid surviving accidents and wars with his integrity and courage intact
is a hero of much higher dignity and status
than some ordinary decorated gatherer of medals.

Thus the small and poorly populated cold and dark old Finland
reached a much more prominent degree of greatness
in resisting the attacks of the world's greatest land the Soviet Union
in two wars and saving independence and her sovereignty
against such an overwhelming superpower,
even fighting back successfully.
That is what I call greatness, the resistance of a young and small democracy
against the hardest tyrannous oppression in the world.
We had more caualties and victims than we could afford,
but at least there also were a number of survivors, carrying on the intrepidity.

The Great Void

When you feel like dead
but have to stay alive
in spite of that you are no good
and feel like having wasted all your life
on vanity of vanities and nothing else,
you are exactly like a living dead,
and all you have is that great void
of emptiness, a hollow nothingness
that is much worse and more unbearable than darkness
since there is no hole in it, no light in nothingness,
no meaning and no challenge, nothing to resist
and fight and overcome, but only the nonentity of silence.
Still you have to stay alive in just a limbo of existence,
and there are ways of escape and means available
for getting out of what is worse than a black hole,
like the relief of living nature, the escape into illusions
of religion and philosophy, and above all the arts,
as you are still alive and capable of some creation –
when all else is gone, your creativity will still be there,
and your primary duty to your life is to go on applying it.

Discarded

Is it then so strange
when you are constantly refused
interminably by all publishers
without motivation nor an explanation,
constantly refused an outcome,
spiritually starved to death by this indifference,
while your manuscripts are never more returned
but probably just shredded into pulp
with never any recognition or acknowledgement
and least of all encouragement nor even any criticism,
just callous murderous indifference for 50 years and more;
and it is like a symptom of the age and our contemporary society
to just don't care, to stick to stubborn ignorance,
to refuse to see and recognize what's obvious
in a permanent refusal of the generosity of creativity,
by demonstratively denying it and turning a blind eye to it,
as if the revelation of the facts of truth and beauty
had become intolerable and unbearable,
like as if to increase and further spiritual death,
which tempted many to consequent and inevitable suicide,
as if the enforcement of humility by destiny was not enough,
– to find yourself directed to the bottle as the only possible appeal?
Thus also a composer was turned down,
his compositions being scrapped as nothing but improvisations;
but does not all composition start with improvising,
and is that not actually the very essence of all musical creativeness?
There are some migrants coming with the highest education
with capacity for being more than only useful to society,
who are shut out, let down, discriminated and ignored,
refused as unacceptable and blocked by doors kept shut
in the society established by incompetence and cheating
where authorities do nothing if there is an income and position to defend.
The fake society is a robotized bureaucracy
where nothing works and nothing is made possible;
and nothing more sustains this established constantly increasing sloth
of a society in its slow inefficiency than the Corona triumph.

The Comfort of Dying Alone

You need no relatives around you,
no sentimentality and tears of hypocritical self pity,
as you only can find peace alone,
and it's a bliss to pass away in that condition.
Is then all that you have left of life
your dreams, your memories of happier days,
those crushed ideals remaining still as mirages of dreams?
But that's the only thing you can take with you
as you leave this mortal battlefield of vain defeats
that only left you incapacitated spiritually, mentally and mortally
while your dreams will carry you across to better opportunities,
or so at least you can imagine in your dreams.

Home

Your home is where you are
no matter where you are,
as only you create your home;
it's only you who can originate
that homely feeling of contentment
as a safe environment of comfort.
It's something you create,
and you go on creating it
as you continue working on it
and filling it with your own dreams,
and that's the very stuff that makes a home:
the spiritual inheritance in your possession
that no one can take away from you forever
of your memories, experiences and dreams
as long as you go on creating them anew.

Turning In

It's time for turning in for winter
in the winter laird for hibernation,
since you anyway won't do much good
as only growing lazy in your lethargy and listlessness
of lacking any energy for love or work or being useful,
since the fact that you are getting old
in spite of your good health cannot be overlooked,
denied, ignored or seen as without consequence.
You have to face it and accept that your mortality
is actually a comfort and relief, as you can blame your age
for everything unpleasant in your life,
thus turning all your inconvenience to convenience,
cultivating your own snugness and complacency.
I would not recommend it though,
but rather recommend that you keep struggling on
and even forcing yourself to continued effort,
as there's no idea in slowing down unnecessarily
for death to catch you up before you have turned in.

It is Not Easy to Accept Defeat

It is not easy to accept defeat
when your entire world is ruined,
when there's nothing left for you
but the disgraceful cowardly escape of suicide,
when you feel your whole life was a failure,
and all that's left for you is to resort to drinking,
which is just the fool's way out to nothing,
the admission of that you are nothing
and you have no comfort left, no work, no will to live,
no appetite, no lust but only emptiness,
the summary of all your efforts being just a void;
as all your best friends have been exiled to the other side,
and you have only ghosts left to associate with,
as all your love, that made your life worth living,
turned into disappointments by betrayal and deceit,
and your idealism proved only fickle dreams and mirages,
like dried up oases turned into a desert of abandonment;
and all you find of life and love is a continuous degradation,
an eternal process of decay and constantly exacerbated death,
that just goes on like torture ever getting worse,
while nothing will survive but maybe some remembrance
of that love that gave some hope in the beginning
only to be hopelessly more lost than anything.

Whenever I Die I Think of You

Whenever I die, I think of you.
Franz Liszt defined life as a perpetual suicide,
you just live to die and start dying the moment you are born,
and all negligence of this fact is just an escapism of vanity,
resorting to the preference of ignorance to realism and truth,
while at the same time you cannot ignore the fact of love,
that it exists and makes life worth the bitterest experience,
as you always will be able to survive whatever happens,

even if it always has to be just temporary,
a respite and an oasis of an island
in the eternal darkness of a universal stormy sea.

The Age of Postponement

It is a troublesome winter
cancelling all activity,
forbidding social intercourse
and closing in on everyone in isolation
not of any splendid sort but rather as some incarceration
of no good to anyone
in the obedience to the laws of superstition,
fear, surveillance and the terror of an alien virus.
Life is at a standstill, all the planet is closed down
while only nature is relieved, rejoicing in the invalidity of man
and breathing out in freedom for a change.
Some draw some weird conclusions from this strange condition,
that it could be an intentional revenge on man by nature
for his recklessness, abuse of nature and lack of economy
in ruthless waste of universal natural resources
putting life itself at risk and leading to the critical extinction
of too many species, of which nature cannot do without a single one.
As usual, the challenge of the difficulty is to keep surviving,
which can be managed at least individually
by keeping a low profile and abstaining from ambitions and pretensions.

Floating as a Wreck

The storms have hacked you all to pieces,
your life is permanently brought to ruin,
you have nothing left but endless bitterness, remorse and tears,
and you lie shackled, shattered, incapacitated as a wreck,
while you notice with some wonder,
although without sails, a slaughtered broken hulk
with nothing left of any navigation skills,
that you keep floating, maybe in a dead calm

just before the final storm, the definite destruction,
but it never comes. Although you feel like dead
and are like dead, you are kept forcibly alive
almost against your will, a most involuntary grace
like being sentenced, not to death, but to what must be worse,
continued life in utterly outrageous circumstances.
And the only thing that you can do about it
is complying with the judgment in subordination
in the inescapable necessity of making just the best of it.

The Poet's Best Friend

The pain of life can sometimes be unbearable
especially if there is no end to it
but it just keeps increasing in outrageous agony
to transcend all the tortures of eternity of hell.
But strange enough, there is a comforter at hand,
a possibility and way out of all vicious circles,
and especially all poets usually found him the best of friends,
 and yet he is the greatest paradox of all as comforter,
inspirer of life and liberator as a way to new life, but it works,
as both John Keats and Pasternak and others found to their surprise,
that there is always a relief of intimacy and true friendship
in the association with the ultimate perdition, death,
as a security alternative if nothing else works out.
The suicidal comfort never has to be accomplished,
but as an idea of meditation and of spiritual rebirth
in a kind if revitalization, it is always handy as a comfort.

How Lonely Are You?

There is no loneliness in loneliness.
The universe is there and waiting for you,
while in company it is closed up for you,
as friends and lovers must have all your main attention.
In order to have concentration for your meditation
and creation, you must needs be alone,
and in that loneliness you then will find the company
of all the world, but only spiritually, never physically,
which could be felt the more releasing and relaxing
if not even as some sort of freedom and important liberation.
This is individual, of course, not everyone was born for loneliness,
and not everyone has known the vital urge for loneliness,
while some are better off alone
especially with their creative freedom,
if that is what they were made for.

Dreams as Symbols of Marriage

They say I am married to my dreams.
They do not harm me. We do not quarrel.
Unfortunately they are not always available.
Like love you have to wait for them patiently,
as they cannot appear except naturally.
Like women their souls have no body,
and what's worse, you cannot even touch them.
So why should you keep them and have them at all?
You just cannot do without them.
They may trouble you and delight you,
but they are always there,
and that's the only certain thing about them.
So just tolerate them, accept them
as an inevitable part of your life,
and the best thing of all, they cost you nothing;
so just live with them
and make the best of them as they are.

The Vanity of Poetry

It's a trap.
The poet writes a poem
and is pleased with it
and is fooled into some self-complacence,
a delusion of a narcissistic character,
and if he cultivates this self-love,
this self-satisfaction, he is lost
and drowns in mirroring himself.
A writer's occupation is a lonesome business,
he can only write alone
and has to be alone for concentration,
but if he then writes for others
and about real people of some interest to him
like of love, the most constructive object,
he is safe and will not drown

but keep on floating on the waves of love for others
if he just keeps up the outlook
and forgets himself
as he is actually and only an observer.

The Incompatibility of Truth and Love

When you are in love
it's natural for you to idealize your love
and see her in an aura of some magic beauty,
thus presuming her to have the best of qualities,
as love is generally most creative,

making your imagination carry you away with fancies,
as you couldn't love her without also dreaming of her.
Then the truth turns out to be something entirely different,
like an alien dimension, as you notice she has pimples,
there's an opposite and different side to everything,
and even the most ideal love will prove to have a different side.
When hard reality starts importuning,
cruelly imposing practical demands and difficulties,
practically love becomes an awesome enterprise,
involving worries, problems and adversities,
and that's not the love you bargained for.
The problem of this incompatibility
is, you have to trick and wind your way through this new jungle
which could even prove a minefield prompting necessary caution;
and you find yourself obliged to compromise
with both your love and with reality
to find the most delicate and difficult of balances.
If you can keep that balance, you will have succeeded
in maintaining both your love and save it through reality
by endurance, by sticking to it
and by never quite forsaking your idealism,
but keeping all that magic of your true original creative love
in sight, as any captain never must neglect his compass.

The Fascination of Evil

This is the weirdest kind of mystery,
as it is practically omnipresent
in all public media, above all:
most movies loaded with atrocities,
the domination unavoidable of sex and violence,
and literature even mostly being dominated
by intrigues of crime and murder;
while the opposite is rare
for the apparent reason that it does not sell.
It's a phenomenon that started already from the beginning,
the Homeric poems being all about the Trojan war,
the Bible being full of death and dramas of destruction,

Dante's divine comedy being nothing without hell,
and Shakespeare filling up his stage with corpses.
This is actually a challenge, the absurdity of evil
being the supreme adversity
which you must overcome like any trial of survival,
even if to only prove the natural doctrine and thesis,
that what does not kill you has to make you stronger,
and that is possibly the only meaning of it.

Dreams A Necessary Compensation For Reality

When you wake up in the morning sometimes
there is something of a dream still lingering
and actually providing the most lovely memory
of sweetness, beauty and exquisite happiness;
but it will only last for one brief moment:
as you open up your eyes and have reality

take over brutally, all lasting bliss of dreams is gone,
and all you have is the outrageous hardness,
ugliness, brutality and horror of your practical mundanity.
Are all those dreams of beauty then just falsehood,
delusions and illusions to deceive you,
tempting you to any form of escapism
just to get out of mortal traps of practical ordeals?
The contrast is too sharp between those dreams and facts of life
to be acceptable, and any escapism appears quite necessary.
Holding on to sweet remembrance of delicious dreams
will tempt you to abandon real life altogether;
but it is in fact a question of two different realities
and even different dimensions. In your dreams
you are transported to another better world, it seems,
but it is as real as the concrete world, although abstract.
Many are convinced their dreams are truer than reality
and that reality is just all humbug, lies and vain deceit,
and they cannot be proven wrong, while on the other hand,
your dreams can also never be considered evidence of any truth.

The Indispensable Comfort of Memories

The archive of your memories
has the inevitable tendency
to constantly increase in volume, depth and value,
wherefore also you grow more reluctant with the years
to do without them, and especially when you with terror
feel them naturally fade away and disappear,
the archive getting over-loaded,
like a room or home that never is cleaned up.
The harder then you stick to them from fear of losing them,
while at the same time you fail to observe
that they are dragging you behind and cluttering your mind
to pull and slow you down, and that is difficult to remedy.
It will then gradually become more difficult to start new enterprises
and to start at all, as it is comfortable and convenient to just sit back
and live on glories past. There is the danger and the death trap.
It is a bog, and you must constantly be careful not to get bogged down;

and then the dire necessity occurs to constantly compel yourself
and force yourself to never stop committing yourself to new efforts.
That is how old concert pianists keep constantly at work and fit,
like Rubinstein and Horowitz still giving concerts in their 80s,
but by constant urgent practicing and forcing themselves to hard work
for hours every day not to get bogged down
in the comfortable trap and flattering dreams of pleasant memories.

When You Get Drowned in Love

When you get drowned in love
there is no way out but to let it go,
to let yourself get drowned in it
and if possible to just enjoy it,
until you are smothered and can't bear it any longer;
and that is the moment when you come to think of suicide
as the only possible and definitely certain cure;
but even that is just a gamble:
you don't know what is beyond the grave,
while staying on in the unbearable condition
of your being buried, sacrificed alive
with no end to the torture, is like being on the operation table
in an operation which will never finish but just carry on
to cut you up in slices for no purpose as it seems,
just can't be tolerated in the long run.
Death could then be a deceptive liberator,
but he always will have the advantage over you
since it's impossible to make him out
as the supreme and ultimate remaining mystery,
the only certain thing about him being that he's always there
and waiting for you in the end for good or worse;
and since he is inevitable anyway
you might as well get lost in love while you are at it
and just let it do with you whatever it may please
while you had better make the best of it and just enjoy it.

Delusional

It could happen to anyone
Who falls to the temptation
To get too involved and fixed in his own ego,
Thereby losing all detachment and perspective
To reality in something of a wishful thinking effort
To replace the undesirable elements of this reality
With their own or to at least impose their own
By driving over and ignoring facts.
They get immersed in what they think must be reality
But which is actually just castles in the air of their own fancy.
No harm in this, but danger will occur
If they gain power or some influence with many followers
Who let themselves be tricked into believing
The attractive and seductive character of his conviction,
Falling like himself for the convincing and idealistic mirage.
They get caught in their own spider's web
Of irresistible illusions, actually believing they are true,
While their materialization generally proves a fatal self-deceit,
Especially to followers of credulous naivety who end up victims.

The Exhibitionist

– a practical solution (essay)

An artist exhibits his paintings
and pays the gallery for his exhibition,
hoping the gallery visitors will pay for his paintings
by generous appreciative buys,
and sometimes this could be profitable.
Another does the same but without money
and with music and literature only,
presentinghis creations on the web
to be downloaded free of charge for anyone.
There all his works of literature and music are found
directly accessible for anyone with access to the web,
themost open university to all theworld
for people universally regardless of language and nationality,
exposing himself to criticism for doing this for nothing
without any other explanation than that he has no choice,
internet being the poor intellectual's redemption,

especially since all other means have been closed to him,
being socially shut out on no other grounds than formalism,
being musically also excluded for insisting on consistence
inmelodiousness, tonality and harmony,
exposed as well to frauds, deceits and even robbery
by exorbitant taxation leading hopelessly to bankruptcy and ruin,
forcing him to live consistently under subsistence minimum;
so he has no other choice than to present his life's work
in a permanent continuous all comprising exhibition
on the web, for anyone to visit and collect by downloads,
while everything remains intact by digital continuity anyway.

The Lost Soul of Nikolai Gogol

He wrote a novel called "Dead Souls",
a grandiose social satire spiced with humour,
and a poignant clever insight and analysis
of his contemporary social order and society
with a brilliant eye for human idiosyncracies;
and he was widely read, appreciated and successful,

publishing the first of part of his "Dead Souls" without problems;
but he then came under the precarious influence of a fanatic,
who seduced him to exaggerated piety as an extreme ascetic,
breeding second thoughts about his writings
bringing his self-criticism to fatal levels,
which induced him to commit the second part to flames,
his doubts thus turning self-destructive,
which he came to bitterly regret,
exacerbating his religious fervour and asceticism
to make him starve himself to death.
He was Ukrainian, writing "Taras Bulba" as his first and greatest novel,
a heroic and romantic family account of a rebellion
against oppression of the Cossacks,
one of the most brilliant masterpieces of the Russian literature,
a kind of manual and gospel universally for insurrection
against any power of inhuman and political repression.
We are there again today, as the Ukrainians have to struggle for their life
against intolerable force of terror by the greed of an oppressor.
Gogol's novel thus became prophetic giving him immortal status
as a compensation for his early and untimely death.

The Enrichment of Love

You are that kind of person
of whose love you cannot tire,
but you just must go on loving
and adoring for the sake of lovableness
of the subject, and the more you love her,
the more motivated you will be
to just go on enjoying, loving and persisting
to hold on to the exquisite moment
of a beauty seeming unable to fade
but only to increase with wisdom and maturity,
like an old wine only growing finer with the years
and increasing only by consuming it.
This is not wishful thinking,
This is true love when it works,

pure magic if you like but purest of all sorts,
which only needs protection, careful cultivation
and profound sincerity of tenderness
of some infinity of generosity
to just be able to go on forever.

The Splendour of the Underdog

As a paria he is untouchable,
protected by the honesty of his humility,
as he has no capacity for hubris,
being always beaten down, suppressed and chastised
by his fate of static and perpetual poverty
and no mundane ambitions for career or power,
being a philosopher by nature and allergic against vanity,
as the innate humanist has constantly been driven over
and ignored, rejected and despised by history,
which all since 1914 only has concerned itself
with the perpetual continuity of its own recklessness

of bolting in derailment stuck in its own force
of running wild in senselessness and voluntary blindness
listening to only noise and madness of the demagogues,
who only scream of thirst for blood and violence
in apocalyptic hubris of destruction
on a universal massive scale;
while the despised, ignored, forgotten underdog
keeps dodging in the underworld security
and labouring in peace and quiet
for the possibility of better times.

Without an Audience

Without an audience you can work alone
in peace and quiet and constructive concentration
to get something done without disturbance,
while an audience actually is only a distraction
making noises, sneezing, coughing, snivelling
and cutting patronising deprecatory remarks
to only show their ignorance and lack of understanding.
The most isolated artist therefore often proves
to be the purest and most skilful valuable craftsman
in his genuine ability of perfect and creative concentration.
Going public is to make yourself ridiculous,
a fool's desire to exhibit his own folly
by debasing his own work to mundane vanity
and exposing his own soul to ridicule.
A drunk is wiser in his loneliness
in keeping all his weakness, sorrows and regrets
in secret honest diligent expression to himself.

Latest update: 31.3.2022

Still to be continued.

Note to the Reader

Thank you for journeying with me through these pages of *Echoes of the Heart, Volume II*. Each reflection, story, and verse carries a part of lived experience—sometimes personal, sometimes universal—but always offered in the hope of finding resonance in your own heart.

If these words have awakened even a faint echo within you, then the purpose of this work has been fulfilled.

For readers who wish to explore the same collection under its earlier title, *October Harvest, Volume II*, it remains available here:

https://clanciai.wordpress.com/wp-content/uploads/2022/04/october-harvest-ii.pdf

With gratitude,

Christian Lanciai

www.ingramcontent.com/pod-product-compliance
Lightning Source LLC
Chambersburg PA
CBHW030539080526
44585CB00012B/201